Mother Knows Best

Talking Back to the "Experts"

T0159795

Mother Knows Best

Talking Back to the "Experts"

Edited by
Jessica Nathanson and Laura Camille Tuley

DEMETER

DEMETER PRESS
TORONTO, CANADA

Published by:
Demeter Press
726 Atkinson College, York University
4700 Keele Street
Toronto, Ontario M3J 1P3
Telephone: (416) 736-2100 x 60366
Email: arm@yorku.ca Web site: www.yorku.ca/arm

Demeter Press logo based on Skulptur "Demeter" by Maria-Luise Bodirsky
<www.keramik-atelier.bodirsky.edu>

Printed and Bound in Canada

Library and Archives Canada Cataloguing in Publication

    Mother knows best : talking back to the experts / edited by Jessica Nathanson and Laura Camille Tuley.

Includes bibliographical references.
ISBN 978-1-55014-487-1

    1. Motherhood. 2. Mothers. 3. Child rearing. 4. Child rearing — Handbooks, manuals, etc. — Evaluation. 5. Mothers — Life skills guides — Evaluation. I. Nathanson, Jessica Ann II. Tuley, Laura Camile, 1964-

Dedicated to our sons, Dylan and Koan
without whom this book would not have been written and,
without whom, it would have been written more quickly.

Table of Contents

**Section Four:
Mother Guilt: Being "Good" Mothers**

Acknowledgements

We are grateful to Andrea O'Reilly, who not only supported this project before Demeter Press was even founded and offered us repeated and unwavering encouragement, but who has also, through her prolific writing and her work with ARM, helped to validate work on mothering and create significant space for it. We wish to thank Renée Knapp, as well, for her assistance. Of course, we are indebted to the authors of this collection, without whose work we would have no book. We also thank our partners and our children (Jessica: Dan and Koan; Laura: Chris and Dylan) for refreshing, challenging, and nurturing us in this effort. Finally, we thank all the mothers we have met while working on this book who expressed interest and enthusiasm: we hope you like it and find it helpful.

Introduction

Knowing Best and Talking Back

Jessica Nathanson and Laura Camille Tuley

In the popular imagination mothers are commonly considered to be omnipotent, with the power to single-handedly determine the success or failure of their children's futures by their parenting skills.[1] For example, the Victorian era's Cult of True Womanhood positioned mothers as the spiritual center of domestic life, responsible for providing nurturance and morality in family life. In the twentieth century, dominant theories of schizophrenia held (incorrectly) that the disorder resulted from having had a cold, emotionally unavailable mother. We call men who have never learned to live independently "mama's boys," blaming this deficiency on their mothers' influence and interventions. And currently, breastfeeding is portrayed as indispensable to the development of infants' immune systems. In the same vein, mothers who choose to work full-time rather than stay at home with their infants are subject to scrutiny by those "authorities" who continue to essentialize and privilege the role of the biological mother over that of alternative care-givers. Thus, mothers are still constructed as the most powerful influence in a child's life.

Given this persistent trend, it is not surprising that a significant amount of advice literature is directed toward mothers. Such literature is based on the assumption that mothers need to be both corrected and directed, and that, when left to their own devices, mothers will get it wrong. Mothers are perceived as needing guidance, and this guidance, historically, has been shaped at least in part by a political and ideological agenda that would confine women to traditional roles within the family and society.

What is missing from such literature, of course, are the voices of mothers talking back to power. We need a feminist, mother-centered critique of such authoritative messages, one that takes into account the vast socio-economic and cultural differences that mothers experience, as well as our different experiences of privilege and oppression. We also need to filter the messages of so-called "experts" through "mother wisdom." We are, after all, experts on our own lives, and, as mothers, have our own wisdom to share.

Like many other feminists who focus on theory that is rooted in lived experience, we came to write about mothering because we were living it. This book follows in the tradition of scholarship and narrative writing about mothers' resistance to authoritative messages. Paula Caplan's *Don't Blame Mother: Mending the Mother-Daughter Relationship*, for example, is one of this book's foremothers. Caplan resists mother-blame and exposes its deep entrenchment in the larger culture and in psychotherapy, in particular. Caplan not only reveals the bias of "expert" knowledge that assumes that mothers are at fault for their children's problems, but she also challenges the notion that such knowledge is beneficial, claiming that "expert" knowledge "damages mother-daughter [and mother-son] relationships because it feeds [children's] belief in [their] mother[s'] inadequacy" (106). In other words, "experts" serve to inform children that mothers aren't smart or capable enough to know how to raise their children without being told. Caplan's talking back is done specifically to help readers to heal their mother-daughter relationships by critically analyzing and rejecting the myths that mothers are incompetent or malevolent, and by eventually recognizing instead that mothers are societal scapegoats.

Patricia Hill-Collins' analysis of Black mothering is another example of the tradition of talking back that this book takes up. Rejecting the notion that mothering is labor done only within one's own (presumably nuclear) family, Hill-Collins calls attention to the mothering done by "other mothers," community members who care for the children of their friends and acquaintances; and the ways that Black women's activism, on behalf of the Black community, is a form of othermothering. Hill-Collins' work thus challenges White-centered models of mothers' work and roles that erase Black mothers. Further, Hill-Collins positions Black mothering as an intensely political location, one that both politicizes mothers to become activists and that also invests mothers with power in their communities. Such notions of mothering resist the "expert" assumptions of a White, middle-class, heterosexual model of mothering as a time of intense absorption in one's child, in seclusion from the larger community and to the exclusion of one's ability to be a political actor.

Molly Ladd-Taylor and Lauri Umansky have crafted an invaluable history and analysis of "mother blaming" in their anthology *"Bad" Mothers: The Politics of Blame in Twentieth Century America*. The anthology treats four basic themes: the "elasticity of the 'bad' mother label," that is, its consistent use in relation to certain demographics of women and contextual application to others (18); sources of mother-blaming (among which is "the dominance of childrearing experts," in the twentieth century) (10); the role of feminism in both engendering and failing to address adequately the "bad" mother label, and the deleterious effect of this label and the attitude that it reflects towards women on families. Like *Mother Knows Best, "Bad" Mothers* is fed by a desire to reclaim the authority of women to define "good" mothering and to raise the consciousness of other women about both the labeling and corresponding ideology by which they have been historically victimized and in which they have been at times complicit: "In other words, the labeling of the 'bad' mother narrows for all of us the definition of 'good' mothering, while luring us to participate in the limiting of our own options" (Ladd-Taylor and Umanksy 23).

Ariel Gore (see Susan Driver, this volume) is an activist and writer who also sees mothering as a political act. She, too, rejects the notion that "expert" knowledge is more authoritative than mother knowledge. In *The Mother Trip*, she laments the fact that "the clearest, most consistent message [in the parenting books she'd read] was this: Withhold all of your own knowledge, Mom, and follow *my* rules" (6). Gore encourages mothers to tap into intuition—their own and each other's—and "to transform the energy our culture has taught us to use to scrutinize and blame ourselves, and turn it outward, into something revolutionary" (8). Gore's revolution is built on shifting this critical gaze away from mothers and onto the "experts," themselves.

Katherine Arnup's work also belongs to this same tradition of talking back to "expert" knowledge. Arnup explores the changing messages contained in child-rearing advice directed toward Canadian mothers from 1900-1960, as well as the ways in which these mothers responded (and, perhaps, resisted) to such advice. Arnup examines the way this advice changed over time to contradict itself; for example, rigid and scheduled feeding, sleeping, and toilet training in the early part of the twentieth century was replaced by more relaxed, child-centered approaches to these practices later on. Arnup also notes the larger social issues that affected the particular advice pressed onto mothers, such as the significance of poverty, lack of access to medical care, and child mortality rates, all of which created a need to assist mothers—and, consequently, made them dependent on such advice—in the first place.

Chris Bobel's work (see also this volume) offers a sympathetic critique of the "natural mothering" movement, which she locates in relation to attachment parenting, voluntary simplicity, and cultural feminism. Such analysis helps feminist mothers to understand the conflict between desiring the bond promised by this intense—and intensive—model of parenting and struggling not to lose ourselves in it. While Bobel argues that natural mothering involves its own "expert" knowledge that practicing mothers may not be able to resist, she simultaneously presents natural mothers as inherently resisting dominant messages about mothering (through, for example, extended [and public] breast-feeding or homeschooling). Ultimately, though, Bobel sees natural mothering as enabled by economic and social privilege and buttressed by gender essentialist understandings of motherhood, and thus, its messages about mothering are ripe for feminist response.

Finally, Andrea O'Reilly both lives and argues for empowered mothering as a model of mothering that celebrates women's agency. In *Rocking the Cradle: Thoughts on Motherhood, Feminism and the Possibility of Empowered Mothering*, O'Reilly explains that empowered, feminist mothering rejects what she terms "sacrificial mothering," which assumes that mothering is a biological imperative, that mothers must take on the brunt of the responsibility for childcare, and that children need to be intensely engaged and monitored on a constant basis by their mothers (38). The empowered, feminist mothering that O'Reilly champions "recognizes that both mothers and children benefit when the mother lives her life and practices mothering from a position of agency, authority, authenticity, and autonomy" (45). O'Reilly argues that empowered mothers are also political actors, mothers who are taking radical action through their mothering outside the bounds of sacrificial (or, "normal") motherhood roles. What is liberating about O'Reilly's work is that she gives mothers permission to focus on themselves, to meet their own needs, in the journey toward becoming better mothers.

Mother Knows Best: Talking Back to the "Experts," takes its title from two sources. First, tongue-in-cheek, it alludes to the popular 1950s sitcom, *Father Knows Best*, in which Robert Young, as patriarch, would solve the family's problems by the end of each episode. It also draws on popular notions of mothers knowing what is best for us. But we simultaneously chose this title to challenge the "experts" themselves, to argue that, when it comes to making the right decisions for ourselves and our families, mothers *do* know best: the best mothering practices can only be adopted after careful feminist analysis by and for mothers.

This anthology is by no means exhaustive, and we regret that we were not able to solicit a deeper discussion of race, class, sexuality, gender orientation, and disability in relation to "expert" knowledge. We had imagined that, in response to our call, we would receive several articles that addressed mothering from the conspicuous standpoints of mothers of color / queer mothers / mothers with disabilities—in other words, that identity politics would show up in the collection in a very powerful (and positive) way. While we received excellent manuscripts, many of the pieces did not focus in a self-conscious way on these issues, though some, such as Janni Aragon's and Damien Riggs' pieces, do. Fortunately, as the academic discipline of mothering continues to grow, the analyses of queer and radical parents of color are also shifting from the margins to the center. We'd like to point to some works that do focus on just these issues.

Thomas Beatie's April 2, 2008 appearance on *Oprah* to discuss his pregnancy sparked much discussion about transmen giving birth, but Beatie is not the first, nor the only, transman to bear a child. As we write this, the most recent issue of *Hip Mama* features Lucy Marrero's "Sometimes Daddies Do Get Pregnant," a reflection on the author's co-parenting with her "female-bodied butch partner who goes by male pronouns" (12). Marrero writes about challenging dominant understandings of the body when reading to her son; she resists the book's descriptions, such as "All girls have vulvas. All boys have penises," telling her son, instead, "Most girls have vulvas and most boys have penises," (13) thereby making room for their family's gender realities. And Jules Rosskam's 2005 documentary, *transparent*, explores the experiences of 19 transmen who have borne children, an act which, in and of itself, demands that one resist "expert" knowledge about what it means to be a mother. Trans perspectives on parenting deserve a place in the scholarship on mothering.

Lesbian, gay, and bisexual parenting has been more fully explored in this scholarship. One example of work that takes up some of the same challenges we raise in this book is Kristin Esterberg's "Planned Parenthood: The Construction of Motherhood in Lesbian Mother Advice Books," forthcoming in Andrea O'Reilly's edited collection, *Feminist Mothering* (SUNY Press). Esterberg analyzes the advice given to lesbian mothers in books written for this audience, noting that this literature constructs lesbian mothering as a "consumer choice," involving choices such as whether or not to become a mother, whether to inseminate (and what kind of sperm to select) or adopt, what kind of family to create, and what the roles of the legal and nonlegal parents will be. In her critique of this choice-based model of lesbian motherhood, Esterberg rightly points out that certain "choices," such as fertility treatment, are simply not options for poor women or for women who have historically and repeatedly been denied the right to be mothers, such as women of color and women with disabilities. However, she also observes that these books minimize the role of biology in parenting while underscoring the importance of the roles of non-biological parents in family life; this, Esterberg suggests, paints mothering as something that can be done by any parent, a possibility which certainly adds to the challenge to William Sears' and Martha Sears' gender-bound vision of attachment parenting that we present in this volume.

D. Memee Lavell-Harvard and Jeannette Corbiere Lavell's edited book, *"Until Our Hearts Are on The Ground": Aboriginal Mothering, Oppression, Resistance and Rebirth*, focuses on Aboriginal[2] mothering, which inherently involves talking back to dominant knowledge. Several of the articles relate mothering to sovereignty and traditional practice, underscoring the centrality of spiritual and cultural tradition, ritual, and extended family to mothering. The collection also examines the impact of racism and colonialization on Aboriginal mothers and families, pointing to historic conflicts between the state and the Aboriginal family and the ubiquity with which Aboriginal children have been taken away from their families. Sovereignty applied to mothering, then, means the right to bear and raise one's children and to raise them within one's tradition. The editors locate the common experience of Aboriginal mothering squarely in the tension between confronting and being confronted by "expert" knowledge: "we share the experience of being different from (and often fundamentally opposed to) the dominant culture, which has a significant impact on our ability to mother as we see fit, according to our own values, and traditions" (2).

Mother Knows Best is organized into four sections that address fundamental issues in mothering. Section One, "Out of our Bodies: Pregnancy and Birth," explores, from various perspectives, the ways in which mothers understand and react to "expert" advice offered about pregnancy and childbirth. As a result of the backlash against reproductive rights, the medical establishment's approach to pregnancy, and the culture of pregnancy advice books, pregnant women are perceived not only as already mothers but also as vessels for their unborn babies. Such a perception results in stripping women of their agency and personhood, and thereby of their ability to make choices about their prenatal behavior and healthcare. The social policing of pregnant women's alcohol use is one example of this; Denise Copelton addresses the ways in which women explain their decision to drink and to manage their drinking against a backdrop of medical—and common—knowledge that establishes such choices as both dangerous and morally wrong. Amber Kinser, approaching the issue from a different angle, lets pregnant women claim their own experiences by juxtaposing pregnant women's narratives with those of medical experts, creating a mosaic of women's struggle to participate in the depiction of their pregnancies. Likewise, Laura Major works to center women's own experiences of pregnancy by focusing on pregnancy and childbirth poetry. Meredith Nash's examination of ultrasound as a standard procedure raises questions about how we visualize the "personhood" of the developing baby at the expense of that of the mother. Laurie Ousley's analysis of a popular series of pregnancy and childbirth advice books shifts the focus to the way that pregnant women are defined by such texts, highlighting both the way in which they challenge, through their lighthearted, humorous approach, prevalent literature that is deadly serious, as well as the way in which these books also fall into the trap of offering "expert" advice that is, itself, sorely in need of critique. And Susan Racine Passmore turns a critical eye toward the Bradley Method, a "natural" method of childbirth that has given expectant parents the tools to challenge medicalized childbirth but which also positions women as secondary agents in their own childbirth experiences.

Section Two, "Is Breast Always Best?: Breastfeeding," examines the complexities of, obstacles to, and ideologies that shape breastfeeding practices in contemporary western culture. Because of the intense labor breastfeeding requires of mothers, the nutritional and health benefits breastmilk provides to infants, the cultural standards that mark women's breasts as objects of sexual desire, and the refusal of the workplace to adequately accommodate nursing mothers, breastfeeding is a critical issue in any discussion of mothering. Mothers who cannot or choose not to breastfeed frequently experience, not only guilt and anxiety, but censure. Stephanie Knaak argues that because the discourse of contemporary breastfeeding is suffused and constituted by the "ideology of intensive motherhood," mothers' experience of infant feeding is often riddled with conflict, emotional turmoil, guilt and worry. But not all mothers can simply choose to breastfeed, and Catherine Ma outlines the social, political and psychological impediments to breastfeeding for poor and working and women of color. Finally, the social imperative to breastfeed, combined with a simultaneous pressure *not* to breastfeed, results in competing directives to women that negate women's own experiences. Karen Maclean describes how the natural "ecosystem of breastfeeding knowledges and knowing," at the heart of which is the mother's experience, is often obscured and undermined by such "authoritative" or "expert" knowledge of breastfeeding.

In Section Three, "Challenging Practice: Raising Our Children," we tackle the often controversial subject of attachment parenting and its implications for feminist mothers. Demanding round-the-clock, constant mothering, AP promises healthy children and fulfilled mothers but ignores the reality that most mothers require intellectual and professional fulfillment and that children benefit by parenting from other sources (namely, fathers or partners). Chris Bobel critically explores the radical ideological and social potential of "natural mothering." Rachel Casiday investigates parents' right to forgo the medical establishment's recommendations regarding vaccinations and, by extension, to "take back" responsibility for their children's health, an approach that has been popularized by Sears and Sears, Dr. Jay Gordon, and other well-known AP advocates. May Friedman examines the paradox of feminist mothers' attraction to attachment parenting and the confusion and ambivalence that may result. Nélida Quintero interrogates the inadequacy of the workplace's response to AP, emphasizing the professional mother's need and right to adapt both her work schedule and the practices of attachment parenting to accommodate her role as a "multi-faceted" worker. Damien Riggs challenges the biological and "traditional" family-basis of AP theory and its bias against lesbian, gay and bisexual caregivers. Finally, Laura Tuley proposes a model of equal parenting that would both cater to the needs of academic and other creatively working mothers and facilitate a healthier relationship between fathers and children.

Our final section, "Mother Guilt: Being 'Good' Mothers," explores the impossible role that all mothers are expected to fill and the resultant guilt we feel when we fall short of this expectation. As we have stated, mothers are generally perceived as the main caregivers, the ones on whose shoulders rests the ultimate responsibility for parenting and therefore, the ultimate blame. Janni Aragon explores the powerful impact of racism, ethnicity, and class on the mothering experience. Kimberly Chisholm's narrative prose offers a striking yet common tale of the disconnect between expert advice about childrearing and the gritty reality of life in the parenting trenches, taking us with her into a moment of child-parent warfare in which we experience some of the worst, and the best, mothering moments. Susan Driver explores Ariel Gore's unique contribution to mothering advice books, one which invites her readers to challenge any authoritative opinion and to reject the notion that there is any one particular way to be a good mother. Angela Hattery's investigation of "intensive motherhood ideology" reveals the tension between the necessity for most mothers to work out of the home and the notions of "good" mothering that expect mothers to stay at home, and the ways in which these tensions foster divisions between women rather than a combined effort to create a more equitable division of labor. Marsha Marotta examines the white, middle-class standards of motherhood that are prescribed through the mainstream, and the ways in which mothers attempt to meet these standards through selflessness and self-sacrifice; not surprisingly, she notes that, without substantial critical analysis of such prescriptive ideals, mothers are left feeling incompetent. Finally, Jessica Nathanson draws upon personal experience to argue that mothers need an intellectual, creative life apart from their children in order to be functional, and "good," mothers.

Moving beyond our current culture of mother-blaming and empowering all those who mother to make informed and self-confident choices requires radical social change. The extension of affordable and quality healthcare to all families; the accommodation of caregivers in the workplace; the legal recognition and societal affirmation of all family units; the availability of resources, from the basic necessities for survival to the ability to live free of poverty, violence, and oppression; the restoration of indigenous lands and cultures—all of this is necessary if mothering is to be understood as a feminist and affirmative practice. In order to get from here to there, we who mother need to come together to critically examine those "expert" messages that direct us and ask ourselves to what end or in whose interest they do so. We need to plot our own journeys through mothering, based on these critical reflections and on the wisdom we acquire through our own experiences of parenting. This book is, we hope, a step in the right direction.

---

[1]Paula Caplan writes, "the mother [is] always assumed to be responsible for the problem" (275).

[2]The editors use this term to refer to the diversity of indigenous peoples of the world, not specifically to any one group or groups.

Works Cited

Arnup, Katherine. *Education for Motherhood: Advice for Mothers in Twentieth-Century Canada.* Toronto: Univeristy of Toronto Press, 1994.

Caplan, Paula. *Don't Blame Mother: Mending the Mother-Daughter Relationship.* New York: Harper & Row, 1989.

Caplan, Paula. "Don't Blame Mother: Then and Now." Andrea O'Reilly, ed. *Mother Outlaws: Theories and Practices of Empowered Mothering.* Toronto: Women's Press, 2004: 275-283.

Esterberg, Kristin. "Planned Parenthood: The Construction of Motherhood in Lesbian Mother Advice Books." Andrea O'Reilly, ed. *Feminist Mothering.* SUNY Press, forthcoming.

Gore, Ariel. *The Mother Trip: Hip Mama's Guide to Staying Sane in the Chaos of Motherhood.* Seattle: Seal Press, 2000.

Hill-Collins, Patricia. *Black Feminist Thought.* 2nd Ed. New York: Routledge, 2000.

Ladd-Taylor, Molly and Umanksy, Lauri. *"Bad" Mothers: The Politics of Blame In Twentieth-Century America.* New York: New York University Press, 1998.

Lavell-Harvard, D. Memee, and Jeannette Corbiere Lavell, eds. *"Until Our Hearts Are on The Ground": Aboriginal Mothering, Oppression, Resistance and Rebirth.* Toronto: Demeter Press, 2006.

Marrero, Lucy. "Sometimes Daddies Do Get Pregnant." *Hip Mama* 12-13 #39 2008.

O'Reilly, Andrea. *Rocking the Cradle: Thoughts on Motherhood, Feminism and the Possibility of Empowered Mothering.* Toronto: Demeter Press, 2006.

Rosskam, Jules, Dir. *transparent.* Frameline, 2005.

1.
Out of Our Bodies

Pregnancy and Birth

Neutralization and Emotion Work in Women's Accounts of Light Drinking in Pregnancy

Denise A. Copelton

In the U.S., both medical and lay experts vehemently warn against the dangers of alcohol consumption in pregnancy. The intensity of warnings has increased as scientific evidence linking prenatal drinking and fetal alcohol spectrum disorders has accumulated.[1] For example, while the 1981 Surgeon General's Advisory on Alcohol Use in Pregnancy cautioned pregnant women to "limit" alcohol consumption, a 2005 Advisory urged both pregnant women and women who might become pregnant to "abstain" completely (United States Department of Health and Human Services 1-2). Similarly, most popular pregnancy books warn that there is no safe level of alcohol consumption in pregnancy, and often conflate any amount of drinking during pregnancy with fetal alcohol syndrome (FAS)—the most serious of the fetal alcohol spectrum disorders. This article examines women's responses to expert advice on drinking during pregnancy. I summarize expert advice on prenatal drinking in a sample of nine pregnancy books and explore pregnant women's responses to this advice. Specifically, I examine respondents' views of pregnant drinkers, and for those who drank during pregnancy (knowingly or unknowingly), I explore the techniques they use to neutralize suggestions of bad mothering.

Methodology

I completed a textual analysis of nine popular pregnancy books, and interviews with 55 pregnant women in their second or third trimester who had read or were in the process of reading at least one pregnancy book. I compiled a list of twenty popular books by consulting Amazon.com's listing of pregnancy bestsellers and personnel at two large bookstores. From this list, I chose a purposive sample of nine books—two written by mothers, three by physicians, two by childbirth educators, and two affiliated with medical organizations.[2] I recruited participants between January and July 2002 through childbirth education classes at Prairie View Hospital, a non-profit serving an urban center in the upper

Stoppard, Miriam. *Conception, Pregnancy and Birth.* New York: Dorling Kindersley, 2000.

Sykes, Gresham, and David Matza. "Techniques of Neutralization: A Theory of Delinquency." *American Sociological Review* 22 (1957): 664-670.

United States Department of Health & Human Services, Centers for Disease Control & Prevention. 2005. "Surgeon General's Advisory on Alcohol Use in Pregnancy." 9 February 2007 <http://www.cdc.gov/ncbddd/fas/documents/Released%20Advisory.pdf>

A Mosaic of Pregnancy Expertise

Amber E. Kinser

This is not just an angry fracturing and breaking of unwanted images and positionings—though it is also that—but the bursting forth of the bud from the death of the female winter.

—Bronwyn Davies

When medical discourses claim that pregnancy is primarily an experience of the body, and "family" discourses claim that pregnancy is primarily an experience of the fetus and for the fetus, there need to be augmenting discourses that speak of pregnancy as a significant experience of the pregnant person. Focusing on the lived experience of pregnancy precludes the reduction of pregnancy to gestation. It allows women to speak in the public domain about all that it means to live out the forming of another human life while simultaneously crafting one's own, to understand oneself to be accomplishing this, and to be understood by others to be accomplishing this. It is likely that what many women want pregnancy to mean to others, as well as to themselves, is not what it has come to mean. By strengthening the discourses that give voice, not only to what it presently means but also to what it could and should mean, we facilitate more humane conceptions of, and therefore, responses to and experiences of, pregnant life.

Such understandings have implications that reach beyond pregnant life. First, cultural conceptions of pregnancy as subjectively meaningful process rather than merely baby production make significant contributions toward redefining women's place. Woman-as-body becomes a more complicated reduction to accomplish when childbearing—understood to be women's essential place—is accepted as significantly more than physiological experience. When women are not reduced to what their bodies do, but are viewed as mind-body and sociality, they assume subject positions that allow significant and critical participation in the construction and change of social meaning. Second, such understandings may enable partners, perhaps particularly men, to share in a level of connectedness with their pregnant partners that they may not have achieved before. To conceptualize pregnancy as a meaningful process beyond its work of making a child precludes others, especially partners, from dismissing the process as "merely" biological and consequently not meriting relational involvement or intersubjective work. Partners' participation in and connection with pregnant life can make pregnancy an experience that pregnant women are able to share with their partners. Finally, partners' deep involvement with pregnancy might well encourage their symbiotic association with the work of creating a child that can extend to the work of raising a child in ways that it often does for women, and often fails to do for partners, men in particular.

The subject positions from which persons act greatly determine the kinds and amounts of contributions they can make to the meanings that comprise their social world. Being a subject means, as Michel Foucault argues, being both "subject to someone else by control or dependence, and tied to [one's] own identity by conscience or self-knowledge" ("Subject and Power" 212). Human selves are collectively constituted as subjects through language, discursive practices, social institutions, and power relations.[1] How persons *speak* and *embody* such discourses are critical components of that collective activity. Individuals participate in constituting their own subjectivity in particular ways through "each moment of speaking and being" (Davies 73-74). However, the fact that a pregnant person becomes constitutively subjected in particular ways is typically kept hidden behind a veneer of the "natural" and "free choice." Yet the subject is not acting out of self-created or "natural" desires; nor is power emanating from distinct points imposing those desires on her. Rather, power should be recognized as networks and practices that come from all around, under, within and above subjects who participate by enacting particular subject positions (Foucault, *History of Sexuality*). And the point of any treatment of power relations must ultimately be, following Foucault, to understand the positioning and objectivizing of the human subject.

To the extent that their own speech and practice are informed by dominant discourses, women's pregnancy discourse functions to strengthen women's positioning as subjects in ways defined by discourses of power. For example, if pregnant women and conversational others allow pregnancy talk to be dictated by these discourses of power, and if they conceive of and talk about pregnancy predominately in terms of birth and children or in terms of physiology, then they participate—I hope unwittingly—in trivializing pregnant life. Yet, anywhere power operates, so also can resistance (Foucault, "History" 95). Pregnancy talk can and does have the capacity to displace privileged metaphors for the pregnant experience. If the dominant discourse is to be changed and women's experience of pregnancy is to be claimed as valid and significant, the subjugated language of women must be given voice. Kathy Ferguson articulates well the significance of such a project:

> By unearthing/creating the specific language of women, and comprehending women's experience in terms of that linguistic framework rather than in terms of the dominant discourse, feminist discourse is articulated as a voice of resistance . . . . To articulate a substantially different voice for women is to break into the dialectic of speech and social structure, changing the relation between them, and thus altering the process by which the identity of individuals is formed. (154)

The following brief mosaic of pregnancy voices is designed, not only to amplify women's pregnancy talk but also to illuminate women's struggle to wrestle through the complexities of pregnant subjectivity, particularly given the capacity for powerful medical discourses to drown out that talk and the subjective meanings that might emerge. It represents only a small part of pregnant women's struggle to participate in the naming of pregnant truths. In the mosaic, I have positioned the pregnancy expertise of several women in dialogue with the medical expertise of one physician, William G. Birch, M.D., who authored a book distributed by two-thirds of the OB/GYNs in the Midwestern, college-town community where I lived at the time. Various versions of Birch's book have been in publication since 1963, and it continues to be widely distributed, endorsed by obstetricians around the country, as evidenced by their name and office address stamped on the cover and their free distribution of it to their pregnant patients. This book continues to be published with only minor revisions. As of its 2003 printing, none of the excerpts featured in this mosaic have been changed.

The women's voices in my mosaic are drawn largely from personal interviews I conducted with several women from that same community about their current or past pregnancies who also were likely recipients of this book during their pregnancies. I have used pseudonyms here and in my previous works from which I draw excerpts; two of the excerpts I've included are from published prose and poetry. The women's voices are identified by italics.

My hope is that these few pages might play a part in the larger cultural performance represented by *Mother Knows Best,* in resisting and insisting: resisting mightily the primacy of medical expertise in articulating pregnant meaning, and insisting mightily that women's experience of pregnancy be honored in all of its fullness.

* * * * *

Grace is four months pregnant.... Grace has an amniocentesis in Los Alamos and a midwife in Taos. As a maternity outfit she is wearing a lot of red lipstick.... Grace has gained twenty pounds from eating cake.... Mary Ann will have her baby at home in three weeks. It is a good way to frighten her mother-in-law. Mary Ann is an ex-heroin addict which now makes her very suburban.... She is wearing a purple mumu and a migraine headache. Mary Ann has gained sixty-five pounds and her husband won't let her cut her hair. (Sagan 51)

The best way to get the most out of your pregnancy—to insure an enjoyable experience—is to obtain the most accurate information. (Birch 1)

Actually, I believe that I wasn't as scared of the pain as I was scared of this thing with which I was so unfamiliar. I mean, I just didn't know what to expect. And so in order to be prepared, in order to feel like you know what to expect you read up on everything, you take childbirth class, you ask everybody, and then you've got all these experiences, many of them scary, and you still haven't sorted out what to expect. And it's all just quite overwhelming... (Elaine[2])

Being informed will prevent anxiety and worry and will make your nine months more pleasant and secure. (Birch 1)

...but that's pretty much what the worst part was, was the fear of the birth. And that didn't become salient until I took my childbirth classes and I was faced with all this information that I almost sometimes wish I hadn't been faced with. (Elaine[3])

There is no substitution for your doctor's advice, and this is a good time to caution you against well-meaning friends who are dying to tell you about their road to motherhood. (Birch 9)

My brother's wife, Debbie, she wrote me almost every month with stories of her pregnancy and she had two babies in January. She'd say "Oh, I love winter babies and you're gonna enjoy your little baby." Talked about how kids don't need all this stuff, they just need a lot of love. And all these little philosophies.... (Liz[4])

The old wives' tales and free advice are worth exactly what they cost—nothing! (Birch 9)

...and I would write her back. And then the first I saw her after all this letter writing, I just felt like, oh, you know, thank you so much. Really. (Liz[5])

If you do have any fears or misgivings, confide them to your doctor or nurse. (Birch 9)

I talked with my mother-in-law more during this pregnancy. It was during the beginning, I think, when I was afraid for a while that I was gonna miscarry again. I was really worried about that ... (Tammy[6])

confide them to your doctor or nurse. Only they are equipped to give you the facts. (Birch 9)

...I was worried, you know. And real unsure and I called, I think, for a lot of support from my mother-in-law because you know, she was a friend of mine anyway. And so you know, I would call her up just to, just to talk, and tell her, and I knew she was actually interested in me as a person. (Tammy[7])

All these anxieties can be easily assuaged by bringing them out into the open. An intelligent rather than emotional look at the answers to these questions will help you put an end to any apprehensions. (Birch 22)

against bone. rubbing. pressure against bladder
i pee and pee and pee
and drink water and more water. never enough water
it twists in my womb
my belly a big brown bowl of jello quakes
twenty pounds and climbing
eat eat eat. milk. got to have ice cold milk.
vitamins and iron three times daily
cocoa butter and hormone cream
infanstethescope
sex sex sex. can't get enough of that funky stuff (Coleman 69)

What about the relationship between you and your husband? Will it change? Will it undergo some stress? (Birch 22)

They'd say like you shouldn't lift anything, and you should always sleep, and your husband or whoever should do everything for you, and you shouldn't lift a finger you know. And I'd try that. And he'd be like, fuck you. Yeah sure. (Andrea[8])

Unless you are most unusual, it will, of course. For one thing, sex patterns may change. And you both my find yourselves growing impatient for it to be over with, especially toward the end. (Birch 22)

I remember telling him lots of times that I wanted to strap a bowling ball around his belly and let him walk around for a day. Just so he would know, like, when I did complain, that it was legitimate. I think he knew that I was uncomfortable sometimes, but that he got tired of me saying it. If there's nothing he can do about it, then, then he doesn't really want to hear it all the time. Which is, I mean, that's fair, I guess. I kept saying that I wanted, I wanted him just for a little while, just for an hour, to be able to carry the baby around just so he would know. (Beth[9])

This impatience may some times be released against one another. But again, unless you are unusual, most of these problems can be ironed out with goodwill and common sense. (Birch 22-23)

If I had any common sense I wouldn't be pregnant! I've done this twice already. Do you think that if I had any common sense I would do this to myself again? (Rebecca[10])

But again, unless you are unusual, most of these problems can be ironed out with goodwill and common sense. (Birch 22-23)

His idea of, like, helping, he would help me wash dishes even. I mean maybe in reality he only helped maybe two or three times a year. To actually even wash dishes in the sink. But in his mind, he was talking like two or three times a week. Or more. I mean, that's what he saw that as. And, I wasn't prepared for that. I mean, being pregnant or not, I wasn't prepared for the fact that he would have this idea so much that this is her work, and this is mine. My job is to go to work and bring home the bacon, and hers is to do everything else, at the house. And you know, he just wasn't there to support me, I guess, very much. (Lori[11])

Anytime such groundless fears loom on your subconscious mind, simply remember that having babies is a perfectly normal and natural function. (Birch 23)

You know, uh, I don't think he understands the factor of, you know, sometimes sex hurts. Sometimes, you know, you get these little aches and pains during it and, and it's like a total turn off. I'm wondering "Oh my god, what was that?" you know. And that, that for me is a total turn off whenever, you know, my mind isn't into it, I'm wondering, "What was that?" Afterwards, whenever the next day I'd wake up, and there'd be blood there, things like that and I mean, all the way through he's been really good about understanding things, but I don't think he understands that part. (Marie[12])

an intelligent rather than an emotional look at the answers to these questions will help you put an end to any apprehensions. (Birch 22)

To my husband, it's technical. It's physical. Um, you know, these are the stages of development, this is what she should be going through. And, he doesn't, it's frustrating that he does not attach the emotional issue to it.... I'm not sure he understands. Like the issue when I was crying over a dream I had about my mom because my mom would never be able to see my daughter, you know. And he's like "Well, why are you crying over your mother? She's been dead for years." You know, it was like he doesn't understand. He's a very logical person. But it was like, "Why don't you understand?" (Stephanie[13])

simply remember that having babies is a perfectly normal and natural function. (Birch 23)

I was just thinking this morning that nobody ever told me that being pregnant was like something you would see on Star Trek or an Alien kind of thing. I mean, like, nobody ever told me that's what it would feel like. ... I kept thinking that I was just gonna pop open and out was gonna come this thing out of me. (Jamie[14])

...simply remember that having babies is a perfectly normal and natural function. (Birch 23)

*   *   *   *   *

Most of the women with whom I have spoken about pregnancy had no doubt that they spoke the language of "pregnantness" proficiently. They were interested in enriching their own renderings by learning from medical discourse. But they were thwarted in their efforts to negotiate the "terms" of pregnancy with others. When their articulations of pregnant experience were not considered an integral part of the ongoing cultural conversation, they had to work at sustaining the

31

belief that it was *they* who spoke the mother tongue of pregnancy.

May women always resist the primacy of medical discourse in defining all that pregnancy is. May we react in our talk against the disregard for and deprecation of our own unique knowledge of pregnant meaning, and the ways in which pregnant living has brought us to this knowing place. May women insist on talking about pregnancy in languages that emphasize subjective experiences of pregnancy that embrace, and value, and wonder about pregnant selfhood.

[1]See Foucault, *Discipline and Punish: The Birth of the Prison* and *The History of Sexuality: An Introduction,* Volume 1. See also feminist poststructuralist work in Davies, "Women's Subjectivity and Feminist Stories." See also Foucauldian feminist work in Ferguson, *The Feminist Case against Bureaucracy.*

[2]Kinser, Amber E. "The Politics of Pregnancy Discourse." Presented at the Speech Communication Association Convention. New Orleans, LA. 1994. 14-15.

[3]Kinser, "Politics" 14-15.

[4]Kinser, Amber E. "Tension and Fluidity: Self and Relationship Change in Pregnancy." Presented at the Speech Communication Association Convention. Miami, FL. 1993. 20.

[5]Kinser, "Tension" 20.

[6]Kinser, Amber E. Unpublished interview notes. "Tammy," 1993. 11.

[7]Kinser, Unpublished interview notes, "Tammy" 11.

[8]Kinser, Amber E. "Pregnant with Meaning: An Interpretive Analysis of Women's Pregnancy Talk." Doctoral dissertation. Purdue University. 1997. 238.

[9]Kinser, "Pregnant with Meaning" 239.

[10]Kinser, Unpublished interview notes, 1997. "Rebecca" 4.

[11]Kinser, "Pregnant with Meaning" 236.

[12]Kinser, "Pregnant with Meaning" 242.

[13]Kinser, "Pregnant with Meaning" 256.

[14]Kinser, Amber E. "Tension" 14.

Works Cited

Birch. William G. *A Doctor Discusses Pregnancy.* Chicago: Budlong Press Company, 1993.

Coleman, Wanda. "Giving Birth." *Cradle and All: Women Writers on Pregnancy and Birth.* Ed. Laura Chester. Boston: Faber and Faber, 1989. 69-70.

Davies, Bronwyn. "Women's Subjectivity and Feminist Stories." *Investigating Subjectivity: Research on Lived Experience.* Ed. Carolyn Ellis and Michael G. Flaherty. Newbury Park: Sage, 1992. 53-76.

Ferguson, Kathy. E. *The Feminist Case against Bureaucracy*. Philadelphia: Temple University, 1984.

Foucault, Michel. *Discipline and Punish: The Birth of the Prison*. New York: Vintage Books, 1977.

Foucault, Michel. *The History of Sexuality: An Introduction*. Volume 1. New York: Vintage Books, 1978.

Foucault, Michel (1982). "Subject and Power." *Beyond Structuralism and Hermeneutics*. Eds. H. Dreyfus and P. Rabinow. Chicago: University of Chicago Press, 1982. 208-226.

Kinser, Amber E. "Tension and Fluidity: Self and Relationship Change During Pregnancy." Paper presented at the 1993 Speech Communication Association Convention, Miami, FL, 1993.

Kinser, Amber E. "The Politics of Pregnancy Discourse." Presented at the Speech Communication Association Convention. New Orleans, LA. 1994.

Kinser, Amber E. *Pregnant with Meaning: An Interpretive Analysis of Women's Pregnancy Talk*. Doctoral dissertation. Purdue University, 1997.

Sagan Miriam. "Heroines." *Cradle and All: Women Writers on Pregnancy and Birth*. Ed. Laura Chester. Boston: Faber and Faber, 1989. 51-52.

Creative Gestation

Escaping Polarization in Pregnancy and Childbirth Poetry

Laura Major

One needs to listen, more carefully than ever, *to what mothers are saying* today through their economic difficulties and beyond the guilt that a too existentialist feminism handed down, through their discomforts, insomnias, joys, angers, desires, pains and pleasures....
> —Julia Kristeva, "Stabat Mater"

When we consider the words "mother knows best," we instinctively think about a mother's intuition and feeling. Intuition and feeling indeed contribute to why mother knows best, but if we are to offer a rational defense for this knowledge, we cannot appeal solely to these affective states. My defense for mother knowing best grows out of the polarization that the binary of nature/culture has engendered. This binary reveals itself, on one hand, in advice books that appeal solely to the "natural" view of parenting, and, on the other, in the medicalization and objectification of reproduction and the critique thereof. Moreover, this binary is ever-present in the everyday choices that mothers need to make. I want to argue that the nature of a theoretical discussion on the issues of reproduction, whether in academia or in popular culture, is polarizing. The theorist or pregnancy and childbirth expert must take a stand in relation to the culture/nature binary if s/he is to make a lucid argument or present coherent advice. When mothers talk, however, *especially through the genre of poetry*, the binary opposition is transcended.

The above epigraph does not strike one as startling on first reading. In fact, it seems rather commonplace, certainly not one of Julia Kristeva's more complex or sophisticated theoretical musings. Yet it is the very simplicity of her suggestion—to listen to what mothers are saying—that is so surprising, for it reveals the preeminent theorist recognizing the limits of theory "to approach the dark area that motherhood constitutes for a woman" (179). The personal, the autobiographical, the experiential, and, I argue, the poetical, express more than theory, articulating those very "discomforts, insomnias, joys, angers, desires, pains and pleasures" that Kristeva mentions. Pregnancy, according to Kristeva, is "the threshold of culture and nature" (183). To enunciate this unique position, women need to tap into its potentialities, into what has been repressed, and bring their individual experiences to the fore. Lyric poetry is a powerful avenue for this expression.

Unlike in theory, where consistency is necessary for coherency, in lyric poetry poets contract ideas rather than expanding on them. The poet can critique culture and society, make psychoanalytical insights, provide phenomenological descriptions, construct subjectivity, and enact relationality all at once. Poetic language, according to E. Warwick Slinn, has the unique potential to expose or disrupt the norms reiterated by the speaker: "Through fixing cultural process in language ... poetry may enact that confusion of reference or exposure of incoherence which is at once formalist display and cultural critique" (68). Thus the poet can both present and undermine a single viewpoint.

Poetry cannot replace advice books or theoretical discourse, nor does it purport to, but it can offer us a different mode of seeing ourselves as mothers. Indeed, the reader of poetry will be drawn into intersubjective relations with the "I" constructed in the text. Eleanor Rosch, an evolutionary psychologist, suggests the enormous potential for the reader inherent in narrative art forms, including poetic self-narrative. Art forms, "by the very fact of being perceived as representational rather than real," loosen up something within us and enable us to see differently (244).

My emphasis on the personal, especially in the genre of poetry, not only opposes the purely theoretical, but also opposes the nature/culture divide within theory. The nature/culture, origin/representation, cause/effect divide, or more specifically the essentialist/anti-essentialist divide, continues to dominate and polarize feminist discourse. But *"culture" and "nature" inadequately describe the lived bodily experience of pregnancy and childbirth.* Rather, culture (the intersubjective), nature (the objective) *and* personal experience (the subjective) concurrently and interactively determine who we are and what we do, make and mean. Pregnancy and childbirth poetry transcends the culture/nature binary by insisting on the third axis, and celebrating the personal, the individual, yet social and embodied subject.

The Cultural Construction Side of the Binary

Cultural construction theory, which aims to expose the ways in which culture determines much of how we think and behave, is a useful tool for beginning to discuss threats to pregnant subjectivity, such as the objectification of the pregnant woman by the medical and legal establishment. One cannot, after all, change the way one sees one's body unless one first recognizes the ways in which one daily inscribes cultural messages on it. What cultural construction does well[1] is discuss the objectification and appropriation of the pregnant subject in relation to the medical and legal community. According to Susan Bordo, a practitioner of cultural construction theory, pregnant women do not enjoy the same legal protection of bodily integrity as do other embodied subjects; on the contrary, their reproductive lives are often nonconsensually controlled. In fulfilling the role of fetal incubator, explains Bordo, "the pregnant woman is supposed to efface her own subjectivity, if need be. When she refuses to do so, that subjectivity comes to be construed as excessive, wicked" (79).

While this analysis may seem old-fashioned in its attack on patriarchal institutions, the woman-as-fetal-incubator ideology does manifest itself today mostly in social and legal concerns over the habits and lifestyles of pregnant women (81).[2] On a socio-political level, cultural construction theory suggests exposing the contradictions in a legal system that denies the pregnant woman's bodily autonomy. Bordo also suggests challenging the fetal-container model by *reclaiming the view of pregnancy as an "experientially profound"* (94) event.

The poetry of pregnancy and childbirth does just as Bordo exhorts; it celebrates the personal experience of pregnancy and childbirth. For example, in Sharon Olds' "The Language of the Brag," the centrality of the "I" as the center her own experience is explicit: "I have lain down and sweated and shaken/....and/ slowly *alone in the center of the circle* I have/ passed the new person out" (my emphasis) (lines 21-24). In her 35-line poem, Olds uses the personal pronoun and personal possessive 26 times. The effect of the constant repetition of "I" and "my" is to draw attention precisely to the individual, experiential profundity of pregnancy and birth.

Objectification in the Medical Establishment

      i tried to tell the doctor
      i really tried to tell her
      tween the urine test & the internal exam
      when her fingers were circling my swollen cervix. (lines 1-4)

            —Ntozake Shange, "Oh, I'm 10 months Pregnant."

Oh, it was something giving birth
When my water bag splattered
And I screamed, the neat green anesthesiologist
Said "Why don't you shut up?"

            —Lucille Day, "Fifteen"

The frustration, emphasized by Shange's repeated attempts—"I tried," "I really tried"—to communicate with her doctor in "Oh, I'm 10 months pregnant," results not from the internal exam, but from the deafness of the doctor to her experience. Similarly, Lucille Day's quotation of her "neat green anesthesiologist" saying "why don't you shut up?" is an extreme silencing of the pregnant and birthing mother. To be told to "shut up" during the travails of labor is one rather acute way of becoming objectified.

Shange and Day are not alone in their objection to the silencing of the mother's voice. Rather, numerous theorists and practitioners have undertaken the critique of the medical establishment.[3] Iris Marion Young's version of this critique is most useful for she theorizes the problems in philosophical terms of alienation and pregnant subjectivity, while also recognizing the centrality of the personal or phenomenological viewpoint.[4]

Young sees the model of mother-as-fetal-incubator, or as Sylvia Plath puts it in "Metaphors," a "fat purse" (line 6) or "bag of green apples (line 8)," as only one manifestation of the denial of pregnant subjectivity. Other expressions of this denial include the view of pregnancy as an "objective, observable process coming under scientific scrutiny" (45), or as Plath expresses "a means, a stage, a cow in calf" (line 7). Whichever of these models dominates, it is clear to Young that the "discourse on pregnancy omits subjectivity" (45) and produces alienation (55).

Shange feels alienated from her doctor because the doctor has made decisions without listening to the voice of the mother-poet. Other poets express a feeling of alienation as growing out of the interventionist and instrumental orientation that dominates in Western obstetric practice. Linda Pastan, in "Notes from the Delivery Room," for example, describes herself being "strapped down" (line 1) in "this place where pain winces/ off the walls/ like too bright light" (lines 4-6) but unable to "produce the rabbit/ from my swollen hat" (lines 23-24). Poets, like Shange and Day, react to these threats and re-imagine their experience in defiance of them.

The Nature Side of the Binary

A woman expresses herself in childbearing. Without this experience she feels she has missed something, that she is incomplete, in some way, wasted.

— Sheila Kitzinger, *The Experience of Childbirth*

These above words of Sheila Kitzinger, possibly the most prominent figure in the natural childbirth movement, starkly exemplify the final threat to pregnant subjectivity, the equation of women, birthing, and mothering with nature.

The natural childbirth movement thus unwittingly perpetuates the age-old women=nature, men=culture dichotomy. That the contemporary home-birth movement in America is made up both of feminists who critique the patriarchal medical institution and traditionalists who want to return to family and home centered values (Cosslett 35) reveals the paradox built into an embrace of the natural.

The equation of "woman" with "mother" in Sheila Kitzinger's phrasing may lead one to biological determinism and perhaps even to the traditionalist view of "a woman's natural role." Alicia Ostriker in "What Actually" re-imagines this equation explicitly, saying: "I believe that some of us are born to be mamas,..., some born not to be. Some in/ the middle" (lines 30-31). To replace the medical model, however, with "primitive woman" (Cosslett) or nature models is to play into another fallacy. The "natural childbirth" philosophy can be "as tyrannical and prescriptive as the medical model -- perhaps more so, because it pretends to be ideologically free and supportive of individuality" (Treichler 135).

Also, the philosophical view of giving birth as primarily natural or biological, rather than human and individual, further places the subjectivity of the pregnant and birthing woman at risk. As Virginia Held argues, "the tradition of describing birth as a natural event has served the normative purpose of discounting the value of women's experiences and activities" (362). This is seemingly the risk that Sylvia Plath expresses in "Three Women" when she says: "I do not have to think, or even rehearse./What happens in me will happen without attention" (lines 9-10). When the poet places herself at the center of the event of childbirth, she re-imagines birth as something that does not happen "*arbitrarily or inevitably, without the conscious participation of the person giving birth....*" (Held 370), but rather as a distinctly human act in which she plays the center.

Transcending the Binary through Poetry

The discourse on pregnancy and childbirth is indeed polarized, and the experts on each side continue to battle it out in advice books or in the academy. Lucille Clifton's short poem "She Understands Me," in which in which Clifton praises her creative muse Kali, shows how poetry says in a compact stanza that which theory labors to convey over many pages:

> it is all blood and breaking,
> blood and breaking, the thing
> drops out of its box squalling
> into the light. they are both squalling,

animal and cage. her bars lie wet, open
and empty and she has made herself again
out of flesh out of dictionaries,
she is always emptying and it is all
the same wound the same blood the same breaking. (lines 1-9)

The poet describes a birth process that is also a creative process. It is a birth process that is natural and cultural, physical and mental, that entails bodily pain and blood, that is animalistic yet strangely human, and that encompasses a range of moods from interested distaste to triumph. The title of the poem—"She Understands Me" - seems to express the feelings not only of the poet regarding Kali, but also of the reader regarding the poet. She understands the complex and often contradictory experience of childbirth.

Clifton opens her poem with "it is all blood and breaking/ blood and break-ing" (line 1) in order to emphasize right from the outset that childbirth is not a sanitized, sentimental, or even "poetic" event, but rather one that involves bleeding, violence, pain, and tearing. The poet immediately foregrounds the physical body at its most exposed and unaesthetic, appealing to the view of the birthing body as natural. The product of this "blood and breaking" is "the thing," described as such because it refers to both baby and poem. Calling it a "thing" also hints at its strangeness and even animal-like quality, "squalling" as it is and covered in blood.

While the child is the animal, the mother is the barred cage. Yet even though the mother is "box" and "cage," the presence of her blood and *her* ani-malistic squalling undermines these images of her as an object. In this poem the affirmation of the poet's pregnant subjectivity becomes clear as the poem progresses, and the uniquely human capabilities to use both mind and body temper the animalistic or natural elements of the birth process. The body/mind interplay becomes explicit in the most crucial words of the poem: "... and she has made herself again/ out of flesh out of dictionaries." In these lines the mother transforms from cage and "squalling" creature - from the "natural" - to poet, birthing a child, birthing poetry, and rebirthing herself. All these births exude from "flesh" or nature, but also from language and culture. With every child she births and with every poem she writes, she "has made herself again." Indeed her double-bearing powers constitute her ongoing construction of self. Clifton manages to convey the complex experience of birth-giving without subscribing to any particular ideology or theory. For her, birth is an event that is natural, cultural and individual.

Clifton's mother and baby unit is isolated from any intervention. Indeed, this birth takes place far away from a sanitized hospital room with enemas, epidurals and monitors. Rather, "it is all blood and breaking/ blood and breaking." In contrast, Muriel Rukeyser in "The Poem as Mask" describes the sort of highly interventionist birth mentioned earlier—a caesarean section:

> ...there is memory
> of my torn life, myself split open in sleep, the rescued
> child
> beside me among the doctors, and a word
> of rescue from the great eyes. (lines 9-13)

What is interesting here, is the acceptance of and even admiration for what the doctors did for her. The word "rescue" appears twice in these lines to emphasize that the medical staff saved her child from danger. Rather than criticizing the intervention, which included an unauthorized hysterectomy (!), Rukeyser looks at the doctors' eyes and sees greatness. Her individual situation demands that she transcend the expected critique of the medical establishment and recognize the centrality of the "rescued child." On the other hand, that Rukeyser describes herself in childbirth as "split open" and having a "torn life" points powerfully to the potentially fragmenting impact of the operation. That it was necessary does not make it any less painful for her.

As a final example of the blurring of the nature/culture polarization, Sharon Olds' "Language of the Brag" is illuminating. In this poem, Olds elevates both the creative and procreative abilities of herself as a woman, celebrating her achievement as mother and poet. The speaker opens the poem by enumerating the achievements that she has aimed for: "excellence in the knife-throw" (line 1), to use her "exceptionally strong and accurate arms/ and my straight posture and quick electric muscles" (lines 2-3) in order to "achieve something at the center of a crowd" (line 4), "heroism" (line 8) and "epic use for my excellent body" (line7). These feats are characterized by bodily perfection and almost violent force. The speaker associates this kind of achievement with the boasting of the "cock," (line 6) the male bird known for its self-importance and arrogance. To be able to perform with the body, as does the rooster with its "cock-a-doodle-doo" or its "language of the brag," is to use the body and its language as a boast. Perhaps even more significantly, Olds rather coarsely uses the double meaning of "cock" to associate this language of bragging, bodily performance, and achievement with the male sexual organ and act. Indeed, her measure for extraordinary has always been male. Thus she emphasizes the bodily attributes, such as strong arms and quick muscles, stereotypically associated with men. The concept of epic or heroic acts is also distinctly male, with the epic hero always being a man.

The speaker has desired "courage" (line 12) to perform a heroic quest and has dreamt about the physical challenges that the hero traditionally faced. But her reality is remote from the heroic imagination. Olds constructs her third stanza to maximize the contrast between the heroic desire and the reality:

> I have wanted courage, I have thought about fire
> and the crossing of waterfalls, I have dragged around
>
> my belly big with cowardice and safety (lines 12-14)

The run-on line, which is also separated by a break in the stanza, causes us to compare the courage of crossing waterfalls with the slow dragging of the speaker. The dragging out of the line over the break in stanza further emphasizes the act of dragging the belly. Also contrasting the courageous heroic feat imagery is the "cowardice and safety" with which she drags her belly. The pregnant woman cannot take the risks that the epic hero takes; the constant fear for the baby's well-being necessitates a cautious stance.

In the fourth stanza we depart completely from the heroic domain and move into the territory of intimate pregnant biology or the nature side of the nature/culture binary. In these lines, Olds acknowledges that there are biological and not just cultural differences between men and women. She describes:

> My belly big with cowardice and safety,
> My stool black with iron pills,
> My huge breasts oozing mucus,
> My legs swelling, my hands swelling,
> My face swelling and darkening, my hair
> Falling out, my inner sex
> Stabbed again and again with a terrible pain. (lines 14-20)

These lines paint a picture that does not resemble the "typical" blooming expectant mother or the cultural ideal of the pregnant woman. Rather, we encounter the unsightly, uncomfortable, taboo aspects of the highly material pregnant body: the dark stools, the enormous leaky breasts, the water-retaining swollen limbs, and pigmented, swollen face. We also encounter the "terrible pain" of labor. The knife that she had dreamed of flinging in excellence reappears only to stab her "again and again." The speaker seems less proud of her pregnant body than of her non-pregnant taut and strong body. Yet or perhaps therefore, she assumes possession over this body. The anaphora she uses, repeating "my" through this stanza seven times, acts to claim these attributes, unaesthetic as they may be.

The stanza ends with the line: "I have lain down." (line 21)

I have lain down and sweated and shaken
and passed blood and feces and water and
slowly alone in the center of the circle I have
passed a new person out... (lines 22-25)

The speaker describes the painful, traumatic, and highly unaesthetic act of giving birth. As she does this, she understands that her earlier wish "to achieve something at the center of a crowd," to perform and be recognized, is being realized. Here, however, as she gives birth "slowly alone at the center of the circle," the crowd becomes irrelevant. The act of birth that she accomplishes alone is at the forefront; she has become a different type of hero, indifferent to comparisons with and praise of others.

At the beginning of "The Language of the Brag," the speaker is trying to contend with men on their terms. Her body is manly, and she dreams of being an epic hero. She believes that her gender should not influence her ability to attain these stereotypically male achievements. She soon realizes, however, that her body *is* different from theirs; it may be as "strong and accurate," but, more importantly, hers is a body that carries and delivers life. Olds also goes further than simply representing the two sides of the essentialism/anti-essentialism debate: while she seems to appeal to a sense of biology determining a woman's success or lack thereof in the public realm, thus undoing her previous determination to achieve in the manner of men, she comes to realize that she can achieve in the public realm in a different and even superior fashion to men.

Thus she proudly claims:

I have done what you wanted to do, Walt Whitman,
Allen Ginsberg, I have done this thing (lines 29-30)

The poet realizes that her procreative powers have direct influence on her creative abilities. She understands that if she is to be successful she must create on her own terms, as a woman, not in the language of the cock, but in the "language of blood and praise" (line 28). Olds not only has "done this thing" that poets Whitman and Ginsberg can only imagine, but she has conscripted their poetical methods to create with her experience a poem in which a pregnant and artistic self is asserted. The poet equates childbirth and poetry: "this giving birth, this glistening verb" (line 33). Although she describes the act of "giving birth" as a verb, the line also works when "giving" is read as an adjective and "birth" as a noun. Not only does she give birth, but the birth is also "giving;" it is literally an act of giving life to a child, but it simultaneously gives women the ability to experience themselves and thus write themselves in a way that is unique to them. Olds' equation of birth and poetry serves more than to metaphorically signify poetry by the vehicle of birth. She insists that the literal act of giving birth is connected in a concrete manner to writing poetry from the body and one's experience of it. To know oneself as a woman, to speak as a woman and construct an identity as a woman, requires a knowledge of the body in even its most painful and unaesthetic revelation.

The poem ends with the "I" proudly coming to see her pregnancy, her birth, and her poem as a genuine achievement:

> And I am putting my proud American boast
> Right here with the others. (lines 34-35)

She has achieved something procreative and creative that can be offered up to find its place "right here with the others." Rather than claim herself completely separate or even superior to her poetical "others," she rejoins them as American poets retaining her otherness. Olds then takes the issue of nature and culture to a different level. She insists on the nature component, sexual difference and female biology, yet she emphasizes the impact of culture and language on the achievements of a woman. She comes to understand the interplay between these elements by re-examining her own prior definitions of success and achievement, by listening to her voice and body.

Conclusion

These examples provide only a small taste of the rich body of pregnancy and childbirth poetry that continues to burgeon. The poets, for the most part, are not attempting to prescribe a formula for pregnancy and childbirth but rather to represent their own authentic experience of these events. And we see that these representations subtly critique both cultural assumptions about pregnancy and childbirth and the idealizations of the natural school of thought. This critique does not emanate from a position of expert or theorist however, but rather from the individual voice of the mother. When other mothers listen to these poetic voices, we receive little guidance on how to avoid an episiotomy or on the pros and cons of fetal monitoring. Rather, we attain a sense of the importance of the mother's voice, the mother's creative abilities, the mother's (inter)subjectivity in the representation of an authentic experience of these transformative events.

[1]It is beyond the scope of this paper to launch a critique of cultural construction, although it has been criticized for marginalizing the lived experience of

individuals, not recognizing cultural trends that empower individuals, and for privileging Western culture.

[2]Bordo cites many examples of everyday social sanction and legal action taken against pregnant women. As an example of the former, Bordo tells of a waiter who refused to serve a pregnant woman one cocktail in a restaurant. The waiter was widely supported after the case became public.

[3]These include Adrienne Rich, Ina May Gaskin, Anne Oakley, Barbara Katz Rothman, Emily Martin, Iris Marion Young, Rosalind Perchesky, Paula Treichler, Tess Cosslett, Robbie Kahn Pfeuffer and Naomi Wolf.

[4]Although Young's article is quite dated (1984), its continued citation and anthologizing in recent theoretical collections and essays is an indication of its sustaining relevance. Although dominant medical practice in the United States has indeed changed since then, and alternatives in obstetrics exist, it has not changed enough to invalidate Young's central points.

Works Cited

Bordo Susan. *Unbearable Weight: Feminism, Western Culture, and the Body.* Berkeley: University of California Press. 1993.

Clifton, Lucille. "She Understands Me." *An Ordinary Woman.* New York: Random House, 1974.

Cosslett, Tess. *Women Writing Childbirth. Modern Discourses of Motherhood.* Manchester: Manchester University, 1994.

Day, Lucille. "Fifteen." *MotherSongs.* Eds. Sandra Gilbert, Susan Gubar, and Diana O'Hehir. New York: W. W. Norton and Company, 1995. 51.

Held, Virginia. "Birth and Death" *Ethics* 99: 2 (Jan 1989): 362-388.

Hernadi, Paul. *Cultural Transactions: Nature, Self, Society.* Ithaca and London: Cornell University Press, 1995.

Kitzinger, Shelia. *The Experience of Childbirth.* London: Gollancz, 1962.

Kristeva, Julia. "Stabat Mater." *The Kristeva Reader.* Ed. Toril Moi. New York: University of Columbia Press, 1986. 160-186.

Leedy, Jack. *Poetry Therapy.* Philadelphia: Lippincott, 1969.

Michie, Helena and Naomi Cahn. *Confinements: Fertility and Infertility in Contemporary Culture.* New Jersey: Rutgers University Press: 1997.

Olds, Sharon. "The Language of the Brag." *Satan Says.* Pittsburgh: Pittsburgh University Press, 1980.

Ostriker, Alicia. "Once More Out of Darkness." *Once More Out of Darkness and Other Poems.* Berkeley: Berkeley Poets Workshop and Press, 1974.

Ostriker, Alicia. "What Actually." *Mother/Child Papers.* Boston: Beacon Press, 1980.

Pastan, Linda. "Notes From the Delivery Room." *MotherSongs.* Eds. Sandra

Gilbert, Susan Gubar, and Diana O'Hehir. New York: W. W. Norton and Company, 1995. 45.

Plath, Sylvia. "Metaphors." *Collected Poems*. Ed. Ted Hughes. New York: Harper Collins, 1981.

Rosch, Eleanor. "'If You Depict a Bird, Give it Space to Fly': Eastern Psychologies, the Arts, and Self-Knowledge." *SubStance* 30.1&2 (2001): 236-253.

Rukeyser, Muriel. "The Poem as Mask." *The Collected Poems*. New York: McGraw-Hill, 1978.

Shange, Ntozake. "Oh, I'm 10 Months Pregnant." *Nappy Edges*. New York. Bantam, 1978.

Slinn, E. Warwick. "Performativity and Critique" *New Literary History* 30.1 (1999): 57-74.

Treichler, Paula. "Feminism, Medicine, and the Meaning of Childbirth." *Body/ Politics: Women and the Discourses of Science*. Eds. Mary Jacobus, Evelyn Fox Keller, and Sally Shuttleworth. New York: Routledge, 1990. 113-138.

Young, Iris Marion. "Pregnant Embodiment: Subjectivity and Alienation." *Journal of Medicine and Philosophy* 9 (1984): 45-62.

3D Fetuses and Disappearing Mothers

Rethinking the Politics of Ultrasonography

Meredith Nash

Pregnant women actively consume and interpret the meanings of fetal imagery such that 'seeing' the fetus on the screen has become a routine part of pregnancy. Although one of the positive outcomes of ultrasonography is the enhancement of the maternal-fetal relationship, the Western cultural assumption that *all* pregnant women *should* be 'bonding' with their visualised fetus and treating it like a 'baby' is inherently problematic. Rayna Rapp argues that the proliferation of this technology in 'the West' naturalizes the agency of the fetus. I do not intend to suggest that all pregnant women are passive 'victims' of a patriarchal techno-scientific culture. There are many pregnant women (primarily white and middle class) who do not see ultrasonography as diminishing their rights or 'erasing' their subjectivity. However, in this article, I problematise the proliferation of maternal and fetal surveillance, both culturally and medically, through technologised interventions during pregnancy. I contend that ultrasonographic technology encourages the adoption of a unique fetal subjectivity that is imperative in envisioning the fetus culturally and politically, often at the expense of the mother.[1]

In creating a more nuanced reading of women's relationship to medicalisation and surveillance methods during pregnancy, I focus on the politics and power relations that are (re)produced with the use of ultrasonographic technologies. I suggest that the embodied fetus as future citizen threatens to displace the mother such that the cultural politics of ultrasonography juxtaposes the roles of subject (mother) and object (fetus) in the language of medical science and popular culture.

Understanding the Clinical Gaze

In the United States alone, more than 80 million ultrasound examinations are performed on women every year, and many women have more than one ultrasound during their pregnancy, even though the safety of the procedure is under investigation.[2] Whereas it was once used only in 'problematic' pregnancies, ultrasound is now routinely used in 'normal' pregnancies as a precautionary measure. Through ultrasound, the fetal photograph confirms the existence of a fetus and the status of the obstetrician as medical expert. There is a strict dichotomy between doctor-knowledge and patient-knowledge such that the obstetrician controls access to medical information to maintain the authority of professionalized knowledge (Oakley 46). Medical dominance is sustained by the 'clinical gaze' that regulates most women's experiences as 'patients' (see also Martin; Davis-Floyd). During pregnancy, women are constantly surveilled. For example, ultrasound machines penetrate deeply within the womb where "…what one cannot see is shown in the distance from what one must not see" (Foucault, 'Birth' 164). This androcentric or male-defined subjectivity often fails to acknowledge the pregnant, objectified woman metaphorically as well as literally in the fetal photograph. Instead, the mother's body is treated as one of quantifiable processes, or merely a contingency in the process of gestation. The 'clinical gaze' represents medical 'seeing' and surveillance so that ultrasonography recasts the uterus as a public space. This "socially embedded seeing" contains what it also produces: a fetus without a mother (Hartouni 25). I suggest the perception of pregnancy as risky and in need of surveillance normalizes medical intervention as an objective process rather than a multidimensional and subjective process.

Although ultrasonographic technology is useful as a diagnostic tool in determining fetal abnormalities and sex, it also carries with it limitations surrounding the agency and empowerment of pregnant women in making reproductive decisions. Rather than being merely an informed choice, Janice Raymond equates reproductive technology rhetoric with "technological determinism" for the reason that it makes moral and social judgments in favor of 'expert' opinions and not necessarily the concerns of women (125).

The dominant paradigm of "fetus without mother" I draw upon is conceived from the expectation that ultransonography is used as a means of defining and realising pregnancy. By gathering more detailed knowledge about the fetus through technology, the fetus is placed in opposition to the mother as patient. Whereas early diagnosis of pregnancy was external and visible with a growing belly, in contemporary obstetrics, the 'diagnosis' of pregnancy is reliant upon sophisticated imaging techniques which centre on the fetus. Due to the historical construction of pregnancy as a "condition of the woman," and continuing in recent decades, "the technology that makes the baby/fetus more 'visible' potentially renders the woman *invisible*" (Rothman 113). In the photograph, the fetus is no longer an 'object' of the pregnant woman's body, but rather is constituted as a 'subject.' As advancing medical technology alters our perception of what being 'human' is, the social recognition of fetus as person has come at increasingly earlier stages of pregnancy, and this humanisation has only come with the negation of maternal bodily space. In contemporary ultrasound imaging, the fetus exists alone in a black hollow shelter representing no connection to its mother. Through ultrasound, women become 'uterine environments,' sites for public inspection and surveillance (Duden 24). At twelve weeks (and often much earlier), it is possible to explicitly 'see' the fetus in the womb with human movements, resulting in the recognition of fetal personhood much earlier in development than ever before (Blank 104). In our culture of 'choice,' it seems paradoxical that this embedded sense of individualism confers personhood without the community and interpersonal relationships that forge persons as truly 'human.' As a routine part of medicalised pregnancy, ultrasonography is necessary and desirable in providing a window to fetal development. Thus, the fetus becomes less of a biological abstraction and more of an individual before actually being born.

Photographic 'Seeing' as 'Truth'

In examining the perception of the fetus as complex and personified, it is necessary to investigate the ways in which a certain 'truth' or 'reality' is produced by photographic images, similar to those used in ultrasound. Ultrasound, as a radical technology, challenges our basic assumptions about 'seeing' both politically and aesthetically. The significant role that the visual plays in Western culture is indicative of the paramount importance extended to information derived from seeing. This is often more useful than information gained through other senses. As photographs are an attempt to appropriate reality, cement it in history, and "furnish evidence," it is under the 'presumption that something exists' that fosters the belief that we know more about the world so long as it has been visualized (Sontag 5). Lisa Mitchell and Eugenia Georges claim this phenomenon exemplifies the "cultural valorisation of the visual" (378). The use of photography during ultrasound is a means of contending with the unknown. Photographs strategically transform fetuses into "found objects" with the seemingly unproblematic insistence that fetuses have always 'existed' as 'persons.' This increasing disarticulation between maternal environment and fetus has been cemented in law with discourses of fetal rights (Stabile 74). Feminists have become increasingly concerned with the emergence of fetal rights discourses because the privileging of fetal rights potentially encourages the subordination of women's reproductive rights in protecting the survival of the fetus at all costs. On the other hand, not recognising fetal identity can alienate many women who do see fetuses as babies.

Obstetrical science encourages the perception that fetal photography is unpremeditated, impersonal, and objective. Paradoxically, with use of photos as evidence for what is 'real,' less emphasis is placed on experience or lived bodies. For example, 'seeing' a fetus in the ultrasound photo is all that is necessary for its existence despite it being unable to survive easily outside of the womb. The isolation of the fetus from the maternal environment in contemporary imaging renders the pregnant body as sacrificial to fetal subjectivity; if the mother is represented in the photo, the fetus cannot exist as a subject (Newman 88). For example, when Susan described her 20-week ultrasound to me, she mentioned that the ultrasonographer altered the sonogram photographs to make for more visually pleasing images:

> *This guy came in and used Photoshop and got rid of the placenta. The photos were really nice so we're thinking about going back for an entertainment ultrasound. I don't know if I can handle not seeing it for another 20 weeks. They got rid of all the mucky stuff. It kind of freaked me out because it [the fetus] looked very skeletal. They took so much of the flesh away.*

As the mother, Susan's body, represented by the placenta was literally *erased* from her sonogram images. In this sense, 'seeing' a fetus in the ultrasound photo is all that is deemed necessary for its existence without any connection to a maternal body. Susan actually liked having a more aesthetically pleasing image of her unborn baby, despite her body or the 'mucky stuff' being erased. As a result of this erasure or 'cleaning up,' she told me she felt more comfortable showing the images to friends and family as baby's 'first photo'.

Visualisation through photography is empowered by the Enlightenment notion that "more knowledge of objects equals progress" (Evans 109). The idea that sight is extended by photographic 'seeing' is palatable to Western culture for the reason that it is the ultrasound photographs which make pregnancy vulnerable to advancing technology. In our capitalist culture, 'seeing' a fetus before its actual birth is an affirmation of a Western "impatience with reality" in that we trust machines to predict the future and reassure us of our own bodily knowledge (Sontag 65). For instance, some women appreciate 'seeing' their fetus in the ultrasound as reassurance because they have not yet felt it move. In this sense, the technology can actually supersede a woman's own bodily knowledge by providing access to information about the fetus that has not yet been derived corporeally.

The medical professional is imperative in the interpretation of ultrasound images. As many pregnant women look forward to 'seeing' their fetuses on the screen and rely on 'expert' knowledge, biomedical estimates often take precedence over that of the woman (Mitchell and Georges 379). A woman's subjective feelings about the pregnancy are often less credible in comparison to the high level of credibility displayed in and credited to photography. For example, the issue of credibility arises most commonly around 'dates' such that a woman's prediction of when she conceived is often different from the prediction of the machine. Women may be anxious about their changing bodies during pregnancy and the ultrasound photograph of the fetus provides a reassurance that the fetus is 'real.' In seeing the visual image of the fetus, pregnancy is authenticated and often women feel more comfortable telling their friends and family after 'passing' this preliminary screening (Mitchell and Georges 380).

That humanness is attributed to the fetus can be seen in such references to fetal movement in the images as 'dancing,' 'swimming,' 'yawning,' or 'waving' (Mitchell and Georges 377). The emotional attachment and social relationship between the mother and the visualized fetus is emphasized as the fetus is given an identity distinct from the mother. The woman is often referred to as 'Mom' to signify the start of her pregnancy (Mitchell and Georges 380). Similarly, learning fetal sex and assignment of gender also makes women feel more closely attached to the fetus, now thought of as a 'baby' (Rothman 123). For example, in my current longitudinal research into experiences of pregnancy in public,[3] a number of pregnant women have told me that the pregnancy does not feel 'real' until they can actually 'see' the fetus during the ultrasound. For example, Lucy[4] says:

> *I like ultrasounds. I think you get a chance to get a sense of being really pregnant. No one actually checked [confirmed the pregnancy] so when I got to 12-13 weeks and they put the ultrasound on me I thought, 'I hope I really am pregnant. I hope there's something there. I would feel really stupid if nothing was there'. Someone telling you your baby is okay, seeing it with your own eyes, it's quite a powerful medium.*

In this example, Lucy regards ultrasound technology as a tool in confirming that she is pregnant and that there is nothing 'abnormal' about the pregnancy. Lucy is also a doctor and performed her own pregnancy test; that her own 'diagnosis' of pregnancy was not confirmed by her obstetrician based on her similar position as medical 'expert' made her think that there could be a possibility that she was not, in fact, pregnant. This lack of confirmation caused Lucy to perhaps doubt her own bodily knowledge of pregnancy, despite being a medical doctor herself.

With increasingly sophisticated 3D and 4D technology, a fetus is no longer a fetus—it is a son or daughter. Despite its positive bonding benefits and my suggestion that there is no singular experience of ultrasound of fetal personhood, I argue that women are still positioned in the subordinate role in the newly formed duality with the fetus as they are encouraged to sacrifice themselves for the well-being of the fetus. Many women with *wanted* pregnancies are perfectly happy to sacrifice their bodies for 40 weeks for the health of the fetus. However, risk avoidance becomes especially problematic in the United States as pregnant women can be charged for 'abusing' a fetus (especially in the case of drugs, alcohol or smoking) but not necessarily for aborting the fetus (Blank 100). Again, I am not attempting to frame all women as passive victims. Rather, I would like to argue that it is not the technique or the 'choice' itself which creates the devaluation of women's bodily experiences during pregnancy, but the social and cultural context which subordinates women to the fetus and medical science. For example, medical-legal discourse of fetal rights, abortion rhetoric, and public health campaigns encourage the representation of fetuses as 'babies' and pregnant women as merely incubators. This is directly linked with the scientific and cultural imaging of the fetus. Of course, American women experience their relationship to the politics of fetal rights differently on the basis of class, race, sexuality and religious background. For example, the rules of self-sacrifice in pregnancy are commonly seen as the inevitable path to motherhood for many middle-class women. In contrast, poor women are seen as ill-equipped to make responsible choices simply because they do not have the means to finance a legal battle. In addition, whether the pregnancy is planned or not can affect a woman's perception of the fetus as a 'baby' or 'parasite' (Oaks 2001).

'Seeing' and Surveillance

The observational mechanisms of the Panopticon, the famous circular prison architecture created by Jeremy Bentham, can be used to articulate the process of ultrasound and ideas of surveillance. Panopticism has been used as a theoretical basis by Foucault and is one I utilize to explain the emergence of visualising technology as it is defined by shaping the conduct of its subjects and the regulation of bodies.[5] Additionally, panopticism is a useful means of understanding why pregnant women willingly regulate their own behavior.

According to Bentham, the essential purpose of surveillance is "that the persons to be inspected should always feel themselves as if under inspection" (43). Using this framework, as an increasingly public experience, pregnancy demands self-surveillance. In particular, the threat of impending 'risk' is a cultural construction that encourages women to avoid pregnancy complications (Lupton 80). To explain why individuals submit themselves to self-surveillance, Deborah Lupton suggests that we pay attention to "the ways in which individuals voluntarily … discipline themselves … turn the gaze upon themselves in the interests of their health" (11). Failure to conform to 'expert' advice or the tenets of 'good' health is more threatening to pregnant women and this ultimately motivates many women to consider visualizing technologies in their prenatal care. For instance, Sally told me her 12-week ultrasound was more a moment of relief than a time for bonding:

> *I was just excited and somewhat relieved to see there's a heartbeat there because only two days before we were having dinner with friends and at that stage I was only 11 weeks [pregnant] and our friends had told of us of someone they know, one of their close friends that lost their baby at ten weeks.*

In this example, even though she was maintaining a healthy diet and exercising, Sally relied on technology to confirm that she was still pregnant and had not miscarried. Lupton reminds us that "in the interests of health, one is largely self-policed and no force is necessary" (10). Thus, the embodiment of fetuses through ultrasonography is a result of the internalization of the disciplinary power of dominant discourses through rhetoric of positive health. Through surveillance techniques like ultrasonography, pregnant women are encouraged to be 'good' mothers through self-sacrifice and avoidance of 'risk.' Technical surveillance shifts the focus of care from the pregnant woman to the fetus as the inherently more interesting patient, both technically and medically.

Good Mother/Good Consumer

For the fetus as fetish, fetal commodification is enmeshed in a spectacle in which the invisibility of the mother's labor—and her body—is central to its importance. Women (primarily middle-class) become mothers and collude in the process of self-surveillance by purchasing goods for the baby, particularly before birth (see also Rothman, 'Motherhood'). Moreover, the advent of 3D and 4D ultrasounds encourages middle-class women to view ultrasonography as 'entertainment' with psychosocial value for themselves and not a strictly medical tool, as a way of bonding with the unborn child.[6] In this sense, commodification of the fetus is inextricably linked with its humanization: pregnant women actively consume and inscribe ultrasonography with their own meanings. Women bring their 'baby' to life by purchasing items for the fetus that not only construct the fetus as a social being but also construct the pregnant woman as a "mother to be" (Clarke 57). The purchase of ultrasound photographs, DVDs set to lullaby music, and even picture frames made especially for ultrasound images suggests that pregnancy is not only a personal experience but one deeply embedded in the marketplace.[7]

In *The Commodification of Childhood*, Daniel Cook argues that when the consumer is the mother, consumerism is "purified" by "imbuing commodities with sentiment" (64; see also Miller). In this sense, buying for the child is legitimated as an act of maternal love and affirms the social bond between mother and baby. As a new cultural form, consumption forges both the identities of the mother and the fetus. Women collude in the commodification of the fetus and their own bodies by purchasing the entertainment ultrasound as a positive affirmation of the 'reality' of a pregnancy. Obtaining goods and using technology for bonding with the fetus and becoming a mother signifies membership in the social group of 'mothers.' Women who do not have the economic means to consume, or those engaged in non-normative mothering practices are at odds with American capitalist culture and defined as outside of the group.

Problematising Fetal Personhood

The propensity of Western culture to perceive fetuses as human through new ultrasound technology privileges fetuses over women. There is no question that fetus as subject has been of historical importance. However, it seems that the visualisation of the fetus has transformed the relationship between mother and child.

Although ultrasonography has the appearance of enhancing the maternal-fetal relationship through 'bonding,' it is problematic because the uncoupling of social and biological birth in the Western world has made it possible for personhood to precede biological birth. In an age in which women "desire and create fetal personhood through their avid consumption of infertility treatments, amniocentesis, ultrasound, and in-utero video services," the cultural construction of the moral primacy of birth is undermined (Morgan 55). Ultrasound disrupts a singular conception of maternity, as it also challenges what constitutes 'life.'

Whereas there are a number of women who identify with the notion of an independent and embodied fetus through ultrasonography, there are also a number of women who do not perceive the fetus in this way. In order to understand the choices that pregnant women make in relation to prenatal screening, it is necessary to reinforce that pregnancy is a unique experience. Many women do not conflate their pregnant identity with the perception that it will lead to the birth of a baby only at the moment of ultrasound (Gregg 65). For instance, some women feel their pregnancy is 'real' when the fetus moves for the first time and it doesn't matter whether they have 'seen' the fetus or not. However, as I have argued, along with other feminist scholars of childbirth such as Barbara Katz Rothman and Rosalind Petchesky, ultrasound does influence women's relationship to the fetus, and they often consider the 'baby' to be an independent entity upon seeing an image on the ultrasound screen.

In discussing the varied ways in which women relate to the fetus, Robin

Gregg argues that "the medical model [of pregnancy] does not address women's social locations or the possible conflict between disparate aspects of a woman's life…the model implicitly assumes the existence of a conflict between the woman and her developing fetus" (79). Emily Abel and Carole Browner also agree that, despite the importance of women's experiential knowledge during pregnancy, there is still an "ongoing and dynamic tension" between women's experiential knowledge and biomedical knowledge (321). Although many women rely on biomedical knowledge for reassurance, I argue there are still spaces for resistance to biomedicine. Pregnant women, as 'patients,' "willingly accept the role of the object of the medical gaze, but seem to actively participate in it" (Cussins 178). In this sense, as much as ultrasound modifies the bodily knowledge of pregnant women, women also modify the technology (see also Haraway). The technology would not exist without women, and women often need technical information to make informed choices during pregnancy. However, ultrasound also exemplifies the ways in which biomedicine is assumed to sharpen women's experiential knowledge of pregnancy to the extent that women's bodily knowledge may be seen as less credible as it competes with technological knowledge.

Due to the routinization of ultrasound technology, the popularisation of visual images of the fetus as well as political movements such as anti-abortionism, the maternal-fetal relationship is constructed as antagonistic. As long as mother and fetus are considered to be separate, sympathy is generated from the fetus as the 'victim' of a hostile maternal environment. This construction does not reflect the individual experiences of pregnant women who construct their relationship to their fetus as dynamic and constantly shifting.

[1]For example, see Lynn Morgan's analysis of Ecuadorian women's experience of fetal imaging, in which she suggests that 'relationality must be reciprocal'; "Fetal Relationality in Feminist Philosophy: An Anthropological Critique" and "Imagining the Unborn in the Ecuadorian Andes."
[2]See also U.S. Food and Drug Administration, which notes, 'Recent reports in the medical literature suggest that an increase in the number of ultrasound examinations during pregnancy may restrict fetal growth and that prenatal ultrasonography may be associated with delayed speech in children'.
[3]Detailed information about my research entitled, *The Baby Bump Project*, is available on my research website, <http://babybumpproject.tripod.com> or on my blog <http://babybumpprojectblogspot.com>.
[4]Names of participants have been changed.
[5]For further information see Foucault's *Discipline and Punish: The Birth of the Prison*.

[6]However, according to obstetrician Stuart Campbell, medical practitioners like himself that encourage bonding to the fetus through ultrasound find the reference to 'scanning for entertainment' to be offensive in as much as it precludes the assumption that parents have a 'natural desire to see and know and love their baby before birth' (2).

[7]See <http://www/mybaby4d.com> for more information and images.

Works Cited

Abel, Emily and Browner, Carole "Selective Compliance with Biomedical Authority and The Uses of Experiential Knowledge." *Pragmatic women and body politics.* Eds. Margaret Lock and Patricia. Kaufert. Cambridge: Cambridge University Press, 1998. 310-26.

Bentham, Jeremy. *The Panopticon Writings.* Ed. Miran Bozovic. London: Verso, 1995.

Blank, Robert. *Mother and Fetus: Changing Notions of Maternal Responsibility.* New York: Greenwood Press, 1992.

Campbell, Stuart. "4D or not 4D: That is the Question." *Ultrasound Obstetrics &Gynecology* 19 (2002): 1-4.

Clarke, Alison J. "Maternity and Materiality: Becoming a Mother in Consumer Culture." *Consuming Motherhood.* Eds. Janelle S. Taylor, Linda L. Layne and Danielle F. Wozniak. New Brunswick: Rutgers University Press, 2004. 55-71.

Cook, Daniel. *The Commodification of Childhood: The Children's Clothing Industry and the Rise of the Child Consumer.* Durham: Duke University Press, 2004.

Cussins, Charise M. "Ontological Choreography: Agency for Women Patients in an Infertility Clinic." *Differences in Medicine: Unraveling Practices, Techniques, and Bodies.* Eds. Marc Berg and Annemarie Mol. Durham: Duke University Press, 1998. 166-201.

Davis-Floyd, Robbie. *Birth as an American Rite of Passage.* Berkeley: University of California Press, 1992.

Duden, Barbara. "The Fetus on the 'Farther Shore': Toward a History of the Unborn." *Fetal Subjects, Feminist Positions.* Eds. Lynn M. Morgan and Meredith W. Michaels. Philadelphia: University of Pennsylvania Press, 1999. 13-25.

Evans, Jessica. "Photography." *Feminist Visual Culture.* Eds. Fiona Carson and Claire Pajaczkowska. London: Routledge, 2001. 105-22.

Farquhar, Dion. *The Other Machine: Discourse and Reproductive Technologies.* New York: Routledge, 1996.

Foucault, Michel. *The Birth of the Clinic: An Archaeology of Medical Perception.* New York: Vintage Books, 1994.

Foucault, Michel. *Discipline and Punish: The Birth of the Prison*. New York: Vintage Books, 1995.

Gregg, Robin. *Pregnancy in a High-Tech Age: Paradoxes of Choice*. New York: New York University Press, 1995.

Haraway, Donna. "A Cyborg Manifesto." *The Cybercultures Reader*. Eds. David Bell and Barbara Kennedy. London: Routledge, 2000. 291-324.

Hartouni, Valerie. *Cultural Conceptions: On Reproductive Technologies and the Remaking of Life*. Minneapolis: University of Minnesota Press, 1997.

Lupton, Deborah. *The Imperative of Health: Public Health and the Regulated Body*. London: Sage Publications, 1995.

Maher, JaneMaree. "Visibly Pregnant: Toward A Placental Body." *Feminist Review* 72 (2002): 95-107.

Martin, Emily. *The Woman in the Body: A Cultural Analysis of Reproduction*. Boston: Beacon Press, 2001.

Maynard, Patrick. *The Engine of Visualization: Thinking Through Photography*. Ithaca: Cornell University Press, 1997.

Miller, Daniel. *Material Culture and Mass Consumption*. Oxford: Blackwell, 1987.

Mitchell, Lisa and Eugenia Georges. "Cross-cultural Cyborgs: Greek and Canadian Women's Discourses on Fetal Ultrasound." *Feminist Studies* 23.2 (1997): 373-401.

Morgan, Lynn M. "Fetal Relationality in Feminist Philosophy: An Anthropological Critique." *Hypatia* 11.3 (1996): 47-71.

Morgan, Lynn M. "Imagining the Unborn in the Ecuadorian Andes." *Feminist Studies* 23.2 (1997): 323-51.

Nash, Meredith. Online posting. 15 February. 2007. Essential Baby. <http://members.essentialbaby.com.au/index.php?showtopic=334249&hl=ultrasound>.

Newman, Karen. *Fetal Positions: Individualism, Science, Visuality*. Stanford: Stanford University Press, 1996.

Oakley, Ann. *The Captured Womb: A History of The Medical Care of Pregnant Women*. Oxford: Basil Blackwell, 1984.

Oaks, Laury. *Smoking and Pregnancy: The Politics of Fetal Protection*. New Jersey: Rutgers University Press, 2001.

Petchesky, Rosalind. "Foetal Images: the Power of Visual Culture in the Politics of Reproduction." *Reproductive Technologies: Gender, Motherhood, and Medicine*. Ed. Michelle Stanworth. London: Polity Press, 1987. 57-80.

Rapp, Rayna. "Constructing Amniocentesis: Maternal and Medical Discourses." *Uncertain Terms: Negotiating Gender in American Culture*. Eds. Faye Ginsburg and Anna Lowenhaupt Tsing. Boston: Beacon Press, 1990. 28-42.

Raymond, Janice G. *Women as Wombs: Reproductive Technologies and the Battle*

Over Women's Freedom. San Francisco: Harper Collins, 1993.

Rothman, Barbara Katz. "The Meanings of Choice in Reproductive Technology." *Test-Tube Women: What Future for Motherhood?* Eds. Rita Arditti, Renate Duelli-Klein, Shelley Minden.London: Pandora Press, 1984. 23-34.

Rothman, Barbara Katz. *The Tentative Pregnancy: Prenatal Diagnosis and the Future of Motherhood.* London: Pandora, 1988.

Rothman, Barbara Katz. *Recreating Motherhood: Ideology and Technology in a Patriarchal Society.* New York: W.W. Norton & Co, 1989.

Rothman, Barbara Katz. "Motherhood under Capitalism." *Consuming Motherhood.* Eds. Janelle Taylor, Linda Layne, Danielle Wozniak. New Brunswick: Rutgers University Press, 2004. 19-30.

Sontag, Susan. *On Photography.* London: Penguin Books, 1977.

Stabile, Carole. *Feminism and The Technological Fix.* Manchester: Manchester University Press, 1994.

United States Food and Drug Administration. "Ultrasound Bioeffects: Effects on Embryonic Development and Cardiac Function." 2005. <http://www.fda.gov/cdrh/ost/reports/fy95/ultrasound.html>.

Welcome Laughter

Vicki Iovine's *The Girlfriends' Guide to Pregnancy*

Laurie Ousley

At the time that my sister gave me her copy of Vicki Iovine's *The Girlfriends' Guide to Pregnancy; or, Everything Your Doctor Won't Tell You. Practical, Humorous & Comforting Advice On: "Morning" Sickness, Maternity Underwear, Bladder Control, Pregnancy Insanity, Stretch Marks, Sex?!! Postpartum Dementia*, telling me how much she enjoyed the book, I was in the third month of my first pregnancy and had already read or skimmed through a shelf of books on pregnancy and childbirth. I had already determined that I wanted a natural birth, and had already enrolled in classes with a Bradley natural childbirth instructor. I was very happy about my pregnancy, and fairly well informed, but I was anxious, and most of the books about childbirth—conventional or natural—scared the heck out of me. After a certain point, what I needed was not information, but a good laugh so that I could relax and make it through my pregnancy as gracefully and comfortably as possible.

I also wanted to read something that acknowledged that the daily experience of pregnancy could be unpleasant—and a sense of humor would be entirely welcome. To some degree, *Girlfriends'* made clear the void I needed to find some way to fill. And judging by the fact that it has been in print since 1995, that Iovine has followed it with a new, updated edition (January 2007), *The Girlfriends' Guide to Surviving the First Year of Motherhood* (1997), *The Girlfriends' Guide to Toddlers* (1999), *The Girlfriends' Guide to Getting Your Groove Back* (2001), and that many other books have come along since 1995 that address the social issues and experiences of pregnancy, such as the *Hip Mamas* series by Ariel Gore (1998-2004) and even Jenny McCarthy's *Belly Laughs* (2004), others felt this need as well.[1]

The Girlfriends' Guides were a valuable addition to the literature about pregnancy, not because they offer good medical advice—because they really do not, and I'll get to this—but because they address the daily practicalities of living with a pregnant body, and the social experience of pregnancy that no other source really offers.

Providing Sorority

Iovine asserts from the outset that *Girlfriends'* addresses the pregnant woman's interaction with society and all that entails as well as a woman's emotional reaction to the truly astounding experience of pregnancy that is just not addressed elsewhere:

> … the experience of pregnancy is so much more than medical; it is emotional, physical and social, and I never found a book, in seven years of searching, that addressed those aspects of the experience in the way a good, experienced and, most important, *candid* Girlfriend could. … [The other books are] too detached, too calm, too neat, too *moderate* for what I was experiencing. To me, pregnancy is an alarming, charming, sloppy and sentimental affair. (xv)

This was exactly my experience at the time, and it proved more true as the weeks and months passed. *Girlfriends'* contribution to the literature on pregnancy is an important one, and its sole intention is really to offer sorority, and address the social concerns and daily practicalities of pregnancy. This sorority was exactly what appealed to me. I live far away from my family, and my women friends are scattered throughout the country. I had access to good sources of information, so it was not a question of knowledge for me, but of *commiseration*. I had wonderful conversations with the people in my Bradley class, but they just weren't the same kinds of conversations I could have with my sister or a close friend. One of the things that attracted me to the book was its gossipy, knowing, reassuring tone. I wasn't looking for medical advice, but for that missing sorority—and a good laugh.

Furthermore, I didn't think that the books with the sound medical advice actually conveyed the information with as much drama as is necessary to make their real meanings clear. When the books noted that I might be fatigued in the first trimester, for example, I had no idea that "fatigue" could mean that I might literally fall asleep while in the middle of a conversation; or that if I sat down in a quiet place in the afternoon—which, as a graduate student, I was very likely to do—I might find myself waking up several hours later. That is not my definition of the word "fatigue," or, at least, it wasn't previous to that time. Perhaps it is "profound fatigue" or "FATIGUE" or "on the verge of a coma," but there was no way that just a passing word about "fatigue" could prepare me for the real experience. Somehow, the other books never actually expressed what those experiences really felt like—or even what they really were. It's just a different thing to get clinical information or advice from a doctor or a midwife than from a friend or sister; and the sorts of literature available are generally of the medical or midwife variety. From the very beginning, *Girl-friends'* acknowledges how overwhelming the experience of pregnancy can be as well as how demanding it is on the body.

Recognizing the real void of sorority, *Girlfriends'* also addresses the daily practicalities of dealing with the pregnant body, from determining how to dress, to what pregnancy can do to a sexual relationship, to what to bring to the hospital if a hospital is the intended destination for the birth. I am not a person who is very concerned with fashion, high or low. I have always thought that if I could wear comfortable clothing that was basically clean, neat, and fit properly, I would be just fine. However, I had real issues with dressing myself every morning, managing to clothe a body that was always somehow in flux, and seemed to be sensitive to fabric, and on which clothes fit in a way they never had before.

The detached way that I write here about my body, as separate from me, was exactly how I felt at the time because this new body was not the one I had inhabited for the thirty odd years before I conceived my child. It is a pretty wild experience to see a reflection in a window and only realize once you're a block down the street that that reflection was your own. I laughed out loud reading Iovine's explanations of what the pregnant body can look like in a bathing suit, and at the descriptions of the strangeness of maternity shops in the chapter "Looking the Best You Can." I took Iovine's advice about purchasing maternity bras and underwear, as well as the "core outfit" she maintains is essential. My doctor and midwife did actually offer me advice about what sorts of positions my partner and I could try in our attempt to maintain a sexual relationship, but it would have been inappropriate for them to discuss it with as much candor or humor as Iovine does. Most of the literature just tries to assure the reader that sex is generally safe without providing much in the way of real information. I was a well-educated pregnant woman, but that did not mean that I had a handle on the practicalities of the daily experience—and, frankly, the funny anecdotes helped to relieve some of my anxiety.

Another aspect of *Girlfriends'* that should not be overlooked is its straight-forward way of addressing the reader's vanity. The chapter on clothing is only the most obvious of these addresses. I do not have an unhealthy relationship with my body, but I am not accustomed to having so much of my intellect at its service. I had to think more about getting dressed because it became a real challenge. I was always sweating. My face was always red, and I was often quite literally unable to think. On a number of evenings, my partner came home from work to find me waiting in the kitchen for him to tell me what we could eat for dinner. This was unbearable. I did not enjoy pregnancy, and everything I continued to learn about it and birth just made me anxious. Iovine's repeated assurances accompanied by the personal anecdotes really helped me to put some of my anxiety and vanity aside. *Girlfriends'* makes funny these indignities of pregnancy that may be noted in passing in the other books as physical symptoms but not as part of the emotional challenges of pregnancy. While the books and experts might note that the vitamins may change the color of your stool, they do not indicate that you might actually have an emotional reaction to that fact. They do not note that you may *feel* something about the brown line on your abdomen or the fact that it is not only your belly that is growing. Frankly, there was no way I could have known that I would have had emotional responses to such things. As Iovine states repeatedly, pregnancy is a "total body experience," and addresses it as such. Yes, I would have stretch marks. Yes, it would take nine to ten months to have my body (mostly) back again.

I did not find the book as funny upon returning to it to write this essay, and I did not make it through the *Girlfriends' Guides* that followed, but I laughed again through the descriptions of life after leaving the hospital. I particularly laughed about the fear of moving one's bowels after such an ordeal; and the fear and astonishment of having a newborn with only a vague idea about how to care for him. My own "girlfriends" (a word I would not ordinarily use, but more on this later) and the women in my family have confirmed every one of the fears Iovine lists. They're rational and they're real, and the only way to deal with them is to relax a bit and laugh.

Girlfriends' Medical Advice and Bias

Now that I have spent so much time explaining the void that *Girlfriends'* filled, I think it important to make very clear what is problematic about the book, and it is certainly problematic. While Iovine repeatedly insists that she is no expert in medical matters and that the book is not intended as a manual,[2] it does, in fact, pose as a manual, and the medical advice implied in the book supports without question many of the contemporary medical conventions of birthing that midwives and advocates of natural births are wont to oppose—for good reason. First, Iovine seems to support some of the invasive testing, such as amniocentesis and Chorionic Villus Sampling, that many of the natural birth proponents and most midwives recommend against, in most cases, because of the risk involved in the procedures. In what she asserts will be the most contested chapter, "Pregnancy and Exercise," Iovine argues that women should not exercise during pregnancy, which, she admits, is opposed to the advice women get from every other source. This seems to be a personal issue with her as she explains that she had some difficulties with two of her own pregnancies, during which she damaged her placenta while lifting weights (99). She does change the rather militant stand against exercise in the final section of the chapter, recommending walking and swimming, relating a story about a friend who exercised to help with sciatic pain related to pregnancy, but the weight of the chapter certainly argues against exertion.

Most importantly, the part of the book with which I have the most argument is the repeated assertions that one would be a fool to refuse an epidural or even choose to see a midwife. In fact, there are several pages of Iovine berating the reader who might determine (with sound medical reason) that an epidural brings with it unnecessary risk to her baby and herself and increases the risk of a caesarian section, which rational people might want to avoid (69-71). The woman who has studied her options, and has consulted with a midwife and a doctor who support natural childbirth is informed that she has been misguided by the "Pregnancy Police"; and perhaps even "those nazis in your prepared childbirth class" (67). In this case, rather than reassuring the reader, as she usually does, that she and her child will more than likely be fine, and that she will be able to handle the most frightening part of having a child (the labor and birth), she belittles the women who wish for natural birth as "frontier women" with "something to prove." She also declares the epidural "*great*" (228; 67, emph. orig.). Iovine's stated intention is to reassure the reader that "A healthy mother and baby, achieved under *any* conditions necessary, are the ultimate goals of labor and delivery," and that if labor and delivery do not go according to plan, women shouldn't feel that they have somehow failed (67). These assertions are basically true. However, there are sound medical reasons for choosing a natural birth, and these are carelessly dismissed and the women who choose them derided.

The book emphatically supports the model of conventional birth that I really did not want; and more importantly, that has been fairly well-proven to be unnecessarily harmful to women and babies. Iovine, although tongue-in-cheek as is her mode, does not seem to have fact-checked her medical advice, however qualified it might be. She also does nothing to support those who resist the medicalization of their pregnancies.

Finally, *Girlfriends'* is relentlessly gender biased and hetero-centric. The gender bias is strongest in the addresses to the reader's vanity, which I have claimed to like about the book—and I will insist that this is not a contradiction. The assumption is that the readers are married to men. These men are generally referred to as unknowing, ignorant parties, who, if they sympathize with their wives, are doing so out of their own needs, wanting to draw women's attention from their bodies and their babies to care for their now-ignored, uncared-for husbands (Chapter 11, "Husbands of Pregnant Women"). "Husbands" are interested in their wives when they find them "attractive" and fun, so remaining attractive is a real concern that becomes a recurring theme throughout the book. I think, as I said, the attractiveness quotient is an important one, not because of the "husbands," but because, when one is pregnant, much of the world seems to be focused on one's body in a way that is entirely new to many women; and because one's *own* focus on one's body is entirely different. I was never all that focused on my own appearance until my body co-opted *me*. Furthermore, *Girlfriends'* consistently asserts that men are basically useless throughout pregnancy and birth, becoming important only after the baby is born, and likely after the baby is weaned. These images of women and men are objectionable in so many ways, but, of course, the bias and stereotypes are announced in the title—it's the Gir*lfriends' Guide*, after all.

Sorority: Putting Girlfriends' to Its Proper Use

After I read Iovine's book, I asked a group of my friends who are scattered about the country if we could put together an e-mail distribution list of pregnant women and new moms so that we could be "girlfriends" and go through this together. We had friends, friends of friends, and cousins and sisters of friends join us. It was a wonderful thing to check my e-mail every morning to find a message from one of my new collection of Girlfriends about some of the physical afflictions of pregnancy, such as passing gas or belching in a crowded store; or leaving the house with spit-up on the shoulder of a black shirt only to notice it during a meeting; or falling asleep in the middle of a conversation with a disapproving mother-in-law. While it's not likely that I would share with a doctor, or midwife, or birthing class, the problem I had fitting into the booth of my favorite neighborhood restaurant or dressing for job interviews in my eighth month, these were great stories to share with the women who understood and shared their own embarrassing stories. We put everything in perspective together. When someone who was approaching her due date didn't write for a few days, we all had a good chat about whether she was in labor. And those, like me, who were more than two weeks late, provided updates on the waiting which made the waiting a little more bearable. But the group also allowed for some of the women who hadn't studied pregnancy as if they were studying for the medical boards (as a number of us did) to learn some of what they really needed to know—and allowed us to encourage at least one of the girlfriends to insist that her doctor address some of her very real medical concerns. We did what a sorority would do—we protected our own.

The Girlfriends' Guide to Pregnancy was less an advice manual than a good idea in and of itself; and that is how I and my own girlfriends made use of it. The publication of *Girlfriends'* seems to have inspired the same sort of use among other readers, judging by the many websites on pregnancy that seem to take *Girlfriends'* and its followers as a loose model. What is important about *Girlfriends'* is less the book itself than the need to which it pointed—a need which is now better met by more recent publications. The value of that cannot be overstated.

[1]I do not intend to equate Gore's series with Jenny McCarthy's books in any way other than that they address the social aspects of pregnancy with humor. The books really could not be more different. See Ariel Gore's *The Hip Mama Survival Guide: Advice from the Trenches on Pregnancy, Childbirth, Cool Names, Clueless Doctors, Potty Training and Toddler Avengers*; *The Mother Trip: Hip Mama's Guide to Staying Sane in the Chaos of Motherhood*; *The Essential Hip Mama: Writing from the Cutting Edge of Parenting (Live Girls)*; among her other books, collections, and related websites. See also Jenny McCarthy's *Belly Laughs: The Naked Truth about Pregnancy and Childbirth*.

[2]In the introductory chapter, "Why I Wrote This Book," for instance, Iovine states several times that her readers should consult their doctors regarding medical advice: "Desperate as you may be at this point in your life for someone to tell you what to do, I would feel a whole lot better if you would run any of my suggestions by your doctor before adopting them" (xvii); "It is never my intention to undermine the role of doctors in any way, and I would be forever relieved if you would think of this book as a 'supplement' of sorts to the very serious advice and counsel of your obstetrician" (xix). Iovine does remind the reader to discuss her medical situation with her doctor, but this is equivalent to any other warning provided in small print on a far more appealing, larger package.

Works Cited

Gore, Ariel. *The Essential Hip Mama: Writing from the Cutting Edge of Parenting (Live Girls)*. Emeryville, CA: Seal Press, 2004.

Gore, Ariel. *The Hip Mama Survival Guide: Advice from the Trenches on Pregnancy, Childbirth, Cool Names, Clueless Doctors, Potty Training and Toddler Avengers*. NY: Hyperion, 1998.

Gore, Ariel. *The Mother Trip: Hip Mama's Guide to Staying Sane in the Chaos of Motherhood*. Emeryville, CA: Seal Press, 2000.

Iovine, Vicki. *The Girlfriends' Guide to Pregnancy; or, Everything Your Doctor Won't Tell You*. New York: Pocket Books, 1995.

McCarthy, Jenny. *Belly Laughs: The Naked Truth about Pregnancy and Childbirth*. Cambridge, MA: Da Capo Press, 2004.

Natural Rites

The Culture of Natural Childbirth

Susan Racine Passmore

On the first night of my Bradley Method® natural childbirth class, our instructor read aloud a familiar passage. It was from Robbie Davis-Floyd's, *Birth as an American Rite of Passage*, which is a deconstruction of American childbirth in the 1980s as a hegemonic cultural process. At first, my only thought was that, "it's not every day you hear a feminist anthropologist quoted to a group of non-feminist, non-anthropologists." As a feminist anthropologist myself, I can say such an event is highly unusual. The product of this stimulus was that I began to consider the culture of the "natural" childbirth in which I was being instructed. I had read Davis-Floyd as a graduate student and I could say that her work had led me to natural childbirth. Davis-Floyd described the Bradley Method® as an example of an alternative, "wholistic" model of a birth and I knew I wanted to avoid the iatrogenic effects of a "medicalized" birth. However, I discovered that, although I avoided a medicalized birth, I did not escape cultural construction. In fact, the rite of passage I experienced was one encoded in different, and, at times, surprisingly similar, cultural messages as the medicalized one that Davis-Floyd described.

Birth as an American Rite of Passage was published in 1992. Since then there has been a shift toward greater choice in childbirth for many women and, as some have argued, a shift in the way in which motherhood itself is constructed. In October of 2003, Lisa Belkin of the *New York Times* reported on an "opt-out revolution" which found professional, highly educated and upper and upper middle class women dropping out of the workforce in significant numbers to devote themselves full-time to motherhood. These women are not driven to housewifery by unaffordable daycare options or insufficient maternity leave policies but happily chose to leave high powered positions for the same domestic sphere that feminists not long ago struggled to break away from. At the same time, feminist authors Susan Douglas and Meredith Michaels, announced the emergence of a new cultural force. "Momism," spurred on by media and commercial culture, entails

[T]he insistence that no woman is truly complete or fulfilled unless she has kids, that women remain the best primary caretakers of children, and that to be a remotely decent mother, a woman has to devote her entire physical, psychological, emotional, and intellectual being, 24/7, to her children. The new momism is a highly romanticized and yet demanding view of motherhood in which the standards for success are impossible to meet. (4)

Thus, women, especially women from middle and upper class backgrounds, are driven to new definitions of success which privilege their roles as mothers.

The question I repeatedly came to while I learned the Bradley Method® and prepared for the birth of my daughter was, what is the connection between the rituals of birth I was learning and the role of motherhood? If a medicalized model of birth embodies specific cultural values, what do "natural" models of childbirth teach about new models of motherhood or momism? The following is a discussion of my Bradley Method® experience and thoughts about a new relationship between birth and American values and, especially, a new construction of the familiar feminine identity of motherhood.

Birth as a Rite of Passage

Davis-Floyd's argument was both strong and straightforward. Birth is a cultural, as well as physical, process. As a rite of passage, birth functions "to align the belief system of an individual with that of the social group" (Davis-Floyd 10). Although in popular discussions rituals are often seen as atavistic cultural artifacts, in anthropology, rituals have long been recognized as having a significant role in the creation and maintenance of culture. Rites of passage are particularly interesting and important rituals for two reasons: (1) they are points in time that, theoretically, each individual (or type of individual) passes through; and (2) they are, often, at the intersection of the cultural and biological worlds. They are opportunities for culture to overwrite biology and for biology to lend a sense of concreteness to culture. Thus, rites of passage are lessons about the cultural world and accepted norms. Rituals work

to convey, through emotions and the body, a series of repetitious and unforgettable messages to the initiate concerning the core values of the society into which he or she is being initiated through the carefully structured manipulation of appropriately representative symbols, and thereby to integrate those values as well as the basic premises of the belief system on which they are based, into the inmost being of the initiate. (Davis-Floyd 17)

Essentially, rituals are one of those cultural mechanisms that create the difference between things that "feel right" and "make sense" and things that do not.

Davis-Floyd argues that medicalized birth serves to reinforce and reify "American core values." These make up what Davis-Floyd calls the "technocratic model." The cultural values that are transmitted through the ritual of birth are those of science, technology, patriarchy and institutions. Women and nature are managed and minimalized through the use of medical procedures such as the use of the lithotomy position, continuous fetal monitoring, epidurals, and extraction methods, which take the emphasis away from women and babies and create a situation in which medicine and doctors seem to be dominant actors. Most importantly, the technocratic model remolds a seemingly obviously feminine event into a process of science, culture and patriarchy.

The opposing set of cultural values to the science/ technology/ patriarchy/ institutions of the technocratic model are nature/ individuals/ families/ women which Davis-Floyd sees as represented symbolically through "alternative" birth (Davis-Floyd 47). In contrast to the technocratic model, this "wholistic" or "natural" model of birth is marked by a lack of medical intervention in which the mother is "awake, aware and active" in birth (Davis-Floyd 160). Davis-Floyd recognizes that the wholistic models of childbirth are cultural constructions. However, these cultural messages are perceived to be more positive and supportive of greater autonomy for women. Davis-Floyd argues that "where hospital rituals seek to impose a belief system often alien to the woman, today's home birth rituals develop out of the belief system she consciously chooses to espouse" (294).

The Bradley Method® as a Wholistic Model of Childbirth

The Bradley Method® was developed in 1947 by Dr. Robert Bradley. Grounded in ideology that values nature over science, the technique is based on Bradley's childhood observations of pregnant and birthing farm animals rather than his medical training. The basic premise of the method is that by sticking closest to nature, parents ensure the safest birth and healthiest newborn. In fact, the Bradley Method® is critical of the "artificial" breathing patterns encouraged by the Lamaze method. In his book, *Husband-Coached Childbirth*, Bradley outlines the dangers of attempts to "fool Mother Nature" through technology and medical intervention. Additionally, Susan McCutcheon, who wrote *Natural Childbirth the Bradley® Way*, argues that the method is "family-centered" rather than "doctor directed" (5). Thus, the Bradley Method® is constructed in direct opposition to the technocratic model.

Today, the Bradley Method® is an intensive childbirth preparation course taught by instructors trained by the American Academy of Husband-Coached

Childbirth® (AAHCC). The method promises the possibility of a pain-free "natural childbirth" and natural childbirth is defined as, "totally unmediated and without unnecessary medical intervention" (McCutcheon 4). The students of the Bradley Method® are trained for birth without drugs, cesarean section, labor induction, episiotomy, the lithotomy position, and continuous fetal monitoring. Essentially, the Bradley Method® seeks to avoid a hospital birth, preferring instead a freestanding birth center or home birth attended by a midwife rather than an obstetrician. The front cover of McCutcheon's *Natural Childbirth the Bradley® Way* proclaims that the method is "the most successful natural childbirth method ever—over 90 per of all Bradley births are completely drug-free!" In order to "achieve" their own "successful" birth, readers are encouraged to prepare for birth through intensive childbirth "training."

There are several components to the training for a Bradley birth. Initially, there is the idea that any medical intervention is dangerous to mother and child during birth and pregnancy. Interventions such as ultrasounds, x-ray, Chrorionic villus sampling, amniocentesis, and all drugs (including over the counter drugs) are to be avoided during pregnancy. The Bradley Method® student also strictly monitors the expectant mother's diet. Bradley believes that a good diet creates a healthy baby and a healthy and strong mother prepared for the rigors of childbirth. A good diet is defined as one high in protein which has been related to low risk of toxemia during pregnancy and may help women to avoid labeling as a "high-risk" pregnancy which may lead to medical intervention. Pregnant women are to eat a minimum of 100 grams of protein daily and abide by a set of other guidelines including daily consuming:

1. One quart (4 glasses) or more of milk.
2. Two eggs, (hard boiled, in french toast, or added to other foods).
3. One or two servings of fish or seafood, liver, chicken, lean beef, lamb, pork, beans or any kind of cheese.
4. One or two good servings of fresh green leafy vegetables: mustard, collard, turnip greens, spinach, lettuce, or cabbage.
5. Two or three slices of whole wheat bread, cornmeal, cornbread, or tortillas.
6. A piece of citrus fruit or glass of juice of lemon, lime, orange, tomato, or grapefruit.
7. Three pats of butter.
8. Other fruits and vegetables. (Pregnancy Diet)

Additionally, Bradley mothers-to-be are to have:

1. A serving of whole grain cereal such as oatmeal or granola.

2. A yellow or orange-colored fruit or vegetable five times a week.

3. Liver once a week. (if you like it)

4. Whole baked potato three times a week.

5. Plenty of fluids, water, juice, etc.

6. Salt food to taste for a safe increase in blood volume. (Pregnancy Diet)

Finally, pregnant women are to account for their diet by turning in a daily nutrition log to their Bradley instructor weekly who provides suggestions, comments and approval.

Like an athlete in training, pregnant women are also to exercise regularly. The Bradley Method® involves two types of daily exercise. The first of these is to increase the overall health, strength and stamina of the pregnant women and may include walking or swimming or any type of exercise that the woman may enjoy that is not discouraged during pregnancy. Additionally, there are specialized exercises to prepare for the rigors of childbirth. These include tailor (cross-legged) sitting, squatting, and Kegel exercises among others. These are also practiced daily and with even more regularity. For example, pregnant women are encouraged to choose between squatting or tailor sitting every time they sit. Pregnant women also practice relaxation twice daily—once alone and once with their partners—to aid in pain management during birth. Relaxation involves mediation scripts, massage, and positioning to maximize blood flow.

Finally, Bradley students prepare by increasing their knowledge to become mini-experts on childbirth equipped to take charge and challenge health care professionals who may suggest routine but unnecessary medical procedures. Unlike other childbirth preparation courses, the Bradley Method® includes a full trimester (twelve weeks) of classes. Each week there is also a considerable amount of homework. For my class, we were to read: Bradley's *Husband-Coached Childbirth*; McCutcheon's *Natural Childbirth the Bradley® Way*, The *Bradley Method Student Workbook* by Hathaway et. al.; and the *Thinking Woman's Guide to a Better Birth* by Henci Goer. Recommended for the class was Sears and Sears' *The Pregnancy Book*. To prepare for the arrival of the baby, Dr. Bradley also suggests *The Womanly Guide to Breastfeeding* by La Leche League; *The Baby Book* by Sears and Sears; *How to Raise a Healthy Child in Spite of Your Doctor* by Mendelsohn; and *The Family Bed* by Tine Thevenin (193).

Lessons in Motherhood

Gender Roles and Family. Who's in Control?

Rites of passage are always about shifts in status and role. In the case of birth, women are moving into the social position of mother. The lessons they learn are about how they are to fulfill this role. Davis-Floyd depicted the wholistic models of birth as "women-centered," and it is true that natural childbirth focuses attention on the mother rather than on technology and health care professionals. However, does woman-centered necessarily imply greater autonomy? Does natural, alternative or wholistic childbirth actually challenge the status quo as regards gender roles?

The Bradley Method® does make remarkable assumptions about pregnant women in these days of shifting and contested definitions of gender and family. Pregnant women are consistently presented as straight and married. They are also presented as holding a generally traditional role in the family. Indeed, Bradley did not divert the authority during birth from doctor to woman but brought in a middleman—the husband/coach. Bradley was the first to introduce the idea that fathers could contribute to birth and should participate in the process as the mother's "coach." Thus, the Bradley birth is family-centered but still managed by masculine authority.

Bradley employs two analogies to explain the concept of the husband/coach. They are both trainers of athletes and farmers who have sown seeds that require ongoing nurture and support (Bradley 111). In either case, they are actors in childbirth while women are not always presented so. In the 1980s, Colemon Romalis argued that the Bradley Method® encouraged an infantilization of the pregnant woman (100). Actually, the analogy is not woman to infant but rather, as noted, woman to barnyard animal. Romalis quotes the 1965 edition of *Husband-Coached Childbirth* in which Bradley refers to the childbirth class as a "hen party" and pregnant women as "nuttier than a fruitcake" who require the management of their husbands and doctors, termed "pregnancy policemen" (82).

Although more politically correct today, there continues through all the Bradley materials a sense that the pregnant or laboring woman is not quite able to manage herself. For example, coaches, not women, are ultimately responsible for adherence to the training schedule. McCutcheon encourages coaches to

> Keep your wife out of all the soft, cushy chairs at your house. When she sits in a soft chair, her bottom sinks down and her knees come up [inappropriate sitting] … If you catch her complaining to friends about how you make her do her exercises, perhaps she's actually bragging about how much she is cared for and about your active part in getting ready for birth. (62)

The ultimate symbol of the coach's authority may be the "official coach card" distributed only to male students in Bradley classes although both mothers and coaches are responsible for the same curriculum.

The Work of Pregnancy: Lessons in How to Succeed in Motherhood

If Douglass and Michaels are correct and momism requires that mother-hood be an intensive 24/7 job, then the first training session could be a Bradley Method® birth. A Bradley birth is certainly work. In fact, a natural childbirth is almost always talked about as something that is "achieved." Davis-Floyd uses this language as women who espouse the wholistic or natural model of childbirth feel "devastated" by unplanned medical intervention and see their medicalized births as "failure" and "personal weakness" (176). In the Bradley Method®, mothers-to-be work hard towards "success." Relaxation and exercise are to be practiced twice a day. They must practice tailor-sitting (cross-legged) or squatting continuously (a particular challenge in the workplace). The

Table 1: The Work of Preparing a Bradley Birth

Activity	Duration	Frequency	Time per Week
Relaxation/Meditation	40 minutes	Daily	4.7 hours
Nutrition (recording intake in daily log)	40 minutes	Daily	4.7 hours
Regular Exercise (i.e. walking, swimming, etc.)	30 minutes (two 15 minute sessions)	Daily	3.5 hours
Pregnancy Exercises (i.e. squatting, pelvic rocking, kegel exercises etc.)	20 minutes	Daily	2.3 hours
Reading (only mandatory)	30 minutes	Daily	3.5 hours
Bradley Class	150 minutes	Weekly	2.5 hours
Total			21.2 hours

Bradley pregnant woman is also on the constant alert about what she is eating. It's hard to think of eating—even "good food"—as work, but the Bradley student must also record everything she eats and count every gram of protein by researching nutrition information in protein charts or on the internet. This process can take a considerable amount of time and is subject to the approval of a Bradley Method® instructor. In addition, Bradley students still have to spend time reading mandatory texts and going to class. Table 1 on the previous page outlines all of the work expected of the Bradley mom-to-be. At 21 hours per week, pregnancy is at least a half-time job if you don't include all the extra work of preparing for childbirth such as painting nurseries and installing car seats or doing that extra reading that Bradley suggests. The schedule is somewhat daunting.

At all times the Bradley mom is cognizant of her "job" (and if she isn't, her coach is to remind her)—every time she eats or relaxes or steals some time to do her paying job. Our Bradley Method® instructor told the story of how one irresponsible former student expressed a desire to get a combination nanny/nurse right away when her baby was born. Our instructor disapprovingly quipped, "She didn't know that babies are a *full-time* thing." That is, motherhood is a "full-time thing" in which no substitutes can be accepted. The full-time pregnant woman is in training to be a full-time mom. As the opt-out mom, who devotes extra time and effort to motherhood, the Bradley® mom-to-be strives for an overachieving pregnancy, labor and delivery.

Responsibility, Blame and the Dangers of Childbirth

Working hard to "achieve" a natural birth also serves another purpose. It gives an illusion of control over a sometimes dangerous and very individual, biological process. Davis-Floyd recognizes that this is achieved in the technocratic model by the "standardization" of birth and medical procedures. With the exception of medical procedures, the Bradley Method® too introduces birth as a regular and predictable process. In fact, Bradley goes so far as to introduce the idea that women follow predictable patterns of emotional responses to birth. McCutcheon introduces an "emotional map of labor" which includes:

> 1. Excitement—The beginning of labor before "serious" contractions begin. McCutcheon includes an illustration of a smiling woman depicting this stage on the emotional map.
> 2. Seriousness—The smile is wiped away and the laboring woman gets down to business.
> 3. Self-doubt—This stage, McCutcheon reports, "Really means that you are almost done." (115)

The final stage in the emotional map of labor, "Self-doubt," refers to the transition stage of labor in which, it is believed, many women "crack" and request pain relieving drugs. This rhetoric reinforces the idea that there is a regular and reassuring process of birth. It is also an example of how the autonomy of laboring woman is curtailed—she is not rationally making a decision but experiencing a "classical shaky moment of doubt" (McCutcheon 12).

Additionally, if pain is experienced, it is often presented as an effect of poor discipline. The laboring woman who feels pain lacks preparation and concentration. McCutcheon reports that, "the woman who has already decided before labor that it definitely will be painful is almost certain to find it so. Like water taking the shape of its container, experiences often take the shape of expectations" (99). Thus, responsibility (and blame) is in the hands of the pregnant woman.

While the technocratic model controls women by encouraging the idea that all births that don't occur in hospitals are dangerous, natural models of birth emphasize the danger of biomedicine (Davis-Floyd 179-184). For example, one evening, our instructor told us that "we live in a world where they have to put an X on you so they don't amputate the wrong arm." She also told a story of a woman who was given a lethal dose of iron in a hospital. McCutcheon also tells fearful stories of the dangers of biomedicine, although one wonders why she uses such outdated examples. She relates a story of how a botched administration of the pain reliever Demerol during childbirth caused of cerebral palsy in child in 1972 (167).

McCutcheon also warns of the dangerous impact of the anti-nausea drug Bendectin on fetuses reported in the 1980s (34). McCutcheon asks, "Wouldn't you rather put up with a little nausea?" (35). This emphasis on the dangers of a medicalized birth and pregnancy has an added effect of, again, making women responsible for controlling the danger of birth and pregnancy. During pregnancy, women control possible dangers by applying discipline and following the rules. "Each woman must realize that she is the final guardian of her unborn child.... The best thing you can do is simply take no chances," warns McCutcheon (39).

Every part of the Bradley Method® is to be strictly followed to evade the dangers of childbirth. Reading and class materials prepare mothers to guard against unnecessary medical procedures. Exercises and relaxation practice are to create a "painless" birth and to get women beyond that "shaky moment of doubt" so that they do not give in to pain medication. Diet during pregnancy, like breastfeeding, is intended to create a healthy and, perhaps, super baby. As McCutcheon cautions, "When your child is born he may be intelligent and healthy enough, but you will never know how much smarter and healthier he could have been if you had eaten properly" (31).

Conclusion

"Natural" birth teaches several lessons about motherhood. The first of these is about traditional family and gender roles. In the Bradley Method® there is not a subversion of patriarchy. There is an assumption of a traditional (married, straight) couple in which there is a more or less traditional balance of power. During birth and pregnancy, women are not in control but rather managed by husband-coaches and their Bradley instructors. The ultimate goal of a natural birth is a healthy baby not a powerful mother. Bradley students learn to put their desires or needs last as they strive to "achieve" that goal.

The Bradley Method® presents a world in which it would seem that through hard work and devotion mothers can control everything from contractions to child intelligence. Ultimately, however, women are themselves controlled and caught in feelings of guilt even before their child's first breath. The women who sought a natural childbirth in Davis-Floyd's sample were "devastated" when their births involved unplanned medical interventions. The formation of a new identity is in play as self-blame leads new mothers to shame and, even, negative feelings about their worth as women and as mothers (Davis-Floyd 243). The artificial conviction that unpredictable events can be controlled means that women have to put enormous energy into the task at hand, whether pregnancy, birth or motherhood (if they love their babies). Failure means that one didn't work hard (or love their baby) enough. Thus, "opting out" and "momism" feel like natural choices to many women amidst a constellation of choices and meanings of motherhood.

Works

Bradley, Robert. *Husband-Coached Childbirth*. New York: Bantam Books, 1996.

Davis-Floyd, Robbie. *Birth as an American Rite of Passage*. Berkeley: University of California Press, 1992.

Douglas Susan, and Meredith Michaels. *The Mommy Myth : The Idealization of Motherhood and How It Has Undermined All Women*. New York: Free Press, 2004.

Goer, Henci. *Thinking Woman's Guide to a Better Birth*. New York: Perigee Trade, 1999.

La Leche League. *The Womanly Art of Breastfeeding*. New York: Plume, 2004.

McCutcheon, Susan. *Natural Childbirth the Bradley® Way*. New York: Penguin, 1996.

Mendelsohn, Robert S. *How to Raise a Healthy Child in Spite of Your Doctor.* Toronto: Ballantine Books, 1987.

"Pregnancy Diet." *The Bradley Method.* 8 January 2007 Online: http://www.bradleybirth.com/PD.aspx>.

Romalis, Coleman. "Taking Care of the Little Woman: Father-Physician Relations during Pregnancy and Childbirth." *Childbirth: Alternatives to Medical Control.* Ed. Shelly Romalis. Austin: University of Texas Press, 1981.

Sears, William, Martha Sears et. al. *The Baby Book: Everything You Need to Know About Your Baby from Birth to Age Two.* New York: Little, Brown and Company, 2003.

Sears, Martha and William Holt. *The Pregnancy Book: Month-by-Month, Everything You Need to Know From America's Baby Experts.* New York: Little, Brown and Company, 1997.

Thevenin, Tine. *The Family Bed.* New York: Perigee Trade, 1987.

2.
Is Breast Always Best?

Breastfeeding

Deconstructing Discourse

Breastfeeding, Intensive Mothering and the Moral Construction of Choice

Stephanie Knaak

In North America today, breastfeeding promotion has become a centrepiece of pre- and post-natal health programming, and most new mothers intend to breastfeed (Health Canada "Canadian Perinatal Health Report" 9; Li et al. 1199). That said, initiation and duration rates remain variable. In general, the highest rates for breastfeeding tend to be found among mothers who are well educated, white, middle class, over the age of 25, and married to men who earn family wages (Health Canada "Canadian Perinatal Health Report" 10; Millar and Maclean 27; Dennis 12, AAP "Breastfeeding" 1036). Higher rates are also found among mothers not employed in the paid labour force—as well as those on maternity leave and mothers working part-time (Lindberg 239; Frank 1082-1083).

This socio-demographic variability raises some questions about the notion of choice in infant feeding. In this paper, I argue that the location of breastfeeding discourse within the ideology of intensive mothering constructs an environment of choice which is morally-based, implicitly judgmental, contradictory and constraining. In such an environment, the very foundation of "choice" collapses, leaving in its wake a decision-making and experiential environment characterized by the emotional burdens of success, failure, and what is required to be a "good" mother.

Today's dominant infant-feeding discourse is organized by a broader belief system about what constitutes "good parenting" in Western societies today. Sharon Hays calls this belief system "the ideology of intensive mothering." She argues that this ideology has become increasingly powerful over the past century. According to Hays, the ideology of intensive mothering "tells us that children are innocent and priceless, that their rearing should be carried out primarily by individual mothers and that it should be centered on children's needs, with methods that are informed by experts, labor-intensive, and costly" (21).

Hays also argues that the tenets of intensive mothering ideology exist in contradiction with contemporary capitalism's logic of self-interested gain: "in a society where the logic of self-interested gain seems to guide behavior in so many spheres of life, one might wonder why a logic of unselfish nurturing guides the behavior of mothers ... in no previous period is the distinction between what is appropriate in relation to mothering and what is appropriate in the outside world at greater odds" (x, 69). Hays suggests the reason *why* intensive mothering has become so powerful in recent decades is because it functions as one of the most powerful counter-discourses to capitalist structures and values.

How, then, is contemporary breastfeeding discourse influenced by the ideology of intensive mothering? First of all, today's dominant infant-feeding discourse—and intensive mothering ideology more generally—draws heavily on science to confirm the veracity of the "good mothering" practices it promotes. It is an "expert-guided" discourse. However, many of the expert claims about breastfeeding are themselves ideologically infused. The current push for exclusive breastfeeding draws heavily on the idea that scientific research is unequivocal: breastfeeding provides myriad significant short and long-term health benefits, and the risks of not breastfeeding could be potentially catastrophic (Law 407-449; Knaak "Shifting Context of Choice" 204-211). However, a critical mining of the research reveals this to be an exaggerated interpretation (Knaak "Breastfeeding Discourse" 413; Law 414; Blum "Mothers, Babies, and Breastfeeding" 295).

For one, studies that *do not* uphold the presumption that breast milk is a baby's "miracle food" often go unrecognized and tend to have little clout in framing the state of the discourse. Take, for example, the popular claim that breastfeeding enhances cognitive development. While this claim is common in the dominant discourse, there is little acknowledgement that most higher quality studies find no significant relationship between the method of infant feeding and IQ or cognitive development (Jain et al. 1044-1053; J Anderson et al. 525-535).

Other "expert" claims about the advantages of breastfeeding are not actually supported by scientific evidence. Take, for example, the popular ideas that breastfeeding leads to improved bonding or closeness (Alberta Health 2; Health Canada "Toward a Healthy Future" 78), and that breastfeeding is "definitely pleasurable for the mother" (Spock and Parker 107). These assumptions are pervasive in the dominant discourse, even though available research suggests that breastfeeding is not necessarily enjoyable or relationship-enhancing, but that experiences *vary*, from pleasurable, to burdensome, to ambivalent (Romito and Lupton 240-246; Schmied and Barclay 329-331; Maushart 145-169; Davies 9-10).

As well, there is little discursive recognition that, even though the weight of the evidence concludes that exclusive breastfeeding *is* healthier than exclusive formula feeding, the relative outcomes between formula fed and breastfed babies are, on balance, less pronounced than the discourse portrays (AAP "Report of the Task Force" 579-584, Law 414-425). Marked at least in part by improvements to the quality of formula (Baker 833-835, U.S. Food and Drug Administration 1), the nutritional comparability of formula to breast milk is such that in industrialized countries "the advantages of breastfeeding over bottle feeding [to infant health] are less obvious" (Angier 168), and "whether infant feeding practice influences childhood or adult health remains uncertain" (Wilson et al. 21).[1]

A final consideration generally omitted from the dominant discourse is proper attention to the variable quality of the research. Specifically, many of the studies that show benefits of breastfeeding fail to properly control for socio-economic variables known to significantly influence health (Bauchner et al. 887-891; Law 413-423; Dewey et al. 696). As such, much of the available research does not actually demonstrate the incremental benefits of breastfeeding, but shows the significance of socio-economic status on babies' differing health outcomes (Kramer et al. 414). In this context, it is important to recognize that the scientific literature itself often overestimates the benefits of breastfeeding by failing to adequately control for other confounding factors (Knaak "Breastfeeding Discourse" 413; AAP "Report of the Task Force" 579).

The second major feature of intensive mothering ideology is the unquestioned assumption that mothers should be—and are—the primary feeders and care providers. This is another indication of breastfeeding's ideological underpinnings, reinforced in the general absence of fathers' and other care providers' potential and actual contributions to infant feeding (Law 407-412). In general, assessments of the benefits and risks of breastfeeding do not consider the degree of father/other partner involvement in childcare as an important consideration (Blum "At the Breast" 1-24). Indeed, much of the current breastfeeding advice actively discourages others from engaging in feeding activities. It is commonly recommended, for example, that babies be exposed *only* to the breast until feeding is thoroughly established, thought to take about six weeks or longer. This ideological connection threatens to further entrench a traditional gendered division of labor in childcare, and obscures the fact that intensive involvement of fathers and/or other care providers in childcare has a number of important potential benefits (for example, in terms of father-child relations, or in lightening mothers' loads and providing mothers more time to engage in their own self-care).

Breastfeeding discourse has also been influenced by the tenets of intensive mothering ideology in its near-exclusive focus on the baby. In general, contemporary infant feeding literature focuses on the advantages that breastfeeding affords babies. Rarely is the health or the interests of mothers–or fathers–discussed. Glenda Wall notes, for example, that "the benefits of breastfeeding and breast milk for the baby occupy the major focus in the literature ... those benefits to mothers that are listed in the literature are often confounded with the interests of the infant and based on the assumption that mothers will gain satisfaction from doing what is best for their babies" (601).

A second example of the child-centeredness of contemporary breastfeeding discourse is the way it calculates the relative costs of breast- and formula-feeding. One popular argument is that breastfeeding is preferable because it is "free," while formula costs approximately $2.50 (USD) per day. This argument forgets about the additional nutrition and calories (about 600 a day) *mothers* require to support the basic function of lactation while preserving their own physical health (Angier 157-175; Billingham 184-186).[2] Furthermore, for mothers who stay out of the workforce until their children are weaned, or who work reduced hours or take longer breaks in support of breastfeeding, there are additional costs to be factored in.

The ideology of intensive mothering also emphasizes that "good mothering" is expected to involve emotionally absorbing and labor intensive methods. Contemporary breastfeeding discourse involves both. As stated by the La Leche League, for example, "the needs of their babies are not only for mother's milk, or mother's breast, *but for all of her*" (White 19, emphasis added). In this context, many of the breastfeeding techniques currently promoted demand concentrated involvement of mothers' time, and physical and emotional energy. For instance, as I've noted, the recommendation for exclusive breastfeeding severely constrains the possibility for others to assist in the labor of feeding, an activity that can occur more than ten times a day in the early months of an infant's life. Another example is the dictum for feeding on demand rather than according to a schedule. Other guidelines include that bottles or pacifiers not be introduced for at least the first six weeks of breastfeeding, and that mothers alter their own diets in support of breastfeeding.

Learning to breastfeed discreetly is another labor intensive and emotionally absorbing practice expected of mothers. Mothers are acutely aware that there is public discomfort with breastfeeding (Mahon-Daly and Andrews 69-71; Stearns 308-325; Rodriguez-Garcia and Frazier 111-114). However, the onus is on mothers to learn how to breastfeed discreetly, rather than on the public to become more comfortable with the act of breastfeeding (Potts 976). As Stearns articulates in this context, "the actual labor of breastfeeding is increased because women must constantly negotiate and manage the act of breastfeeding in every sector of society–in public and in the home" (311).

Interestingly, however, the amount of energy, time and labor involved in breastfeeding—and its associated recommendations and practices—often goes unrecognized. In fact, the popular discourse often emphasizes the *convenience* of breastfeeding, even though the very notion of convenience is a personal, subjective interpretation, and available research suggests that many mothers find breastfeeding to be a physically draining practice (Davies 9-17; Schmied and Barclay 329-332).

The final characteristic of Hays' description of intensive mothering ideology is its general contradiction with capitalist ideals and values. And, like the ideology of intensive motherhood, the prescription of what is and isn't appropriate in terms of infant feeding is at odds with the capitalist logic of efficiency and self-interested gain. This contradiction is acutely pronounced in the general clash between breastfeeding and employment, a challenge that—when addressed in the dominant discourse—is typically framed as a problem for individual mothers to solve by changing the particularities of their work situations (Law 430-432). As one childcare text advises in this context, "you might consider finding part-time work" (Simkin et. al. 285).[3] This stance is also reflected in policy considerations. For example, one recent study found that even when practitioners acknowledge a mother's return to work or school to be one of the main reasons for stopping breastfeeding, fewer than two in ten recommend changes to the workplace to make it more conducive to breastfeeding (Lazzaro et. al 100-101).

In sum, then, contemporary breastfeeding discourse is framed, organized, and filtered through a powerful ideological lens—the lens of intensive mothering. In as much as the current shape of dominant breastfeeding discourse reflects and reinforces the tenets of intensive mothering, it also fails to provide a complete or fully comprehensive understanding of breastfeeding, and of infant feeding more generally. For one, given the issues of scientific selectivity, much of the professional advice and information mothers receive about infant feeding is skewed. The discourse tends to downplay certain ideas (like the labor and costs often associated with breastfeeding) while exaggerating or inappropriately emphasizing others (such as the idea that breastfeeding necessarily leads to improved bonding, or that breastfeeding is inherently convenient or pleasurable).

Finally, not only does this ideological suffusion affect the information, advice, policy and practices associated with breastfeeding, it also organizes the very environment in which mothers must make their breastfeeding decisions, and in which mothers undertake their day-to-day infant feeding activities. In this context, the push to breastfeed has become about much more than finding ways to provide babies with the best nutrition possible, and/or about supporting breastfeeding as a reproductive right for mothers. It has become a discourse intimately connected with notions of morality and "good mothering," creating an environment where mothers (and others) subscribe to the idea that "if you don't breastfeed your baby, you're automatically out of the running for Mother of the Year" (Douglas 244).

The ideologically-infused character of contemporary breastfeeding discourse has created a context of choice that is morally-based, implicitly judgmental, constraining and contradictory. This has profound implications for how mothers make sense of their own infant feeding experiences, and for their ability to mother with authority, agency, autonomy and authenticity (O'Reilly 12). First of all, contemporary breastfeeding discourse frames the notion of choice in judgmental terms, as there is clearly a "right" and a "wrong" choice.

It is also a moralizing discourse in the sense that such judgments lead directly to the syllogism "wrong choice=bad mother," "right choice=good mother" (Wall 592-610; Murphy "Risk, Responsibility and Rhetoric" 295; Murphy "Breast is Best" 188), a sentiment mothers themselves also often express when they have not been successful in their attempts to breastfeed (Romito 25; Lee and Furedi 3; Schmeid et al. 45-46; Badinter 305).

In addition, dominant breastfeeding discourse creates an environment of choice that is highly constraining, where women often feel that exclusive breastfeeding is the only acceptable or "correct" option (Knaak "Shifting Context of Choice" 204-209; Maclean 1-50). The entire notion of choice collapses in such a framework, as the underlying foundation of "choice" implies the existence of at least two comparable alternatives or options. In this respect, breastfeeding discourse shares a certain parallel with the issue of choice in pre-natal testing, in which the selective presentation of information creates an environment of "ought" rather than one of real choice (Beaulieu and Lippman 59-74).

Mothers are thus well aware that there is an expectation to "choose" breastfeeding. They are also often very committed in their desire to breastfeed, and many go to extreme lengths to ensure they are successful, sometimes at the expense of their own physical and emotional wellbeing (Schmied et al. 48) or their babies' (Cooper and Atherton 960, Kwakwa 126). Also problematic is that for mothers who, for whatever reason, *do not* live up to the current prescribed standards,[4] the potential result is blame, guilt, and judgment by self and/or others for failing in one of the major tasks of "good" mothering.

This issue is further compounded by a general discursive presumption that the ability to exercise a "choice" to breastfeed is as simple as making the decision to do so, based on the clarity and persuasiveness of the data in favor of breastfeeding. Arguably, this dominant presumption about decision-making behavior is based in social exchange and rational choice theories of human behavior—approaches which have been deemed inadequate to understand mothering decisions (Hartsock 57-70; England 14-28).

In this vein, research on mothers' actual infant feeding decisions and experiences suggests that their decision-making processes are much more complex than the dominant discourse suggests. Considerations such as financial and family circumstances, health considerations, competing demands on time and energy, issues of bodily privacy and autonomy, health information resources and support, cultural dictates, as well as unforeseen life contingencies all play important roles, as does the adequacy and availability of broader social-structural supports for mothers (Carter 104; Earle "Fathers' Role" 329; E Anderson et al. 396-397). The developed countries with the highest rates of breastfeeding, for example, are also those with the strongest public policies and programs in support of mothers, such as official "baby-friendly" maternity hospitals, generous maternity leave policies, and better supports for low income mothers (Hofvander 1243-1244).

In our current discursive environment, the demands of mothers' everyday lives—the actualities of labor, time and energy involved in exclusive breast-feeding, and the competing demands on mothers' time and energy—thus tend to be denied or downplayed, and infant feeding is assumed to exist largely in isolation of the many other practices of which it is actually a part. This obscures the fact that some mothers are more able to viably "choose" breastfeeding than others. And notably, the resources most significant to mothers' abilities to make a "choice" to breastfeed—for example, health, time, energy, physical and emotional space, financial circumstances, and personal and social resources—vary along socio-economic lines (McIntyre et al. 207-208).[5]

There are a number of problematic consequences of the current state of breastfeeding discourse. The first is that policy considerations tend to favor initiatives which operate from rational choice models of decision-making—such as calls for more education and programs to de-market formula (Kmietowicz 467; Gengler and Mulvey 172)—rather than models which attend to mothers' broader support needs. In this context, many other possibilities remain under-prioritized, including making maternity hospitals officially "baby-friendly," enhancing community supports for breastfeeding (perhaps by using postpartum doulas), improving awareness about mothers' support needs and their signifi-cance to breastfeeding success, improving cultural outreach about mothers' breastfeeding rights, encouraging workplaces and other public spaces to be breastfeeding-friendly, improving family leave policies, supporting mothers' rights, decisions and reasons for non-exclusive breastfeeding, and improving supports for low income mothers.

A second implication deals with the idea of resistance. Given the normal-izing nature of breastfeeding discourse, acts of resistance become muted and their validity undermined. This is particularly the case for women who make conscious, informed decisions *not* to breastfeed, whether because of the histori-cal association of breastfeeding with wet nursing and slavery, because of issues related to personal freedoms or bodily autonomy, or other reasons (Blum "At the Breast" 147-179; Earle "Is Breast Best" 146-147).

A third implication is that the emotional burdens on mothers to ensure success in exercising a "choice" to breastfeed have become increasingly intense and severe, and their infant feeding experiences are often fraught with worry and concern (Schmied and Barclay 325-333; Knaak "The Problem of Choice" 12-16; Maclean 1-52). What impacts do these emotional burdens have on mothers' abilities to mother with agency, authority, autonomy and authenticity? Is it acceptable, for example, that under the influence of today's dominant breastfeeding discourse so many mothers have come to claim breastfeeding as one of their "core beliefs" about good mothering (Knaak "The Problem of Choice" 12-16)? And is it acceptable that such a discourse has created an environment in which mothers feel their decisions about, and degree of success with, breastfeeding fundamentally implicate their moral status as "good" mothers (Murphy "Breast is Best" 187-208)?

How then, should we proceed? First, the blinders that assume objectivity in breastfeeding research and its dissemination must be more critically scrutinized. More comprehensive and more balanced information about various infant feeding options and their relative impacts to short- and long-term health need to be become incorporated into the discourse. Further, more attention needs to be given to the issue of choice and decision-making in infant feeding. As Law argues in this context, "infant feeding decisions ought to be explicitly understood as questions about balancing the labors, pleasures, well-being, development, and opportunities of a household's various members" (422).

In this context, the dominant discourse needs to take into consideration the full complexity of women's lives and decision-making processes, and acknowledge the *validity* of the various competing demands involved in their infant feeding considerations and experiences. Further, for all women to truly have a reasonable choice about how they want to feed their babies, the need for improved social and structural supports is crucial.

Ultimately, infant-feeding dialogue needs to be stripped of its moral and judgmental character. One way to do this is by continuing to examine the various ways that the ideology of intensive mothering organizes the very basis of breastfeeding discourse. Another way to do this is to re-focus our discursive efforts to emphasize breastfeeding as a *reproductive right* to be protected, supported, and respected; not as a measure of good motherhood.

[1]Infant health benefits include lower rates of diarrhea, respiratory infection and ear infection. Many other hypothesized benefits have not been thoroughly established, and much of the research is complicated by methodological prob-

lems (Angier 168; Bauchner et al 1887-92; Law 410).

[2]There is also the cost of nursing bras, breast pumps and bottles (if they are ever away from their babies for a feeding), and clothing appropriate for (discreet) breastfeeding.

[3]This text was distributed free of charge to all parents participating in publicly-funded prenatal classes in a major Canadian city.

[4]The current Canadian recommendation is exclusive breastfeeding for six months with continued breastfeeding thereafter for up to two years or more (Health Canada "Revised Recommendations" 1).

[5] This is not to suggest that, for some, *no* choice exists; certainly agency is always exercised. It is to suggest, however, that the very concept of choice is situated in this nexus of structure and agency.

Works Cited

Alberta Health. *Breastfeeding: The Best Choice*. Edmonton: Author, 1997.

American Academy of Pediatrics (AAP). "Breastfeeding and the Use of Human Milk." *Pediatrics* 100 (1997): 1035-1039.

American Academy of Pediatrics (AAP). "Report of the Task Force on the Assessment of the Scientific Evidence Relating to Infant-feeding Practices and Infant Health." *Pediatrics* 74.4 Supp. (1984): 579-584.

Anderson, E.S., A. Jackson, M.P. Wailoo, and S.A. Petersen. "Child Care Decisions: Parental Choice or Chance?" *Child: Care, Health and Development* 28.5 (2002): 391-401.

Anderson, J.W., B. Johnstone, and D. Remley. "Breast-feeding and Cognitive Development." *American Journal of Clinical Nutrition* 70 (1999): 525-535.

Angier, Natalie. *Woman: An Intimate Geography*. New York: Anchor Books, 2000.

Badinter, Elisabeth. *The Myth of Motherhood: An Historical View of the Maternal Instinct*. London: Souvenir Press, 1981.

Baker, R. D. "Infant Formula Safety." *Pediatrics* 110.4 (2002): 833-835.

Bauchner, H., John M. Leventhal and Eugene D. Shapiro. "Studies of Breast-feeding and Infections: How Good is the Evidence?" *JAMA*, 256.7 (1986): 1887-92.

Beaulieu, Anne and Abby Lippman. "Everything you need to Know: How Women's Magazines Structure Prenatal Diagnosis for Women over 35." *Women and Health* 23.3 (1995): 59-74.

Billingham, H. "The Politics of Breastfeeding." *Health Visitor* 59 June (1986): 184-186.

Blum, Linda. *At the Breast: Ideologies of Motherhood and Breastfeeding in the Contemporary United States*. Boston: Beacon Press, 1999.

Blum, Linda. "Mothers, Babies and Breastfeeding in Late Capitalist America: The Shifting Contexts of Feminist Theory." *Feminist Studies* 19.2 (1993): 290-312.

Carter, Pam. *Feminism, Breasts and Breastfeeding.* New York: St. Martin's Press, 1995.

Cooper, William O. and Harry D. Atherton. "Increased Incidence of Severe Breastfeeding Malnutrition and Hypernatremia in a Metropolitan Area." *Pediatrics* 96.5 (1995): 957-960.

Davies, Lorraine. "Breastfeeding, Motherhood and Maternal Health." Paper presented at the Association for Research on Mothering's Mothering and Feminism Conference, York University, Toronto. Oct. 22-24, 2004.

Dennis, C. L. "Breastfeeding Initiation and Duration: A 1990-2000 Literature Review." *JOGNN* 31.1 (2002): 12-32.

Dewey, Kathryn, M. Jane Heinig, and Laurie A Nommson-Rivers. "Difference in Morbidity between Breast-fed and Formula-fed Infants." *Journal of Pediatrics* 126.5 Part 1 (1995): 696-701.

Douglas, Ann. *The Mother of all Baby Books.* Toronto: MacMillan, 2001.

Earle, S. "Is Breast Best? Breastfeeding, Motherhood and Identity." *Gender, Identity and Reproduction*. Ed. Sarah Earle and Gayle Letherby. New York: Palgrave Macmillan, 2003. 135-153.

Earle, S. "Why Some Women do Not Breastfeed: Bottle Feeding and Father's Role." *Midwifery* 16 (2000): 323-330.

England, Paula. "A Feminist Critique of Rational-Choice Theories: Implications for Sociology." *The American Sociologist* Spring (1989): 14-28.

Frank, Erica. "Breastfeeding and Maternal Employment: Two Rights Don't Make a Wrong." *Lancet* 352.9134 (1998): 1082-1083.

Gengler, Charles E. and Michael S. Mulvey. "A Means-End Analysis of Mothers' Infant Feeding Choices." *Journal of Public Policy and Marketing* 18.2 (1999): 172-189.

Hartsock, Nancy. "Exchange Theory: Critique From a Feminist Standpoint." *Current Perspectives in Social Theory* Volume 6 (1985): 57-70.

Hays, Sharon. *The Cultural Contradictions of Motherhood*. New Haven: Yale University Press, 1996.

Health Canada. *Revised Recommendations for Breastfed Infants*. Ottawa: Canada: Author, 2004. Online: www.hc-sc.gc.ca/fn-an/nutrution/child-enfant/infant-nourisson/breastfed-nourrissons-rec.html. Accessed January 22, 2007.

Health Canada. *Canadian Perinatal Health Report*. Ottawa, Canada, 2003.

Health Canada. *Toward a Healthy Future: Second Report on the Health of Canadians*. Ottawa, Canada: Author, 1999.

Hofvander, Y. "Why Women Don't Breastfeed: A National Survey." *Acta Paediatr* 92 (2003): 1243-1244.

Jain, A., J. Concato, and J. M. Leventhal. "How Good is the Evidence Linking Breastfeeding and Intelligence?" *Pediatrics* 109.6 (2002): 1044-1053.

Kmietowicz, Z. "Breastfeeding Programmes Should Be Targeted." *BMJ* 321.7259 (2000): 467.

Knaak, Stephanie. "Intensive Mothering and the Problem of Choice." Paper presented at the University of Kent School of Social Policy, Sociology and Social Research's Monitoring Parents: Child Rearing in the Age of Intensive Parenting Conference, Canterbury, England, May 21-22, 2007.

Knaak, Stephanie. "The Problem with Breastfeeding Discourse." *Canadian Journal of Public Health* 97.5 (2006): 412-14.

Knaak, Stephanie. "Breastfeeding, Bottle Feeding and Dr. Spock: The Shifting Context of Choice." *Canadian Review of Sociology and Anthropology* 42.2 (2005): 197-216.

Kramer, M.S., B. Chalmers, E.D. Hodnett, et al. "Promotion of Breastfeeding Intervention Trial (PROBIT). A Randomized Trial in the Republic of Belarus." *JAMA* 285.4 (2001): 413-20.

Kwakwa, J. "Don't Push Breast Feeding!" *Midwives Chronicle and Nursing Notes* April (1984): 126.

Law, Jules. "The Politics of Breastfeeding: Assessing Risk, Dividing Labor." *Signs* 25.2 (2000): 407-450.

Lazzaro, Ellen, Jennifer Anderson, and Garry Auld. "Medical Professionals' Attitudes Toward Breastfeeding." *Journal of Human Lactation* 11.2 (1995): 97-101.

Lee, Ellie and Frank Furedi. "Mothers' Experience of, and Attitudes to, Using Infant Formula in the Early Months: Key Findings." School of Social Policy and Social Research, University of Kent, June 2005.

Li R., Z. Zhao, A. Mokdad, L. Barker, and L. Grummer-Strawn. "Prevalence of Breastfeeding in the United States: The 2001 National Immunization Survey." *Pediatrics* May 111.5 Part 2 (2003): 1198-201.

Lindberg, Laura Duberstei. "Women's Decisions about Breastfeeding and Maternal Employment." *Journal of Marriage and the Family* 58.1 (1996): 239-252.

Maclean, H. *Women's Experience of Breast Feeding*. Toronto: University of Toronto Press, 1990.

Mahon-Daly, Patricia, and Gavin J. Andrews. "Liminality and Breastfeeding: Women Negotiating Space and Two Bodies." *Health and Place* 8 (2002): 61-76.

Maushart, Susan. *The Mask of Motherhood*. New York: The New Press, 1999.

McIntyre, E., J. Hiller, and D. Turnbull. "Determinants of Infant Feeding Practices in a Low Socio-Economic Area: Identifying Environmental Barriers to Breastfeeding." *Australian and New Zealand Journal of Public Health* 23.2 (1999): 207-208.

Millar, W. J. and H. Maclean. "Breastfeeding Practices." *Health Reports* 16.2 (2005): 23-31.

Murphy, E. "Risk, Responsibility and Rhetoric." *Journal of Contemporary Ethnography* 29.3 (2000): 291-325.

Murphy, E. "Breast is Best: Infant Feeding Decisions and Maternal Deviance." *Sociology of Health and Illness* 21.2 (1999): 187-208.

O'Reilly, Andrea, ed. *Mother Outlaws: Theories and Practices of Empowered Mothering.* Toronto: Women's Press, 2004.

Potts, Malcolm. "Not in Front of the Children." *Lancet* 345.8955 (1995): 976.

Rodriguez-Garcia, Rosalia and Lara Frazier. "Cultural Paradoxes Relating to Sexuality and Breastfeeding." *Journal of Human Lactation* 11.2 (1995): 111-114.

Romito, Patrizia. "Postpartum Depression and the Experience of Motherhood." *Acta Obstetricia et Gynecologica Scandanavica* 69 Suppl 154 (1990): 3-37.

Romito, Patrizia and Deborah Lupton. "Blurring the Boundaries: Breastfeeding and Maternal Subjectivity." *Sociology of Health and Illness* 23.2 (2001): 234-250.

Romito, Patrizia, A. Sheehan, and L. Barclay. "Contemporary Breast-Feeding Policy and Practice: Implications for Midwives." *Midwifery* 17 (2001): 44-54.

Schmied, V. and L. Barclay. "Connection and Pleasure, Disruption and Distress: Women's Experiences of Breastfeeding." *Journal of Human Lactation* 15.4 (1999): 325-333.

Simkin, Penny, Janet Whalley, and Ann Keppler. *Pregnancy, Childbirth and the Newborn: The Complete Guide.* New York: Simon and Schuster, 1991.

Spock, Benjamin and Steven Parker. *Dr. Spock's Baby and Child Care, 7th Edition.* New York: Pocket Books, 1998.

Stearns, Cindy A. "Breastfeeding and the Good Maternal Body." *Gender and Society* 13.3 (1999): 308-325.

U.S. Food and Drug Administration. "Infant Formula: Second Best but Good Enough." *FDA Consumer Magazine,* June 1996. Online: www.fda.gov/fdac/features/596_baby.html. Accessed September, 2003.

Wall, Glenda. "Moral Constructions of Motherhood in Breastfeeding Discourse." *Gender and Society* 15.4 (2001): 592-610.

White, Mary. "A Worthwhile Career," page 19 in Virginia S. Halonen and Nancy Mohrachen, *Learning a Loving Way of Life.* Franklin Park, Illinois: La Leche League International, 1987.

Wilson, Andrea, et al. "Relation of Infant Diet to Childhood Health: Seven Year Follow Up of Cohort of Children in Dundee Infant Feeding Study." *BMJ* 316.3 January (1998): 21-25.

If the Breast is Best,
Why Are Breastfeeding Rates So Low?

An In-Depth Look at Breastfeeding from
Policy Makers to the Bottom Dollar

Catherine Ma

The consensus on the benefits of breast milk is undisputed on both institutional and individual levels. The most recent statement proposed by the American Academy of Pediatrics (AAP) on breastfeeding and the use of human milk strongly recommend that infants be exclusively breastfed for the first 6 months, continued for at least the first year of life and beyond for as long as mutually desired by mother and child.[1] The combination of breastfeeding education campaigns in putting forth the benefits of breastfeeding and medical research consistently proving that breast milk matches the nutritional needs of the newborn infant better than artificial means (e.g., infant formulas) has resulted in many individuals agreeing that breastfeeding is the ideal form of infant nutrition. Although the list of benefits to breastfeeding are long, few women breastfeed for the recommended first year of their infant's lives as evidenced by national statistics (Taveras, Capra, Braveman, Jensvold, Escobar, and Lieu 108). The equation of "good mothering" with breastfeeding, combined with the social and economic forces that make breastfeeding difficult, affect women's abilities to breastfeed as well as to see themselves as "good mothers" regardless of how they nurture their infants.

Individual and Social Factors

The decision to breastfeed is often erroneously believed to be solely a personal choice but a closer look finds that numerous outside factors influence this important decision (see also Knaak, this volume). Thomas McDade and Carol Worthman even go as far as stating that the majority of maternal decisions are influenced by physical, social, ideological, and political factors that are colored by the culture we live in (290). Women need to realize the numerous outside influences that greatly influence their breastfeeding success or failure. The disembodied recommendations by the AAP and the WHO to breastfeed for one year, rather then helping women, may actually harm them because they imply that a mother is deficient if she cannot reach the goal of exclusively breastfeeding her infant. Gabrielle Palmer's statement, "they all know the mantra that breast is best, which is as useful as knowing that potatoes are edible without ever learning how to cook them," exemplifies the problematic nature of disembodied recommendations to breastfeed (53). For policy makers to put forth the notion that breastfeeding is best without including supportive measures for women is clearly irresponsible.

On the individual level, mothers who decide to breastfeed are wondering why something considered "natural" can be so difficult. The mantra, "the breast is best" can be perceived as judgmental by women who encounter difficulties while breastfeeding because it covertly implies fault on the woman. This pressure is believed to make breastfeeding another mothering chore that offers women little chance of viewing breastfeeding as an empowering experience. Much of the literature on breastfeeding often leaves out the realistic side which may include problems such as soreness, cracked and bleeding nipples, thrush, clogged milk ducts, and/or mastitis. A growing number of studies that have focused on the individualized experiences of mothers are finding many unprepared for a variety of physical and psychological experiences after birth especially silences surrounding breastfeeding difficulties (Hoddinott and Pill 229; Binns and Scott 16; Johnson, Mulder, and Strube 320). Such findings suggest the importance of women gaining access to the true realities of breastfeeding and not just the idealized images often portrayed in breastfeeding literature and the media.

Following the one-year recommendations to exclusively breastfeed set by the WHO and the AAP, many mothers have equated "good" mothering with successfully breastfeeding their infants ("Breastfeeding Research Points to Backlash" 6; Hauck and Irurita 66). Many new mothers also believe that taking a prenatal breastfeeding class and/or reading literature focusing on breastfeeding is adequate preparation for a successful breastfeeding relationship with their newborns (Johnson, Mulder and Strube 320). Mothers who view breastfeeding in this simplistic manner may find the occurrence of breastfeeding difficulties indicative of their own inability to breastfeed. When mothers come across problems breastfeeding, they often blame themselves for being "bad" mothers. Even women who are able to breastfeed but wean prematurely feel like failures for not reaching the guidelines set by the AAP and the WHO (see Knaak, this volume, for a more complete discussion of these issues).

Women living in Western society have the added burden of dealing with cultural values of autonomy and control as young girls are socially conditioned to be independent and to take control of their lives. But once these young girls become mothers, they are expected to set aside those values and to become dependent and focused solely on the needs of their babies if they are to be "good" mothers. In these cases, women often go to great extremes to exclusively breastfeed their infants and the price they pay is often their own physical and mental well-being. Personal disappointments in breastfeeding often overflow into a mother's self concept and her mothering abilities (Hauck and Irurita 66). Current breastfeeding literature often disregards the needs of the mother when educating women on the benefits of breastfeeding. As a result, many women suffer through breastfeeding difficulties because they are socially rewarded for putting aside their own pain for the welfare of their infants. Certain breastfeeding advocacy organizations may also be hurting women since their tenets dictate that breastfeeding be above all disruptive "distractions" such as working out of the home, having personal goals separate from one's infant or caring for other family members. Such an emphasis on increasing breastfeeding rates could easily result in a backlash against women who are trying to balance an equitable relationship that is not based exclusively on the needs of their infant ("Breastfeeding Research Points to Backlash" 6).

In addition, mothers rarely hear words of encouragement since breastfeeding is something that mothers are simply expected to do (Hauck and Irurita 67). With such one-sidedness regarding breastfeeding, many women forego any attempt to breastfeed and formula feed from the start. Palmer notes how many mothers discourage their daughters from breastfeeding to spare them the mental anguish they suffered in their own failed attempts to breastfeed further fueling another generation of women who formula feed their infants (52). Da Vanzo, Starbird, and Leibowitz examined the effect of prior breastfeeding experience on the likelihood of subsequent breastfeeding and found that an initial unsuccessful attempt lowered future attempts to breastfeed—highlighting the importance of helping primaparas breastfeed as this success holds health implications for subsequent siblings (229).[2]

Medical Models, the Workplace, and Challenges to Breastfeeding

According to Suzanne Arms, how we feed a baby is as much a personal and political statement as it is reflective of our own value system (195). Such conflicts stem from breastfeeding advocacy's double bind, whereby breastfeeding is viewed as empowering but at the price of subscribing to an ideological view of proper mothering based on traditionally female roles (Palmer 29). In line with this ideology is the medical model which perpetuates the disembodied notion of breastfeeding. Evidently, physicians are taught to value the rational mind over embodied knowledge and to distrust woman's bodies. Generally speaking, health care professionals are regarded as having the most current information regarding breastfeeding but their credibility is lost if mothers sense they are dispensing inaccurate or confusing advice, which happens more often than not (Hauck and Irurita 72). Breastfeeding misinformation is not isolated to the medical community and can also be attained from well meaning family and friends, or through advertising and the media (McCarter-Spaulding 210). Such findings support Palmer's notion that incorrect information is more detrimental to breastfeeding women than no information at all (53). Women seem to have a better chance of figuring out what works best for themselves by listening to their bodies instead of following medical advice. Moreover, the lack of medical training in breastfeeding management sends a negative message to medical professionals regarding the importance of breastfeeding. This seems ironic since the AAP has largely positioned itself as a breastfeeding advocate.

With increasing numbers of mothers returning to work shortly after giving birth, one may question how a rapid return to the paid workforce affects breastfeeding rates. Currently, Federal civil rights law prohibits employment discrimination on the basis of pregnancy, childbirth and pregnancy-related medical conditions, but a more critical evaluation of such protection yields mixed results. Jendi Reiter offers the most comprehensive research on how the law has failed women in accommodating pregnancy and breastfeeding in the workplace. She questions whether the law should treat breastfeeding as a natural concomitant of pregnancy or a separate lifestyle choice not protected by laws forbidding discrimination against pregnant women (Reiter 2). In many civil rights cases involving lactation, the requests made by the women were modest (e.g., flexible work schedules, clean & private places to express and store milk). But in many court rulings, breastfeeding was not found to be protected under Title VII of the Civil Rights Act and the Pregnancy Discrimination Act because breastfeeding and childrearing are not related to pregnancy, childbirth or any related medical conditions (Reiter 3). The current legal definition of pregnancy is "a biological process that begins with conception and ends with delivery." (Greenberg, as noted in Reiter 13). Such a narrow definition is a disservice to women, as employers tend to view breastfeeding as outside the realm of pregnancy, increasing the likelihood that a breastfeeding employee's requests be denied because it is seen as a personal choice in direct opposition to the public interests of an efficiently run business (Reiter 9). Such narrow legal definitions and comparisons to the male norm make these rulings more common than not.

Reiter finds that such rulings underscore the outdated and ineffectual definitions of gender equality (14). Since women in the paid labor force are still measured against work ethics based on male norms, they are automatically put at a disadvantage because pregnancy and lactation have no male equivalent. In an attempt to challenge male norms, Reiter hopes to change the view of expanded family-leave time as a disability to a view of it as beneficial (21). This small change can benefit breastfeeding mothers by lessening the stigmas attached to lactation, expressing breast milk, and fostering family values; breastfeeding can actually benefit employers with short-term goals (by reducing employee sick time taken by parents who must care for sick children) and with long-term goals (by contributing to a healthier future workforce). An important component in combining breastfeeding and working outside of the home is having adequate time to establish the woman's milk supply. *The Family and Medical Leave Act* (FMLA) was created to give parents up to 12 weeks of unpaid leave to care for a child or a family member. Unfortunately, employees who needed the time off were unable to utilize this provision as the loss of income was too high a price to pay to care for loved ones (Galtry 11). If the United States is truly concerned about the problem of low breastfeeding rates, it needs to focus on the bigger picture of raising the quality of care for both children and parents. Sadly, most mothers in the United States are offered only four to six weeks of unpaid maternity leave.

Recently, there has been a surge of government incentives for employers to set up lactation rooms to help breastfeeding employees. Although this step is promising, we must be careful to note that it does not challenge the underlying assumptions that still need to be changed if women are to combine breastfeeding with paid work. The addition of a lactation room may seem like a bandage on a gaping wound if discrimination prevents women from utilizing these facilities. These possible loopholes lead Reiter to propose a move from the individual rights model toward a pro-family model where emphasis is placed on an equitable distribution of parenting duties (22). Although some states are experimenting with a multitude of ways to assist mothers in combining paid work with breastfeeding, there is still plenty of room for improvement. One may question what constitutes a "reasonable" effort on the employers' part as such vagueness in legal terms often leaves employees the possibility that their requests will be denied. The mandatory nature of certain state statutes can create a hostile atmosphere toward pumping mothers as employers may feel they are being imposed upon without being financially compensated for their efforts. However, if employers invest in the short-term aspects of breastfeeding by offering flexible work schedules and sanitary places to pump, they can reap the benefits of a long-term investment that will include a healthier and more productive future generation of workers. The fact that these issues are open for discussion offers breastfeeding mothers some hope as they are truly pioneers in forcing corporations to see that breastfeeding can also be beneficial to businesses and society as a whole.[3] However, more needs to be done in order for legislation to recognize that breastfeeding should be viewed less as a private family matter and more as a social responsibility (Galtry 6). Judith Galtry states that in order for breastfeeding rates in the United States to increase, major changes are needed at the Federal level which include but are not restricted to paid family leave, paid breastfeeding breaks, supportive work environments, and financial support for employer-provided programs (13).

Impact of Formula Corporations

The manner in which breastfeeding is viewed in corporate America is tied to its monetary value. From an economic standpoint, breastfeeding is one of the most cost-effective ways to feed an infant as it offers short-term and long-term benefits for both infant and mother (Anholm 5). Even though these benefits have been confirmed by numerous researchers, we still live in a time where artificial feeding is considered the norm. Such conceptions have shaped the way we view breastfeeding as unnecessary and formula as the standard way to feed infants (Wolf 2007). Current conceptions can be traced back to how scientific mothering has influenced the manner in which women mother. Jacquelyn Litt examined case studies of three women of differing social, racial and ethnic positions in their conceptions of motherhood and found that medical discourse was often used as a way to distinguish their upward mobility (285). Scientific mothering became a marker in distinguishing social class whereby affluent mothers saw themselves as more educated, socially mobile, financially stable and better assimilated into mainstream American culture than their immigrant counterparts. Costly pediatric visits resulted in class differences where a rejection of traditional health practices symbolized one's own social advancement and a new immersion into an upwardly mobile social group (Litt 290). At these visits, infants were weighed and measured based on standardized growth charts that, unbeknownst to most parents, were based on the growth patterns of a small group of middle class, Caucasian children who were all formula fed and grew at a faster and steadier pace. As a result, many pediatricians advised mothers to supplement their breastfed babies with formula in order to help them "gain" weight, which, in turn, reduced stimulation to the breast, decreased a mother's milk supply, led to insufficient milk syndrome and eventually lowered breastfeeding rates.

As more women followed the advice of physicians, the incidences of insufficient milk syndrome increased, creating a need for infant formula. The marketing of infant formula was initially geared toward women living in industrialized societies where formula feeding was perceived as an activity of the rich and elite (Baumslag and Michels 148). As the link between elitism and formula grew, breastfeeding became a primitive and derogatory activity delegated to women who could not afford formula. Aggressive formula marketing tactics also targeted medical personnel who were lavished with gifts and other "perks" for dispensing free samples among patients. A company training manual for sales personnel highlighted the importance of influencing hospitals because mothers who initially start off breastfeeding but wean prematurely are more likely to use that particular brand of formula given by the hospital (Palmer 314). Aggressive marketing tactics soon crossed economic divides as more mothers began to doubt the traditional method of breastfeeding and buy into the scientific image of infant formula. This move from breastfeeding led to increased infant malnutrition and mortality as mothers in less industrialized countries did not have the hygienic or economic resources needed for formula feeding.

It was only during the 1970s when public outrage at such preventable deaths turned to political action. In 1977, the Infant Formula Action Coalition (IFAC) organized the biggest consumer boycott of Nestle in hopes of ending their aggressive marketing strategies (Baumslag and Michels 157). As the unethical practices of formula manufacturers became public, the WHO drafted the International Code of Marketing of Breastmilk Substitutes (ICMBS) to improve infant nutrition and support breastfeeding. Although this code is currently in action, there have been reports of violations by major formula manufacturers who are still providing free samples, offering donations to health workers, and disregarding standards for labeling (Aguayo 158). Such restrictions have forced formula manufacturers to be more creative in capitalizing their market share. One way is through research where formula manufacturers often give multi-million dollar research grants to medical organizations such as the AAP, the American College of Obstetrics and Gynecologists, and the AMA (Baumslag and Michels 172). A closer look at the major breastfeeding studies show that these studies have been largely funded by leading formula manufacturers under the guise of promoting breastfeeding. Often these "breastfeeding surveys" contain one or two questions regarding breastfeeding while the remainder of the survey consists of various questions regarding formula choice.[4] Formula manufacturers also entice medical students and pediatricians to forge a bond with them. The benefits of these relationships often include individual research grants, payments of student loans, paid trips to conferences, and/or cash grants for product endorsements (Baumslag and Michels 172).

Another way formula manufacturers gain market share is through the marketing of breast pumps. Many mothers are unaware of the differences between effective, hospital-grade pumps and these cheaper pumps that often damage breast tissue, leading to premature weaning and formula use. It is these ineffective pumps that are often the ones aggressively marketed to mothers through their lower prices and availability in stores frequented mostly by women. Marketing tactics highlight the discretion and time-saving abilities a pump will create for the mother who wants to "have it all"—a career and a family. These advertisements appeal to many working women because success within the corporate world necessitates integrating breastfeeding so that it does not interfere with work. Not only do pump manufacturers prey upon mothers with this "superwoman" mentality, but these marketing tactics also reinforce mothers' erroneous thinking that such a juggling act is easily attainable.

Talking Back: Utilizing the Internet in Breastfeeding

With so many issues standing in the way of women who wish to breastfeed, how can women find success in their desire to feed their infants breast milk? One key but often neglected aspect of maintaining a breastfeeding relationship is social support, in this case, mother-to-mother support. In the United States, motherhood is often privatized so that the nuclear family makes it difficult for mothers, who are often the primary caregivers, to receive the social support they need. In many non-Western societies, the mother often receives assistance from extended family members who have had previous experience breastfeeding and raising infants. This assistance was vital for the successful survival of future generations, but with the rise of industrialism and capitalism, this sense of kinship became replaced by an emphasis on individualism and the nuclear family.

One way to re-establish this type of kinship within an individualist society is through the use of the Internet. Although there are organizations, such as the La Leche League, that hold monthly meetings to help mothers overcome breastfeeding problems, they tend to force women into adopting narrow definitions of gender roles in order to be helped. The League's Catholic roots in the sanctity of heteronormative and nuclear family life focuses entirely around the notion of women being the primary caregivers and maternal sacrifice at the core of the mother-infant dyad (Bobel 144). In addition, not all women are able to find the resources (e.g., time, transportation, etc.) to take advantage of these meetings. As a result, the Internet may provide a much needed service to address the needs of mothers who are unable to leave their homes. Breastfeeding and pumping mothers are finding the use of Internet support groups to be quite beneficial by reducing the social distance between mothers and enabling them to find others who have had the same experiences and who can relate to the specific concerns they face (Gribble 14). Mothers who encounter problems in breastfeeding, marital relationships, childcare, and other issues that relate to breastfeeding can connect with other mothers who are going through or have gone through similar problems.

Hauck and Irurita found that the frequency of contact with another person whose expectations were similar with regard to breastfeeding helped alleviate a mother's feelings of confusion, self-doubt, and guilt. By having access to other women, mothers who wish to breastfeed can move beyond the idealized images of breastfeeding and begin to develop more realistic expectations regarding breastfeeding. Hauck and Irurita found this to be imperative to successful breastfeeding and mothering for two fundamental reasons: First, it helps women develop realistic expectations regarding breastfeeding which reduces the attribution that failure at breastfeeding is self-imposed and second, sharing realistic experiences enables new mothers to feel at ease discussing their difficulties which in turn, lessens the stigma attached to seeking help.

One example of realistic expectations regarding breastfeeding was the fact that a successful breastfeeding relationship was not all or none. The combination of breastfeeding and formula feeding can be a sanity saver to many women and puts less pressure on women to exclusively breastfeed. Such a realistic view of breastfeeding is often clouded by the stronghold the medical community's imposition of strict guidelines that women are expected to blindly uphold. Support groups also gave mothers a sense that their own practices of infant-feeding were normal, whether a mother was practicing extended breastfeeding or exclusively pumping breast milk. Also, many breastfeeding women found the support they needed to buffer the negative attitudes they encountered from others who did not understand the importance of breastfeeding. This sense of normalcy was found to be one of the benefits of Internet support groups as it fostered a sense of community among members and facilitated an openness in members sharing experiences (McKenna & Bargh 692). For example, members of the PumpMoms listserv frequently voiced a sigh of relief to learn that there were other mothers who were unable to nurse their infants and had to resort to exclusively pumping.[5] Gribble adds that this form of Internet support is likely to offer the greatest benefit to women who are breastfeeding in unusual circumstances (e.g., exclusively pumping) (16). This affinity can be empowering because mothers will be able to find others who can lend a sympathetic ear and offer real-life suggestions that the medical community has neglected or discredited (e.g., holistic medicine, use of herbs, venting). The use of these listservs also adds an empowering aspect by subverting the patriarchal notion of disembodiment to work for mothers (e.g., socioeconomic, racial categories and other physical differences are less influential on the Internet) by highlighting commonalties as opposed to differences.

The Internet can also help women unite by becoming more informed about breastfeeding legislation. For example, Congresswoman Carolyn Maloney, who was a breastfeeding mother, has set up her own website to enable women who have suffered any form of discrimination for expressing milk at their workplace (e.g., fired, harassed, docked pay, etc.) to find the support they need to challenge these hostile work environments.[6] She is also the only congresswoman who is working on setting breast pump standards so women will not have to tolerate pumps that are painful, ineffective, or damaging. Her website also contains a summary of state breastfeeding laws that lists, city by city, legislation concerning nursing in public. Because Maloney has put this information into a public forum, women who breastfeed in public are able to use the law to support their decision to breastfeed.

Conclusion

To expand our current views of breastfeeding, more research is needed that focuses on the process and experience of breastfeeding as opposed to the end product of whether or not women breastfeed. If the medical community is truly dedicated to increasing breastfeeding rates, researchers need to examine the social, political, and psychological aspects of breastfeeding in order to understand the underlying factors that prevent women from breastfeeding. Specifically, more research is needed to understand the psychological aspects of breastfeeding. It may also prove to be beneficial if researchers focus on the production of breastfeeding knowledge and lend a critical eye to research funding that involves formula manufacturers. Currently, it seems as though the formula manufacturers are the ones shaping how breastfeeding is viewed by society. If this is true, education about all aspects of breastfeeding (e.g., economical, historical, individual, political, societal) is even more crucial as current policies and practices can easily result in further class distinctions in which wealthy, white women and their children will be the ones who benefit from breastfeeding while poor, women of color continue to have children who are plagued with health problems preventable by breastfeeding. A closer look at the marketing of current breastfeeding campaigns shows that policy makers seem to envision women who are white, upper middle class, and financially stable. This leads one to question: who will be the breastfeeding advocates for less economically advantaged women of color? Although there is funding to help raise breastfeeding awareness in disadvantaged groups, how can policy makers reach the needs of these women if they are having problems helping even those women who have the resources needed to breastfeed? Such strong outside influences make the issue of breastfeeding much more complicated than a simple decision of whether or not to breastfeed. Only when women truly understand all that is at stake with regards to breastfeeding and when all the forces that keep breastfeeding rates low are exposed will women have a real choice as to how they feed their infants.

[1] The most updated statement on breastfeeding and the uses of human milk by the American Academy of Pediatrics. <http://aappolicy.aappublications. org/cgi/content/full/pediatrics;115/2/496>.
[2] See also Carter; Blum; and Maher for more discussion of the social and con-

textual factors that affect women's breastfeeding practices.

[3]Employer benefits include increased productivity, company loyalty, employee satisfaction, lower turnover and absentee rates, and fewer demands on employee health benefits; societal benefits include release of scarce medical funds and staff, savings of foreign exchange, less environmental pollution and less demand for agricultural and energy resources (Baumslag and Michels 190). Additional societal and ecological benefits by breastfeeding include saving finite resources and billions in health care costs (Palmer 301); breastfeeding incurs no costly storage or production costs and is a renewable resource (Palmer 285).

[4]Shortly after the birth of my first son, I received numerous mailings from a leading formula manufacturer with the words, "Breastfeeding Survey" across the front of the envelope. Upon closer inspection, these surveys had no more than two questions on breastfeeding but over 25 questions regarding formula choice, how many times do I use formula, was I using a specialty formula, etc.

[5]The PumpMoms Group is a positive, supportive and resourceful environment for moms who want to pump breast milk for their babies. This online group may be found at <http:// health.groups.yahoo.com/group/PumpMoms>.

[6]Congresswoman Carolyn Maloney's website with information regarding her work in Congress regarding breastfeeding can be found at <http://maloney. house.gov/index.php?option=com_issues&task=view_issue&issue=262&parent=20&Itemid=35>.

Works Cited

American Academy of Pediatrics. "Breastfeeding and the Uses of Human Milk." *Pediatrics* 115 (2005): 496-506.

Anholm, P. Cheryl. "Breastfeeding: A Preventive Approach to Health Care in Infancy." *Issues in Comprehensive Pediatric Nursing* 9.1 (1986): 1-10.

Aguayo, Victor. "Widespread Breaking of the WHO Code on Marketing of Breast-milk Substitutes in West Africa." *Midwifery* 19.2 (2003):158-9.

Arms, Suzanne. *Immaculate Deception II*. California: Celestial Arts, 1996.

Baumslag, Naomi and Dia L. Michels. *Milk, Money, and Madness. The Culture and Politics of Breastfeeding*. Connecticut: Bergin and Garvey, 1995.

Binns, Colin W. and Jane A. Scott. "Breastfeeding: Reasons for Starting, Reasons for Stopping and Problems Along the Way." *Breastfeeding Review* 10.2 (2002): 13-9.

Blum, Linda M. *At the Breast: Ideologies of Breastfeeding and Motherhood in the Contemporary United States*. Boston: Beacon Press, 1999.

Bobel, Christina. "Bounded Liberation: A Focused Study of La Leche League International." *Gender & Society* 15.1 (2001): 130-51.

"Breastfeeding Research Points to Backlash" *Australian Nursing Journal*, 5.6 (1997-1998): 6.

Carter, Pam. *Feminism, Breasts, and Breastfeeding*. New York: St. Martin's Press, 1995.

Da Vanzo, Julie, et al. "Do Women's Breastfeeding Experience with their First-Borns Affect Whether they Breastfeed their Subsequent Children?" *Social Biology* 37(3-4) (1990): 223-323.

Galtry, Judith. "Lactation And The Labor Market: Breastfeeding, Labor Market Changes, and Public Policy in the U. S." *Health Care for Women International* 18.5 (1997): 467-81.

Gribble, Karleen D. "Mother-to-Mother Support for Women Breastfeeding in Unusual Circumstances: A New Model for an Old Model." *Breastfeeding Review* 9.3 (2001): 13-19.

Hauck, Yvonne L. and Vera F. Irurita. "Incompatible Expectations: The Dilemma of Breastfeeding Mothers." *Health Care for Women International* 24 (2003): 62-78.

Hoddinott, Pat and Roisin Pill. "A Qualitative Study of Women's Views about How Health Professionals Communicate about Infant Feeding." *Health Expectations* 3 (2000): 224-33.

Johnson, T., P. Mulder and K. Strube. "Mother-Infant Breastfeeding Progress Tool: A Guide for Education and Support of the Breastfeeding Dyad." *Journal of Obstetric, Gynecology & Neonatal Nursing* 36.4 (2007): 319-27.

Litt, Jacquelyn. "American Medicine and Divided Motherhood: Three Case Studies From the 1930s and 1940s." *Sociological Quarterly* 38.2 (1997): 285-306.

Maher, Vanessa. *The Anthropology of Breastfeeding*. Oxford: Berg, 1992.

McCarter-Spaulding, Deborah. "Is Breastfeeding Fair? Tensions in Feminist Perspectives on Breastfeeding and the Family." *Journal of Human Lactation* 24.2 (2008): 206-12

McDade, Thomas W. and Carol M. Worthman,. "The Weanling's Dilemma Reconsidered: A Bio-Cultural Analysis of Breastfeeding Ecology." *Journal of Development Behavioral Pediatrics* 19.4 (1998): 286-299.

McKenna, Katelyn Y. and John A. Bargh. "Coming Out In the Age of the Internet: Identity 'Demarginalization' Through Virtual Group Participation." *Journal of Personality and Social Psychology* 75.3 (1998): 681-94.

Palmer, Gabrielle. *The Politics of Breastfeeding*. Pennsylvania: Pandora, 1988.

Reiter, Jendi. B. "Accommodating Pregnancy and Breastfeeding in the Workplace: Beyond the Civil Rights Paradigm." *Texas Journal of Women and the Law* 9.1 (1999): 1-28.

Taveras, Elsie M, et al. "Clinician Support and Psychosocial Risk Factors Associated with Breastfeeding Discontinuation." *Pediatrics* 112.1 (2003): 108-15.

Wolf, Jacqueline H. "Low Breastfeeding Rates and Public Health in the United States." *American Journal of Public Health* 93.12 (2003): 2000-10.

What My Daughter Knows

Towards an Epistemology of Breastfeeding

Karen MacLean

Scientific knowledge of breastfeeding has increased dramatically in the past 25 years, and during that period, the number of breastfeeding-savvy health care professionals has also grown. Nonetheless, many Western women experience great difficulty 'getting' breastfeeding.

If breastfeeding required no knowledge at all, then any new mother would be able to breastfeed; this is patently not the case. Indeed, it is increasingly clear that the knowledge available to first world women does not necessarily help them breastfeed. What kind of knowledge, then, does breastfeeding require?

In an effort to answer this question, I have mapped the knowing of the breast-feeding experience I shared with my daughter Ingrid. This mapping leads me to suggest that the knowledge required by and created through breastfeeding is fundamentally different from the expert knowledge we rely on today.

My map shows that breastfeeding draws on and creates an eco-system of knowing. This eco-system 'pulls in' a variety of different kinds of knowing and uses them all in concert for the knowing, learning and decision-making processes of breastfeeding. I suggest that the more breastfeeding women are aware of the various kinds of knowing involved in and the nature of this ecosystem, the more actively they will be able to participate in it, and the better able they will be to succeed. By this, I mean that they will be able to breastfeed when, where and for as long as they wish to without experiencing feelings of shame, guilt or failure for their choices.

Expert Knowledge

In my discussion of breastfeeding, I shall be referring to a cousin of scientific knowledge, which I call "expert knowledge." Expert knowledge is related to scientific knowledge in that it borrows some of the facts, processes, and ideals that underpin scientific knowledge. However, expert knowledge is practical or applied; it is a less objective version of medical facts, simplified, mixed with personal experience—including prejudices—and often out-of-date. It is circulated via childcare and parenting books and TV shows, and by parents and health care professionals. Expert knowledge is generally acknowledged as "authoritative knowledge" on breastfeeding.

Authoritative Knowledge

I borrow the concept of "authoritative knowledge" from anthropology, where it was coined by Brigitte Jordan to describe the communal processes of knowing that surround childbirth. In Jordan's view, there are several kinds of knowing going on in any given situation, and to the participants, some of these carry more weight than others. This is either because they are more effective or because they have what Jordan calls a "stronger power base" (55).

In Western culture, expert knowledge is the authoritative knowledge on breastfeeding that we rely on in our society to make breastfeeding work, and which we agree we need to make breastfeeding work. Unfortunately, because of the characteristics it shares with scientific knowledge, and because of its consensually authoritative status, it obscures and disqualifies other knowledge(s).

Expert Knowledge as Authoritative

Expert knowledge on breastfeeding includes such information as how to position the child, how to treat cracked nipples, how to tell if your child is getting enough milk, etc. However, expert knowing is predicated on a division, which it borrows from medical science, between the knower and the known, which allows only one expert in the room, so to speak. The discourse of expert knowing positions the person seeking information (or the one having the problem) as the object of knowing (Bartlett 376). To the extent to which the person seeking information aligns herself with the object position, she increases the possibility that she may consider herself unable to know or even to act.

If, on the other hand, the reader internalizes the expert information, thus positioning herself as a knower, she risks splitting off and objectifying her body and her nursling. Her knowing becomes largely cognitive as her body's knowledge is obscured or impaired. Thus, the knowing that she and her nursling might do is hampered, and the collaboration between them becomes hierarchical. Mother is the subject, who knows best, and the infant is an object, who knows not at all. Finally, if she internalizes the implicit understanding of the body as a defective machine, which needs science and experts to function, she may be hindered in carrying out functions for which her body was in fact, over millennia, honed.

I am not suggesting that we jettison expert knowing, but rather that there exists a different epistemological eco-system for breastfeeding, which accommodates and "draws in" divergent ways of knowing—including expert knowledge—and uses them all for the knowing, learning and decision-making processes of breastfeeding. I would argue that breastfeeding women do a great deal of their knowing in and through such an eco-system, but that it is often dominated, obscured and undermined by authoritative knowledge. Since I think it would be useful to map and investigate that eco-system, and to make it more visible and available to breastfeeding women, I have attempted to map my own experience

What My Daughter Knows

Briefly, this is what my daughter knew at birth. I need not point out that all this knowing is bodily and non-cognitive.

- That she NEEDS;
- How to find the breast;
- How to latch on;
- How to suck: timing suck, swallow and breath;
- How to identify her mother.

What I Know

The knowledge listed here, on the other hand, is all cognitive. I know that my mother breastfed me because I've been told, and I know that my body knows how to breastfeed because I've read that women's bodies are able to do so. The final item, however, will form part of the substrate for the eco-system I am talking about, as it combines various kinds and sources of knowledge (more about this later).

- My mother breastfed me and my brother ten months apiece (and so on back through history);
- That certain percentage of women in my society breastfeed;
- My body knows how to do this;
- My daughter knows a great deal, herself;
- Breastfeeding will be a team effort between us;
- The stories of other women's breastfeeding experiences.

What I Know About Knowledge

The knowledge listed here is meta-knowledge: knowledge about knowledge.

This list highlights how cerebral my knowledge about my body's knowledge was.

- Certain sources of knowledge are reliable
- Some expert knowledge is useless, some actually pernicious
- My body knows, although I don't know how

What We Learn Together

Of course, the first thing we learned was how to breastfeed: How to actually make *her* knowledge dovetail and collaborate with *mine*, in the context of hospital beds with ratty pillows, nursing bras and tops, overcoats and slings, airplane seats and double beds, and states of wakefulness and sleep.

- How to breastfeed, not least lying down
- How to know and relate to one another, to read and respond appropriately to one another's moods
- That there are different kinds of breastfeeding relationships, depending on the needs and the situation; the when, where, and how change contextually and developmentally

In the process of learning to breastfeed together, we were also getting to know one another, learning how to read each others' needs and moods and how to respond appropriately. In the beginning, an outsider might have assumed that I was doing all the knowing and Ingrid all the learning, and that I was teaching her. However, this was most certainly not the case.

My Daughter as an Interactive Knower

Thus, when my daughter was three-and-a-half months old, she started to insist on being breastfed lying down, preferably in our bedroom. The preference was very strong—if we were out and about, she'd simply wait to breastfeed, refusing the breast, sometimes very calmly, despite the fact that she must have been quite hungry. The only exception to the rule was nursing in the sling while I walked. This preference persisted with very few exceptions, well into her second year. As you can imagine, this wasn't always an easy preference to accommodate; however, I did my best.

In retrospect, I saw that Ingrid was responding in part to her need for a calm environment, in part to her need for me to be in a certain state of mind. That state of mind was achieved either by us being alone (which, in her experience was when we were lying down), or by me walking purposefully from place to place with her in the sling. That my state of mind was a pivotal factor is evident, first, since she would not—even at an early age—let me read during breastfeeding, and secondly, since she would easily tolerate noise and chaotic environments when I was walking with her in the sling.

What My Daughter Learns

• To know and respond to her own needs
• To associate togetherness with comfort and food
• To comfort herself (and do most everything else) interactively
• An epistemological template, based on a process of knowing that starts with self/body and proceeds in collaboration with a cooperative responsive other.

What I Learn

• My body knows
• My body out-knows my intellect
• To be in the moment
• My daughter is an active, powerful knower.

The biggest problem I experienced early on in breastfeeding was the fear that letdown was not going to take place. In fact, letdown ALWAYS happened, sometimes even when Ingrid was not present. But letdown was still a great concern to me for many months, until all of a sudden, I realized that I had not thought of letdown for ages, and couldn't remember the last time I had.

Now I knew, rationally, that the milk ejection reflex is purely physiological but didn't trust this knowledge. Six to eight months' worth of letdowns allowed me to transition from the intellectual knowledge and the *belief* that my body knew its business, to resting secure in my body's knowledge.

I first thought that, in Cartesian fashion, my intellect had finally received sufficient proof of my body's knowledge; however, in the classical epistemological view, 'body knowledge' is a contradiction of terms, and such proof could never be obtained.

Rather, what happened was that the ways of knowing that I have internalized and participated in over a life-time began to give way to a more horizontal process of knowing, where several knowledge sources and processes mingled. In this ecology, my body's hormonal knowledge, my body knowledge and my rational knowledge form—so to speak—a small community of knowers.

What We Created

We created between us, then, a matrix of two knowers, in a historical and social context, with access to various kinds of knowledge (intellectual, experiential, bodily) and tools to critique them. Over time, in the evolving eco-system of this epistemological matrix, we learned to know interactively, and, in the process, we expanded my ways of knowing and created an epistemological template for Ingrid.

An Alternative Eco-System

In the map I have sketched for you, I made assumptions that a "classical" epistemologist might take exception to. In addition to expert knowing and rational thought, I assumed the existence of several other processes that I qualify as epistemological, that is, as kinds of knowing.

First, there is the body's neurological and hormonal knowing, the substrate of body knowledge not available to rational cognition: Ingrid's suck-swallow-breathe timing, my body's memory of having been breastfed, etc. Secondly, there is what Carole Browner and Nancy Press have identified as embodied knowing, "subjective knowledge derived from a woman's perceptions of her body and its natural processes" (113).

Thirdly, there is what I call "narrative knowing," namely the intertwining of information and emotional support that goes on in everyday conversations between women. Such knowing draws on other kinds of knowing—embodied and expert knowing, for example—and weaves them together for transmission "as personal stories or narratives" together with emotional support. This third kind of knowing also functions as an eco-system of knowing, drawing in various ways of knowing to create a matrix of shared knowing and emotional support, not unlike, of course, the breastfeeding relationship itself.

Hierarchy vs. Collaboration

In the process of mapping my breastfeeding experience with Ingrid, I came to the conclusion that expert knowledge may actually impede breastfeeding. The reason is that it shares with science the epistemological processes that separate knowers and organize them hierarchically and that disqualify certain sources of knowledge and knowers. Expert knowledge hampers the ability of team members of a breastfeeding project to collaborate, and disorganizes their knowing processes.

It is important for a breastfeeding mother to regard her nursling, not as an object, but as a competent collaborator who brings to the breastfeeding project a great deal of knowledge, willpower, and initiative. This has an emotional and rational impact on the mother's knowing and on their project. Moreover, the baby's knowing is also affected by the mother's attitude, as philosopher Christine Pierce has pointed out: "certain abilities of persons can be manifested only in circumstances of cooperativeness. One cannot, for instance, manifest intelligence in an interpersonal situation with someone convinced of one's stupidity" (Pierce 422).

Body Knowledge

It is also important for the breastfeeding mother to realize that her body knowledge—accessible as well as inaccessible—plays an important part in the breastfeeding process. For example, if a woman's own breastfeeding experience was marked by strict four-hour feeding intervals, short stints at each breast and abrupt switches, then her body memories will be tinged with frustration, powerlessness and a sense of isolation that will inevitably color her experience of giving breast.

Although she cannot rationally remember this experience, the cognitive knowledge of this experience and of its importance can become part of her knowing processes when working with her nursling to breastfeed. Realizing that her apprehensiveness, worry and fear concerning breastfeeding may have other sources frees the mother to deal with her body memory. Something as simple as a relaxation technique may alleviate part of what she feels, and she may now experience less apprehension at the thought of breastfeeding. Relaxation techniques or sympathizing with one's earlier self are not normally considered relevant to knowing, but can in fact be essential to the process.

Bigger Picture

Although beyond the scope of this article, there is a broad body of work to back up this conceptualization of the process of knowing. Scientific knowledge has been critiqued on a theoretical level by feminists and other epistemologists, and many scientists realize, e.g., the fallacy of the ideal of objectivity. Moreover, the work of researchers such as neuroscientist Candace Pert and psychiatrist Stanley Greenspan has demonstrated that emotions and cognition are closely intertwined and that brain and body are not separable into distinct entities.

Conclusion

The significance of investigating and mapping this eco-system and making its processes more present and available to breastfeeding women should not be underestimated. Arbitrary borders and barriers—like the mind/body split—are internalized and put into practice in most of the knowing each one of us does every day. Breastfeeding may actually help us to bring theoretical insights to bear on our day-to-day knowing. We have something to learn from breastfeeding women.

Works Cited

Bartlett, Alison. "Breastfeeding as Headwork: Corporeal Feminism and Meanings for Breastfeeding." *Women's Studies International Forum* 25.3 (2002): 373-82.

Browner, Carole H. and Nancy Press. "The Production of Authoritative Knowledge in American Prenatal Care." *Childbirth and Authoritative Knowledge: Cross-Cultural Perspectives*. Ed. Robbie E. Davis-Floyd and Carolyn F. Sargent. Berkeley: University of California Press, 1997. 113-31.

Green, Cynthia P. 1998. *Mother Support Groups: A Review of Experience in Developing Countries*. Published for the U.S. Agency for International Development (USAID) by the Basic Support for Institutionalizing Child Survival (BASICS) Project, Arlington, Va. <http://www.basics.org/Publications/pubs/msg/program.htm#part>.

Jordan, Brigitte. "Authoritative Knowledge and Its Construction." *Childbirth and Authoritative Knowledge: Cross-Cultural Perspectives*. Ed. Robbie E. Davis-Floyd and Carolyn F. Sargent. Berkeley: University of California Press, 1997. 55-79.

Pierce, Christine. "Philosophy." *Signs: Journal of Women in Culture and Society* 1 (Winter 1975): 422-33.

3.
Challenging Practice

Raising Our Children

Resisting, But Not Too Much

Interrogating the Paradox of Natural Mothering

Chris Bobel

Recently, I invited a local breastfeeding advocate and La Leche League leader named Mary Beth[1] to my "Gender and the Body" class. She framed her talk around "the many obstacles to making breastfeeding work in contemporary Western society." Mary Beth promoted constant mother-baby togetherness and the rejection of the shiny new gadgets that new parents are expected to acquire whether they can afford them or not, and she made a compelling feminist argument for keeping baby close. Women can and should trust their bodies to nourish their babies, she said. Say no to the male-dominated medical establishment. Say no to patriarchal constructions of the sexualized breast. Take it back. And she was effective. As Mary Beth presented her argument, I watched my students process the information. One student caught my attention, angst evident on her face. During the lively Q-and-A she finally burst out with the following:

> *I'm really struggling with this.... On the one hand, I am trying to fight oppression and claim my place in society, get recognized in the work force, get liberated. But now you are telling me that to be really free, I should go back home and take care of babies, breastfeeding them all the time. And it does sound really great. But I feel stuck. I don't know what I am supposed to do!*

As she spoke, I nodded knowingly. This dilemma haunts many feminists as they struggle to define and shape their lives and is the knot at the center of feminist mothering scholarship. Mothering scholar and sociologist Evelyn Nakano Glenn pointed to the conflict between feminists who regard maternally-derived gender differences as oppressive and those who reclaim motherhood as a source of power and status when she wrote:

> We are reluctant to give up the idea that motherhood is special. Pregnancy, birth, and breast-feeding are such powerful bodily experiences,

and the emotional attachment to the infant so intense, that it is difficult for women who have gone through these experiences and emotions to think that they do not constitute unique female experiences that create an unbridgeable gap between men and women (22-23).

My aim in this chapter is to respond to this dilemma by looking closely at the kind of attached mothering practice that Mary Beth advocates as an expression of feminism.

Mary Beth is part of an emerging social movement of women I call "natural mothers." The natural mothers give birth to their babies at home; they homeschool; they grow much of their family's produce, and sew many of their clothes. The natural mothers seem, at first glance, an anachronism, recalling a time when some women derived their identities from raising families, and excelling at the domestic arts. While their contemporaries negotiate daycare, babysitters, and bottle-feeding, the natural mothers reject almost everything that facilitates mother-child separation. They believe that consumerism, technology, and detachment from nature are social ills that mothers can and should oppose.

The natural mothers constitute a counterculture that enacts a particular form of activism, a kind of "everyday activism," to use Jennifer Baumgardner and Amy Richards' term or what New Social Movements scholars increasingly find in contemporary social movements—a focus on the day to day content of personal lives, linked with issues of identity rather than economic grievances characteristic of, for example, working class movements (see Johnston, Larana, and Gusfield). Natural mothers, working at the level of the individual and the familiar, seek to change culture one family at a time. But what is natural mothering's promise for social change? Does this particular kind of mothering trap or liberate women?

Getting to Know Natural Mothering

In the mid 1990s, I grew to know several small intersecting communities of natural mothers. I spent over two years in the field—participating in playgroups with my toddler and attending La Leche League meetings (the international breastfeeding support organization). I joined a food co-op and "Creating Stronger Families (CSF)," an association of those who chose homeschooling, homebirth, and other parenting alternatives. CSF met for monthly potlucks and "working bees" in which members assisted the host family with a house project and held an annual weekend conference that drew families throughout the Midwest. Later, I interviewed 32 natural mothers I met during the course of my fieldwork. Through these observations and interviews, I learned that

Natural Mothering merges two lifestyle practices—Voluntary Simplicity and Attachment Parenting—while taking inspiration from Cultural Feminism.

Consciously anti-materialist and anti-consumerist, Voluntary Simplicity promotes a life freed from, as one of my informants put it, "biggering and bettering." Voluntary Simplicity, also called Simple Living, dictates a lifestyle that derives meaning from relative austerity, minimized consumption and the belief that individual well being is entangled with the well being of society at large (see Elgin; Levering and Urbanska; Lockwood; Longacre; Luhrs; Pierce and St James). Proponents of this lifestyle reject material preoccupations and opt for recycling, and in some cases, bartering and trading in place of traditional market exchange. They seek meaning in "doing it oneself," freed from the constraints of institutions and experts.

The practice of Attachment Parenting (AP), which is related to Voluntary Simplicity, addresses the concerns of parents who seek to depart from what they believe is the norm in a changing, alienating, and child-decentered culture. Family practice physician William Sears, together with his wife, Martha Sears, R.N., popularized AP in their 30 books on pregnancy, birth, infancy, toddlerhood, discipline and nighttime parenting, beginning with *The Baby Book* in 1993. Now, the Sears are joined by their two oldest sons (also pediatricians) who characterize AP as "just doing what comes naturally" (J. Sears). AP, the Sears' argue, is the best way to create and maintain a bond with your children. AP facilitates healthy physical, spiritual, emotional and moral child development by placing a premium on extensive mother-child physical contact: "This style is a way of caring that brings out the best in parents and their babies (W. Sears 2), they say. The Sears' acknowledge that AP is not new, but simply "common sense parenting we all would do if left to our own healthy resources" (2).[2] Notably, while the practice is called Attachment *Parenting* and not mothering, this terminology is misleading. On the popular website AskDrSears.com, it is stated that "for the first year or two, a child is primarily bonded to his mother," and AP practices inscribe and support this bond. Mothers are attached to children, and fathers and other potential caregivers operate merely in supporting roles.

Finally, as a movement that celebrates, rather than denigrates gendered qualities of nurturance and care, Natural Mothering is inspired by cultural feminism's unapologetic reclamation of domesticity and maternity. Cultural feminism, derived from Radical Feminist Theory, is also known as feminine feminism, domestic feminism, and difference feminism. It differs from more popular liberal feminist theory which regards essentialism as the source of women's subordination. Cultural feminist theory, on the contrary, names the devaluing of women's essential differences (whether biologically derived or culturally constructed) as problematic and at the root of sexism. Cultural feminists believe that women have developed their unique social orientation in the context of the domestic sphere, especially through the practice of mothering, as Nancy Chodorow famously argued. Creating a climate that celebrates rather than denigrates difference is the aim of cultural feminists. Natural mothering is seen as a concrete expression of this conceptualization. Nearly 50 percent of the natural mothers I studied explicitly identified as feminists; others expressed ideas compatible with feminist politics but did not call themselves feminists. Many of the mothers expressed frustration with a particular kind of feminism (typically seen as *the* feminism), which they saw as dictating that working outside the home was a measure of a woman's worth; they preferred a feminism that foregrounded their identity as women and resisted male standards. For example, as natural mother Grace Burton stated:

> *I feel that the women's movement of the 1960s robbed me of something. It did get me more pay in the workplace, and I don't mind that, but they also made me be in the workplace, and I mind that immensely.*

In short, natural mothering is cultural feminist theory in practice.

So how does Natural Mothering, the product of these practices and ideologies, make sense of itself? In short, I argue that Natural Mothering is ultimately paradoxical. While it resists both technology and capitalism, it stops short of resisting patriarchy. Natural mothers accept the category 'woman' as it is socially constructed and fail to acknowledge the privilege necessary to enact their lifestyle. Thus, natural mothering's promise as a project of recreating motherhood, and by extension, society at large, is compromised (Bobel). Because it lacks a comprehensive and honest self-critique, its criticism of the institutions it resists is evaporated and its message is left open to co-optation.

Interrogating the Paradox

This paradox demands a closer look. I found it expressed in the form of two key contradictions that each create a distinctive theoretical tension. The first contradiction centers on *choice*. The natural mothers spoke of a conscious and intentional decision to mother naturally, consistent with their identities as feminists and everyday activists for social change. One informant, whom I call Michelle Grant-Jones, is a mother of three with a B.A. in Women's Studies. Early in our interview, she admitted that "[she] might not look like much of feminist trooping around with [her] kids with no goal really before [her]" but was careful to draw a stark distinction between "stay-at-home mothers" of an earlier generation and herself. Her life, she asserted, was freely chosen and, consistent with her feminism, which recognizes the essential experience of womanhood, and by extension, motherhood. The distortion of this particularly raced and classed history of women's labor aside, her generational comment is interesting. Embedded in this discourse of choice lays a contradiction. Note, for example, the following exchange I had with Teresa Reyes, a biologist turned natural mother of four, who shared how her plans shifted after the birth of her first baby. She originally planned to return to work and leave the baby with her husband, but something changed:

> *I just felt I had no choice. . . I suppose I was a little surprised, because after she was born it was not an option for me to leave her.*

Still other mothers responded to my query, why natural mother? with the response: "I just knew." I heard repeatedly how, when the mothers were faced with a decision, they simply followed their instincts and intuition. When I pushed them to provide a rationale for their choices, they paused and looked away wistfully. "I don't know. It just felt right to homebirth, to extend breastfeed, to keep baby in bed with us," they told me in various iterations. Their mothering practice relied on a particular embodied knowledge. But, of course, this begs a question: if knowledge is derived from the body, from a body regarded as natural and unmediated by culture, and if behavior is actually driven by instinctual impulse rather than reasoned response, is this choice? The natural mothers told me in no uncertain terms that they could NOT mother in any other way. Hence, the last rational choice they made was the choice to embrace an ideology of "nature knows best"—an ideology shaped by biologically determinist and historically and culturally gendered understandings of women, mothers, and families. Simply put, natural mothering was the "choice" that chose them.

The second contradiction revealed in the discourse of natural mothering centers on *control*. The natural mothers believe they have wrested control of their personal lives from institutions and experts claiming to "know best." For example, natural mothers push birthing practices, patently resisting the obstetrical medical establishment. Natural mothers were shopping local food co-ops, buying in bulk, and buying shares in Community Supported Agriculture before major "natural foods" chain stores brought such natural, local and whole foods into the trendy, overpriced current in the mainstream. This suggests that natural mothers *do* (or at least *did*) exist on the margins, trailblazing, pushing institutions, and as a result, raising awareness. Natural mothering is radical in the very real ways it questions features of family life in an advanced capitalist society.

If mainstream culture is rejected, does something else fill that void? The mothers spoke passionately of the importance of "taking mothering back" from institutions and "experts," and simultaneously waxed, with a blend of awe and resignation, on the futility of resisting *nature*. Over and over again, I heard stories of the mothers' abiding faith in nature, which served as a model and resource to them. Stacey Thurer McReardon, aspiring writer and mother of four, shared that when she learned to stop, in her words, "tweaking things," she adopted a philosophy of letting nature run its course and she was much happier for it. Ingrid Kitzinger, a mother of three, referred to childbirth as something you don't really control, something "that just happens to you." Clearly, this is a narrative of respecting omnipotent nature. But when the mothers spoke of nature, they spoke of a monolithic and static concept, predating humankind, that remains pure and unadulterated. To them, nature is the perfect model for human behavior because it is separate from and unpolluted by human manipulation. This view, of course, is problematic; it denies the many ways in which nature is indeed culturally constructed and thus dynamic. For these mothers, the "fact" of nature's separation from culture is what renders it so appealing and powerful. Furthermore, the mothers told me, listening to nature led them to tune into the powerful mother-child bond. This relationship, they maintain, fuses mothers and children virtually into a single entity, extending the relationship developed during pregnancy. In this view, maternal self-sacrifice is not at the root of contemporary mothers' difficulties; rather, a culture that casts mothers and children in opposition, in direct affront to "nature," is the root of personal and social dysfunction.

Among the serious repercussions of the merged mother-child identity at the heart of natural mothering is the way it marginalizes fathers. When I pressed the mothers to say why they, as women, were the designated stay at home caregiver, practicing what Sharon Hays calls "intensive motherhood," explanations based on biological difference surfaced. Primarily due to the importance placed on breastfeeding, mothers seldom shared infant feeding with fathers, or other potential caregivers. Over time, these feeding norms established caring patterns that persisted throughout mothers' *and* fathers' parenting careers. When the mother is positioned as the singular food source, and furthermore, when nursing becomes the primary means of comfort for baby, mothers are quickly constructed as irreplaceable.[3] Based on a deeper understanding of the paradoxes of natural mothering, I turn to a brief discussion of this particular style of parenting's potential for social change.

Can Natural Mothering Fulfill Its Promise?

Most of the natural mothers viewed their lives as strategic missions to effect social change. For example, Grace Burton claimed passionately: "I've decided that absolutely everything I do is political." However, the expression of this politicization varies among the mothers. While some natural mothers participate in public actions, such as "nurse ins,"[4] most strive to effect social change through their daily practice of mothering outside the mainstream. But, I ask, can natural mothering reform society, one family at a time, or is it simply a form of narcissistic retreat devoid of impact beyond the empire of the individual family?

Sociologist and mothering theorist Barbara Katz Rothman conceptualizes American motherhood as "resting on three deeply rooted ideologies—capitalism, technology and patriarchy" (26). Katz Rothman argues that the effect of the three ideologies has been to split motherhood apart, forcing it into a series of dysfunctional dualisms such as mind and body, public and private, personal and political, work and home, production and reproduction and masculine and feminine, and I add to this list: nature and culture. Natural mothering, I argue, ably resists two of these three institutions: capitalism and technology, challenging the bifurcations that these institutions forge. But at the same time, its discourses of choice and control, deeply paradoxical at their core, fail to resist the third institution: patriarchy. The mothers' surrender of agency to so-called instinct and a romanticized view of nature reifies an essentialist construction of womanhood. Theirs is a politics of accommodation. Like maternalists of earlier eras who used their femininity to pressure men to take them seriously as moral role models and to exercise some authority, at least in the domestic sphere (see Cott; Epstein; Ryan), the natural mothers push boundaries of their role while embracing specific features of it; they "bargain with patriarchy" (Kandiyoti). Kandiyoti uses this term to convey the complex set of "rules and scripts regulating gender relations to which both genders accommodate and acquiesce, yet which may nonetheless be contested, redefined, and renegotiated" (286). That is, women, given their context-bound existence, strategize within their particular constraints, enabling them to resist where and when possible. Natural mothering, a lifestyle that is simultaneously rebellious and obedient, represents precisely the kind of negotiation within male-dominated and -defined circumstances that Deniz Kandiyoti theorizes.

Given that natural mothering accommodates patriarchy, its potential for social change is compromised. However, I venture that this is not the only reason the movement is limited. The privilege necessary to enact this particular lifestyle constructs natural mothering as the domain of the few, especially because natural mothers themselves seem blind to this privilege. Consider, for example, my conversation with natural mother Jeanette Zientarski who spoke of mothering as "changing the world." She argued for an instinctual basis for her natural mothering much like the intuitively derived practice beyond the scope of rational choice I discussed earlier. When asked, "why isn't this kind of mothering instinctual for everyone?" she met the question with silence. Recall that the natural mothers "just know" what is in the best interest of their children—mothering this way is driven by feeling, by gut level awareness. Thus, intellectualizing their "choices" is impossible, they told me, implying that my question was the wrong one, that I just didn't get it. But how can it be that some mothers operate on instinct while others do not? There must be a deeper explanation, and so, I turn to the characteristics of the natural mothers themselves.

All the informants were white and all appeared to be heterosexual; 88 percent were married; 87 percent owned homes; 75 percent of the husbands were white-collar professionals; 81 percent of the mothers had attended college and 69 percent had completed a degree (many of them advanced degrees); 53 percent had significant and often extended travel experience, including living abroad, Peace Corps and missionary work. Obviously, this demographic does not reflect the general American population. These privileged women have access to resources as wives and homemakers, enjoying the prestige that accompanies their class, race, and sexuality. Since beginning my research on natural mothers, I have learned that the population is a bit more diverse than I first encountered. "Hip Mamas" (typically women in their 20s and early 30s with a political and or Punk edge who identify with the icon of "the next generation of mothers," mother-writer Ariel Gore), lesbian mothers, and working class mothers also number among the women. But, on the whole, the natural mothers still enjoy what Pierre Bourdieu calls "cultural capital."

Most natural mothers are white and college educated, and are thus less likely to come under attack for their alternative "choices." Imagine a poor woman of color spotted publicly breastfeeding an older child—she is vulnerable in a way a woman of more social privilege is not. A mother receiving state aid does not have the option of waiving vaccinations while an economically-secure mother with private insurance does. An immigrant woman known to use herbal remedies to treat illness may be scolded by her child's pediatrician. At the same time, a more privileged mother may meet similar resistance, but her decision will not be seen as a consequence of her assumed ignorance or her "backward" culture. In sum, natural mothering is a parenting lifestyle not possible for everyone.

It is not only the necessity of some measure of privilege that undermines the force of the movement to effect social change. The absence of an analysis advanced by the movement itself is noted, including the relative blindness the mothers have to their own cultural capital. This blind eye became apparent to me when I asked the mothers to describe the "typical natural mother." Their answers ranged from "people suspicious of popular culture," and "Moms attuned to the sense of the natural," to people with "a strong sense of self." No one cited race, class, or sexuality characteristics as meaningful. This silence was profound and raises serious questions about the viability of a movement that does not fully see itself.

As I have shown, while the natural mothers resist technology and capitalism, they fail to challenge patriarchy. Natural mothers work to extract meaning and power from the maternal role, marshalling tremendous creativity and resourcefulness; and framing their choices with pride and a hope for social change. As homeschoolers, homebirthers, and natural health care consumers, they turn their backs on the mainstream. In so doing, they ask important questions about our parenting holy grails. At the same time that the natural mothers live on the margins and swim upstream, they capitulate to definitions of womanhood and motherhood written in the service of patriarchy. Theirs is not a project of rebelling against the expectation that mothers foreground their children's needs. Theirs is not a project of challenging fathers to roll up their sleeves and provide more instrumental care (as both Nancy Chodorow and Sara Ruddick prescribed). Furthermore, because natural mothering fails to see the fundamental place of privilege in enactment of the lifestyle, it is vulnerable to cooptation. Natural Mothering resists, but not too much.

[1]This is a pseudonym as are the names of the informants I will discuss later in the chapter.

[2]Of course, AP is not contained in the affluent "first world." Meredith Small, fore example, takes great care to point out the historical and global practice of AP, demonstrating the anomaly that is Western-style parenting with its premium on independence and mother-baby separation.

[3]This, of course, is neither a new observation, nor an original argument. Over 30 years ago, Michelle Rosaldo and Louise Lamphere pointed to women's childbearing and lactation as impairing their mobility and thus, dooming them to domesticity and subordination.

[4]An activist tactic through which mothers publicly breastfeed their children in protest of policies which ban or otherwise undermine breastfeeding (see Harmon).

Works Cited

Baumgardner, Jennifer and Amy Richards. *Manifesta: Young Women, Feminism and the Future.* New York: Farrar, Straus, and Giroux, 2000.

Bobel, Chris. *The Paradox of Natural Mothering.* Philadelphia: Temple University Press, 2002.

Bourdieu, Pierre. "The Forms of Capital." *Handbook for Theory and Research for the Sociology of Education.* Ed. J. G. Richardson. New York: Greenwood Press, 1986. 241-258.

Brasile, Monica. "Exotics in Labor: The Primitive Body in U.S. Childbirth

Discourse." National Women's Studies Association Annual Conference. Milwaukee, WI. 2004.

Buskens, Petra. "The Impossibility of "Natural Parenting" for Modern Mothers." *Mother Matters: Motherhood as Discourse and Practice.* Ed. Andrea O'Reilly. Toronto, Canada: Association for Research on Mothering, 2004. 75-86.

Chodorow, Nancy. *The Reproduction of Mothering: Psychoanalysis and the Sociology of Gender.* Berkeley: University of California Press, 1978.

Cook, Daniel. "The Mother as Consumer: Insights from the Children's Wear Industry. 1917-1929." *Sociological Quarterly* (1995): 36, 3, 505-522.

Cott, Nancy. *The Bonds of Womanhood: "Woman's Sphere" in New England, 1780-1835.* New Haven, CT: Yale University Press, 1977.

Davidson, J. *The Joy of Simple Living: Over 1,500 Simple Ways to Make Your Life Easy and Content—At Home and At Work.* Emmaus, PA: Rodale Books, 1999.

Elgin, Duane. *Voluntary Simplicity: Toward a Way of Life That is Outwardly Simple and Inwardly Rich* (2nd Ed). New York: William Morrow, 1993.

Epstein, Barbara. *The Politics of Domesticity: Women, Evangelism, and Temperance in Nineteenth-Century America.* Middletown, CT: Wesleyan University Press, 1981.

Glenn, Evelyn Nakano. Introduction. "Social Constructions of Mothering: A Thematic Overview." *Mothering: Ideology, Experience and Agency.* Ed. E.N. Glenn, G. Chang and L. R. Forcey. New York: Routledge, 1994. 1-29.

Gore, Ariel. *The Hip Mama Survival Guide: Advice from the Trenches on Pregnancy, Childbirth, Cool Names, Clueless Doctors, Potty Training and Toddler Avengers.* New York: Hyperion, 1998.

Gore, Ariel. *The Mother Trip: Hip Mamas Guide to Staying Sane in the Chaos of Motherhood.* Boston: Seal Press, 2000.

Gore, Ariel. and Bee Lavender, eds. *Breeder: Real-life Stories from the New Generation of Mothers.* Boston: Seal Press, 2001.

Harmon, Amy. "'Lactivists' Taking Their Cause, and Their Babies to the Streets." *The New York Times.* 7 June 2005. 25 Jan. 2005 <http://www.nytimes.com/2005/06/07/nyregion/07nurse.html?ei=5088anden=0c55cf357d95bd30andex=1275796800andpartner=rssnytandemc=rssandpagewanted=print>.

Hays, Sharon. *The Cultural Contradictions of Motherhood.* New Haven: Yale University Press, 1996.

Johnston, Hank, Enrique Larana and Joseph Gusfield, eds. *The New Social Movements.* Philadelphia: Temple University Press, 1994.

Kandiyoti, Deniz. "Bargaining with Patriarchy." *Gender and Society* 2 (1988): 274-290.

Katz Rothman, Barbara. *Recreating Motherhood: Ideology and Technology in a Patriarchal Society.* New York: W. W. Norton, 1989.

Levering, Frank and Wanda Ubranska. *Simple Living: One Couple's Search for a Better Life.* Winston-Salem, N.C.: John F. Blair Publishers, 2003.

Lockwood, Georgene. *Complete Idiot's Guide to Simple Living.* New York: Alpha Books, 2000.

Longacre, Doris. *Living More With Less.* Scottdale, PA: Herald Press, 1981.

Luhrs, Janet. *The Simple Living Guide.* New York: Broadway Books, 1997.

Pierce, Linda Breen. *Simplicity Lessons: A 12-Step Guide to Living Simply.* Carmel, CA: Gallagher Books, 2003.

Rosaldo, Michelle Z., and Louise Lamphere. *Women, Culture, and Society.* Stanford, CA: Stanford University Press, 1974.

Ryan, Mary. *The Cradle of the Middle Class: The Family in Oneida County, NY, 1790-1865.* Cambridge: Cambridge University Press, 1981.

St. James, Elaine. *Living the Simple Life: A Guide to Scaling Down and Enjoying More.* New York: Hyperion, 1998.

Sears, Jim. "FAQS." AskDrSears.com. 25 Jan. 2007. Online: www.askdrsears.com/faq/ap2.asp.

Sears, William and Martha Sears. *The Baby Book.* New York: Little Brown, 1993.

Small, Meredith F. *Our Babies, Ourselves: How Biology and Culture Shape The Way We Parent.* New York: Anchor Books, 1998.

Stoller, Debbie. *Stitch-n-Bitch: The Knitter's Guide.* New York: Workman Publishing Company, 2004.

Making Decisions About Vaccines

Interactions Between Parents and Experts

Rachel Casiday

Following childbirth, one of the first decisions facing new mothers concerns vaccinating their infants against a range of infectious diseases. The decision to vaccinate is often taken for granted, with vaccines automatically given to protect children's health. Indeed, vaccines have been credited with saving millions of lives around the world and are widely hailed as a vital, safe and cost-effective public health intervention, a 'magic bullet' for achieving control over the suffering caused by infectious diseases (World Health Organization). However, since the first smallpox vaccine was developed in the eighteenth century, the legitimacy and safety of vaccination have frequently been challenged. Parents—especially mothers—are expected to evaluate contradictory advice in order to make decisions about which vaccines to accept for their children and when to administer the vaccines. These decisions rely on evaluations of relative risk, on trust in the 'expert' sources offering advice, and sometimes on social and legal pressures to comply with recommended vaccination schedules. Such pressure may have a detrimental effect on trust and communication between mothers and the other experts (e.g., medical and governmental) responsible for protecting their children's health.

'Expert' Advice on Vaccinations

Popular parenting books and magazines are full of advice on vaccination. Most general-purpose parenting books recommend following standard immunization schedules (Green; Murkoff, Eisenberg and Hathaway; Eisenberg, Murkoff and Hathaway; Stoppard), reminding parents of the devastating effects of vaccine-preventable diseases. A few writers take a less conventional approach, offering alternative, delayed immunization schedules for parents concerned about the potential effects of immunizing very small children (Cave and Mitchell; Romm). There is also a vocal anti-vaccine camp, producing books specifically warning parents of the many dangers that have been ascribed to vaccinations (McTaggart). This paper examines the interactions between expert advice, health policy, and mothers' decision-making about vaccination. It will discuss in detail a recent controversy surrounding the measles, mumps, and rubella (MMR) vaccine in the United Kingdom. This case clearly illustrates the tensions between parents' and other experts' claims and objectives. Such tensions, and important lessons about their consequences, are also salient for other vaccine controversies.

Overview of the MMR Controversy

The question of vaccine safety and advisability rose to sudden prominence and urgency in the United Kingdom with widespread media reports of a suspected association between the MMR vaccine and autism. The ensuing controversy was marked by complex, often fraught, interactions between parents as decision makers and other 'expert' advisors and policy makers.

The initial trigger for this controversy was the appearance of an article in *The Lancet* (Wakefield et al.) by a team of pediatric gastroenterologists treating a small group of children with a complex of digestive and neurobehavioral problems, including autism. Of the twelve children's parents in the study, eight had noted the onset of their symptoms soon after measles, mumps, and rubella vaccination.

Despite other studies' failure to find an association between autism and MMR (Madsen *et al.*; e.g., Honda, Shimizu and Rutter), widespread anxiety emerged among UK parents and in the media, resulting in a marked reduction in MMR uptake rates (Department of Health). Several writers have outlined a progression of events leading from *The Lancet* publication to the public outcry and diminished public confidence in the vaccine (Anderson; Bedford and Elliman; Begg et al.; Bellaby; Elliman and Bedford "MMR Vaccine: The Continuing Saga"; Jewell; Mills). These accounts focus on the roles of the media and of medical 'experts' in shaping the controversy. Parents are portrayed as passive recipients of media images (conveying misinformation about the balance of scientific opinion on the matter) and expert information. Parental challenges to MMR vaccination are presumed to be the result of insufficient information or of risk calculations that are clouded by an unwarranted emotional response to the media images of suffering autistic children (Elliman and Bedford "MMR Vaccine—Worries Are Not Justified"; Jewell; Sporton and Francis; Whyte and Liversidge; Salisbury and Yarwood). However, these accounts have largely overlooked the roles that parents have actually played in shaping the debate about MMR, as well as parents' own expertise in navigating an array of contradictory information to make vaccination decisions for their children.

Understanding Parents' Views

In order to understand the roles of parents in this debate, I undertook a study of parental decision-making about the MMR vaccine, interviewing 84 parents (74 mothers and 10 fathers) in England (Casiday "Children's Health"; Casiday "Risk Conceptualisation"). Parents were recruited at mother and baby groups, through flyers posted at nurseries and community centers, and through on-line message boards. Of the 87 parents who participated, 56 had vaccinated their children with the MMR at the time of interview; 16 had (or were planning to have) separate (single-antigen) vaccines, 10 did not vaccinate for measles, mumps, and rubella, and 5 were still undecided. Parents were recruited from a broad range of educational and socioeconomic backgrounds, but, on the whole, the study group was well-educated and affluent. Throughout this chapter, I have tended to use the term 'parents' rather than 'mothers'; although in the majority of cases it was mothers who made decisions about their children's vaccinations. I found no systematic gender bias in parents' views about the issue, either in this study or in a later, large-scale postal survey I conducted.

Frightening Risks

The following mother's description of her son's autism is characteristic of the reports that parents had heard about the potential effects of MMR vaccination:

> *I am convinced my son's autism was a direct result of the MMR because, prior to having it, there was nothing in his child development book that had given any concern to me or the health professionals... After [the injection], he was so ill with the fever and vomiting, he stayed restless and irritable from that moment on.... Over the next three months he started to self-injure, banging his head on the floor.* (Sheila,[1] immunized her son with MMR and now suing the vaccine manufacturers)

The crucial aspect of Sheila's poignant testimony is the contrast between her son's normal development prior to his MMR vaccination, and the disturbing symptoms and behaviors that followed. As his mother, she knew him well both before and after his autism was manifest. This gave her a special knowledge about her son that nobody else could claim. Other parents' fears were based on having heard similar accounts, both on the news and from personal acquaintances. It was the sudden change, rather than the ill-defined symptoms, that was particularly worrying.

On the other hand, not immunizing was also seen to present serious and frightening risks to children. A number of factors, from the quality of the child's living conditions and diet to the overall level of vaccination in the community, entered into parents' evaluations of the risks posed by the diseases measles, mumps, and rubella. In general, parents recognized that falling vaccination rates meant that their children, if unimmunized, were more likely to catch measles, mumps, and rubella. In fact, children did die in outbreaks of measles resulting from diminished MMR uptake during this controversy (McDonald and Ungoed Thomas 15). A different, but very important, type of risk that parents perceived from not allowing their children to be vaccinated with MMR was the social risk of being seen as a bad or irresponsible parent.

Parents' Decision-Making Process

What is it about the MMR vaccine that made this such a crucial decision for many parents? Certainly, the dramatic consequences, or feared consequences, of this decision made it very important. Uncertainty about the likelihood of those consequences—about risk—also made it a difficult decision for many. But another, perhaps even more fundamental, issue also played into this decision. Parents were being required to make a choice that would have significant consequences, not for their own health, but for the health of their children who are unable to decide for themselves. Getting this decision 'right' came to symbolize what it means to be a good parent (see Alderson):

> *What's hard is knowing that I have the control of the decision for my baby. He can't decide for himself, and what if I make the wrong one? I'm not a gambling man. I can't gamble with something like that. It's all about protecting little David over there.* (Clive, planning to immunize his child with separate injections)

This concern to make the right decision goes deeper than the risk, described above, of being viewed by others as a bad parent. More fundamentally, Clive, and others like him, needed to get the decision right so that they can view themselves as good parents. Not 'gambling' with his son's health was a way of expressing responsibility for something too precious to be treated casually.

Many parents did not find the MMR decision to be a difficult one, but they went on to explain how important it was to immunize children against diseases. In other words, even when it was not a difficult decision, it was still regarded as very important for children's well being. Parents self-consciously evaluated their options in terms of the risks they posed to their children and, to a lesser extent, to the community at large and to their status as responsible parents.

Risk, to these parents, was construed as the likelihood of a *particular* child coming to harm as a result of their decision. Parents weighed possible outcomes, but uncertainty about the relative risks and benefits made their assessments at times ambiguous and difficult. Parents sometimes adopted compromise solutions to minimize the risk from MMR while still conferring protection against the diseases. Two such strategies were delaying vaccination and immunizing with three separate vaccines (as an alternative to the combined MMR) through private clinics. Parents who adopted these strategies recognized the problems that they entailed, but felt that they offered the best solution to the conundrum.

Delaying immunization, by several months or even indefinitely, gave parents more time to make the decision. When appointments (automatically generated by a central office and mailed to parents) arrived, several parents ignored them or made excuses for not coming at the designated time. They were dissatisfied with the lack of resolution that such a strategy offered, but were reluctant to make an irrevocable decision.

Other parents made a more deliberate decision to postpone MMR immunization until their children were older than the recommended 12-15 months. Older, bigger children were presumed to be more capable of handling the challenge to the immune system posed by the vaccine. Another reason relates to one of the 'expert' arguments that had been used to refute the alleged link between MMR and autism. According to this argument, the autistic symptoms frequently begin around one year of age, making the MMR vaccination appear (fallaciously) to be the culprit (NHS Health Promotion England). Some parents chose to wait until their children had passed this age, making sure that they did not display any signs of autistic behavior, before vaccinating them. This way, they were more confident that their children were not in the 'small minority' they thought might be susceptible to problems caused by the vaccine.

Parents who opted to immunize their children with each component of the MMR separately felt that this option was safer than the combined MMR vaccine because giving children one virus at a time 'doesn't place such stress on the immune system' (*Sarah, did not immunize her child because she could not obtain separate vaccines through the NHS*). Sheila gave a more detailed account of why she felt that giving a series of single vaccines was safer than giving them all at once:

> *My understanding of the single vaccines is that studies have shown that it is when the mumps vaccine is given with the measles one that the mumps vaccine damages the gut wall and enables the measles virus to take up residence there. Therefore, the single measles vaccine should be much safer*

than the MMR. (Sheila, immunized her child with MMR and now suing the vaccine manufacturers)

Sheila's explanation is heavily indebted to Dr. Wakefield's research and hypotheses, and offers a molecular-anatomical mechanism for the supposed action of the triple vaccine. Although Dr. Wakefield was a gastroenterologist and not an immune specialist (a fact readily pointed out by his critics), the hypothetical mechanism he offered is based on specific actions of the viruses on specific organs: the explanation conforms to a medical view of the body as being made up of discreet but interrelated parts, even while it challenges widely accepted medical ideas about the action of combined vaccines. It is worth noting here also that Sheila was particularly reliant on Dr. Wakefield's research because she was a claimant in the legal action against the MMR vaccine manufacturers, and Dr. Wakefield's work constituted the principal medical evidence in this case. The MMR debate was not simply a dispute between 'the experts' and 'the public', but involved many contested claims of expertise among scientists and parents alike.

Parents who had opted for the separate immunizations generally perceived these to offer the same protective benefits as MMR, although the child would be delayed in gaining full immunity to all three diseases. However, a serious problem with the course of separate immunizations was the lack of government control over the quality of unlicensed, imported vaccines or those administering them. In other words, opting for the separate vaccines may have been a risky precaution—in trying to protect their children from the perceived risks of MMR, parents instead put their trust behind a vaccine regimen whose safety and efficacy have not been determined, and in largely unregulated clinics.

What Makes for an 'Expert,' and Whom Do You Trust?

Disagreement among the medical experts was a frustrating concern for many parents. Although they knew that the majority of medical experts had put their support behind the MMR, they also recognized as experts the researchers who suggested the risk of autism. The very strong message from the Department of Health and most GPs and nurses led to parents' doubts that their questions were being answered honestly. Health professionals were thought to risk losing their jobs if they openly discussed reservations, and financial incentives for GPs to reach immunization targets (Jewell 876) were also seen to compromise open discussion. Many parents felt that the only reason that the NHS did not offer separate vaccines for measles, mumps and rubella (as an alternative to the combined MMR vaccine) was that it would cost more to do so, although this is not among the reasons given by the NHS for its policy

(National Health Service Immunisation Information). For parents worried that MMR was unsafe, this apparent prioritizing of cost over children's health and well-being was alarming.

In this controversy, many parents took a fundamentally different view of what constitutes 'expertise,' and a fundamentally different epistemological approach than the epidemiological one used to support the government's position that MMR was safe. They demanded a different type of evidence, which would focus on the individuals who had reportedly been adversely affected (rather than population-level statistics). Anecdotal accounts of the dramatic changes observed by other parents were extremely salient, because of the special relationship between parents and children:

> *And to me the clinching thing on why I wanted the single vaccines was the parents on the television that were showing their children… that these parents were so convinced that it was the MMR… Okay, they say that it's just the signs of autism come out at about the same time that MMR is given. But still, to them it was the MMR. They truly believed that, do you know what I mean?* (Dianne, immunized her son with separate injections and later with MMR)

Dianne's hesitation about the MMR stemmed from the parents' genuine belief that the vaccine had damaged their children. That belief was far more important than the scientific evidence, however sound it might be. Parents, I was told, know their own children better than anybody else, and so are in a unique position to notice changes in their behavior and personalities. These parents were often seen as the true 'experts' about the potential dangers of MMR. Another mother expressed to me her frustration at not being taken seriously when her son had a bad reaction following his immunization:

> *When you tell the GP and you tell the Health Visitor and they [say] 'Don't be silly. What do you know?' And yet, I think an informed parent can certainly have a lot more information available in that afternoon about your child but also about what they found out on the web and that they can actually, yes, possibly have more information sometimes than a GP.* (Jo, did not immunize her second child after her first reacted badly to MMR)

This mother was a Ph.D.-level scientist by profession and described herself as 'pro-vaccination'. However, she drew on her experience as a mother and her own research on the internet, more than her scientific training, to make her case to the doctors and health visitor. As a mother, she had access to first-hand information about her son that her GP would otherwise have missed, and was adamant that such experiences were 'not to be dismissed'.

It is interesting to note that often parents arrived at very different conclusions from the intended messages presented by doctors or government officials promoting the safety of the MMR. For instance, the practice of delaying vaccination until after the period in which autistic symptoms were said to originate (regardless of immunization) was viewed by parents as a way of 'playing it safe,' but by public health workers as needlessly exposing children to infection risk for several months. Parents also reinterpreted many governmental arguments against separate injections as an alternative to the MMR. For example, one official argument against using three separate vaccines rather than the MMR was that fewer children would actually receive the full course of immunization if they had to come on three different occasions rather than just once (NHS Health Promotion England). Most parents I interviewed rejected the claim that separating the vaccines would result in lower immunization rates among parents who opted for three separate vaccines, rather than the MMR:

I was very tempted initially to get the single vaccines. The argument about parents not remembering seemed ridiculous. Of course you would remember to come back for the others. (Audrey, immunized her child with MMR)

The parents who had chosen single-component vaccines had all made a considerable investment of time, research, and money to find a provider and pay for the vaccines. The suggestion that parents who wanted single vaccines for their children would not take their responsibilities seriously enough to ensure that their children received the full course was considered offensive.

In the face of high-profile contradictory information, it was generally parents' trust in particular sources of information (especially known doctors and other parents) that helped them to make their decisions about the MMR vaccine. Actions that damaged trust, such as the heavy-handed messages from government authorities, may have resulted in diminished confidence in the vaccine and in the risk-regulating role of the government and its medical experts (see Streefland).

Conclusion: MMR and Other Vaccine Controversies

The UK controversy over MMR is in many ways representative of other controversies about the principles behind, and implementation of, vaccination programs. A classical example is the smallpox eradication campaign launched by the World Health Organization in 1966. The eradication of smallpox is often touted as one of the greatest achievements of modern public health, but vaccinating enough people to eradicate the disease required overcoming significant resistance in different parts of the world. This resistance to immunization was often overcome with heavy-handed coercive techniques for the 'common good'. Paul Greenough described the intimidation and coercion used by physician-epidemiologists employed in the smallpox eradication campaign in South Asia, including containment of unvaccinated individuals and intimidating host-country medical staff (634–642). Although in the short term, these techniques resulted in the elimination of smallpox, such events have contributed to long-term problems of distrust of health workers.

As new vaccines are continually under development, and the received wisdom about old vaccines gets interpreted in new ways, we can expect many more such controversies to emerge in the future. In evaluating these controversies, and in formulating health policies to cope with them, it is vital to appreciate parents' unique knowledge of their own children, diverse interactions with other experts, and strategies for making important decisions about vaccination for their children. The challenge for doctors and scientists is to find ways of taking seriously parental experiences while interpreting other types of evidence.

I am not suggesting in this paper that there is anything intrinsically wrong with 'expert' medical advice, even when it conflicts with parental inclinations. That several children died of measles because parents did not follow the advice of doctors and medical authorities is a sad—and stark—reminder of the important role that medical experts can play in advising parents (McDonald and Ungoed Thomas 15). However, expert advice that does not recognize or understand parents' concerns is likely to damage trust between parents and health professionals. Furthermore, the advice itself may backfire, as parents may draw very different conclusions from those that were intended. And experts must listen to parents' claims about their children in order to develop research that will help to understand what did cause the serious problems that have been attributed to vaccines. Ultimately, children's health depends on effective, trusting, two-way communication between parents and medical experts.

[1]Pseudonyms have been used for informants and their children throughout this chapter.

Works Cited

Alderson, Priscilla. *Choosing for Children: Parents' Consent to Surgery.* Oxford: Oxford University Press, 1990.

Anderson, Pat. "Another Media Scare About MMR Vaccine Hits Britain." *British Medical Journal* 318.7198 (1999): 1578.

Bedford, Helen, and David Elliman. "MMR: The Onslaught Continues." *British Medical Journal* 326 (2003): 718.

Begg, Norman, et al. "Media Dents Confidence in MMR Vaccine." *British Medical Journal* 316 (1998): 561.

Bellaby, Paul. "Communication and Miscommunication About Risk: Understanding UK Parents' Attitudes to Combined MMR Vaccination." *BMJ* 327 (2003): 725-28.

Casiday, Rachel. "Children's Health and the Social Theory of Risk: Insights from the British MMR Controversy." *Social Science & Medicine* (forthcoming).

Casiday, Rachel. "Risk Conceptualisation, Trust and Decision-Making in the Face of Contradictory Information: The Case of MMR." University of Durham, 2005.

Cave, Stephanie, and Deborah Mitchell. *What Your Doctor May Not Tell You About Children's Vaccinations.* New York: Warner Books, 2001.

Department of Health. *Statistical Bulletin: NHS Immunisation Statistics 2003-04.* London, 2004.

Eisenberg, Arlene, Heidi E Murkoff, and Sandee E. Hathaway. *What to Expect the Toddler Years.* Cambridge: Simon and Schuster, 1996.

Elliman, David, and Helen Bedford. "MMR Vaccine--Worries Are Not Justified." *Archives of Disease in Childhood* 85 (2001): 271-73.

Elliman, David, and Helen Bedford. "MMR Vaccine: The Continuing Saga." *British Medical Journal* 322 (2001): 183-84.

Green, Christopher. *New Toddler Taming.* London: Vermilion, 2004.

Greenough, Paul. "Intimidation, Coercion and Resistance in the Final Stages of the South Asian Smallpox Eradication Campaign, 1973-1975." *Social Science and Medicine* 41.5 (1995): 633-45.

Honda, H., Y. Shimizu, and M. Rutter. "No Effect of MMR Withdrawal on the Incidence of Autism: A Total Population Study." *Journal of Child Psychology and Psychiatry* 46.6 (2005): 572-79.

Jewell, D. "MMR and the Age of Unreason." *British Journal of General Practice* 51 (2001): 875-6.

Madsen, K. M., et al. "A Population-Based Study of Measles, Mumps, and Rubella Vaccination and Autism." *New England Journal of Medicine* 347.19 (2002): 1477-82.

McDonald, Dearbhail, and Jonathan Ungoed Thomas. "This Little Girl Was Killed by Measles, a Disease She Should Never Have Had." *Sunday Times* 4 April 2004: 15.

McTaggart, Lynne, ed. *The Vaccination Bible: The Real Risks They Don't Tell You About All the Major Vaccines.* London: What Doctors Don't Tell You, 2000.

Mills, Heather. *MMR: The Story So Far.* London: Private Eye, 2002.

Murkoff, Heidi E, Arlene Eisenberg, and Sandee E. Hathaway. *What to Expect the First Year*. Cambridge: Simon and Schuster, 2003.

National Health Service Immunisation Information. "MMR Information Sheet 3: MMR, Single Vaccines and Choice." 2002. Crown Copyright.

NHS Health Promotion England. *MMR: What Parents Want to Know*. video, London, 2001.

Romm, Aviva Jill. *Vaccinations: A Thoughtful Parent's Guide: How to Make Safe, Sensible Decisions About the Risks, Benefits, and Alternatives*. Rochester, Vermont: Healing Art Press, 2001.

Salisbury, David, and Joanne Yarwood. "Public Perception of Immunization." *The Lancet* 363 (2004): 1324.

Sporton, Rachel K, and Sally-Anne Francis. "Choosing Not to Immunize: Are Parents Making Informed Decisions?" *Family Practice* 18.2 (2001): 181-88.

Stoppard, Dr. Miriam. *Complete Baby and Child Care*. London: Dorling Kindersley Limited, 2003.

Streefland, Pieter H. "Public Doubts About Vaccination Safety and Resistance against Vaccination." *Health Policy* 55.3 (2001): 159-72.

Wakefield, AJ, et al. "Ileal-Lymphoid-Nodular Hyperplasia, Non-Specific Colitis, and Pervasive Developmental Disorder in Children." *The Lancet* 351 (1998): 637-41.

Whyte, Alison, and Kim Liversidge. "Should Nurses Encourage Parents to Take up the MMR Vaccine?" *Nursing Times* 97.6 (2001): 17.

World Health Organization. "Immunization, Vaccines and Biologicals: Advocacy." 2003. 8 February 2005. <http://www.who.int/vaccines/en/advocacy.shtml>.

"Everything You Need to Know About Your Baby"

Feminism and Attachment Parenting

May Friedman

Attachment parenting refers to a series of practices and ideas that focus on the needs of the child to a greater extent than other parenting philosophies. By privileging the needs of the child, however, attachment parenting may result in the subordination of mothers who are asked to meet their children's needs immediately and around the clock. The maternal subordination required by attachment parenting may be particularly confusing to feminist mothers who are struggling to maintain a strong sense of self while suddenly moving their own needs to second place. Since it is often the same women who identify as feminist who are drawn to attachment parenting as a positive break from rigid and schedule-focused alternatives, the misogyny of attachment parenting, as it is presented by William and Martha Sears and others, may cause particular dissonance for feminist mothers. This paper will focus on the complexities and points of opposition that may result from the combination of feminism and attachment parenting.

What is Attachment Parenting?

Attachment parenting is a parenting style that focuses on cultivating a strong bond between children and their primary caregivers, particularly their mothers. While the tenets of attachment parenting have been practiced by some families virtually forever, "attachment parenting" as a designated title was introduced by Dr. William Sears and Martha Sears, a well-known pediatrician and nurse team who are also prolific authors of books on parenting. Following on the writing of the Sears' is *Attachment Parenting: Instinctive Care for Your Baby and Young Child* by Katie Allison Granju. Most of the information on attachment parenting presented here will be drawn from Granju's book and *The Baby Book* by the Sears'.

William Sears argues that attachment parents are more confident and enjoy parenting more than non-attachment parents, and that children of attachment parents are easier to discipline than are children of non-attachment parents (in Granju xx). Numerous other benefits are ascribed to attachment parenting, including increased physical health for babies and children and lower incidence of hyperactivity. Sears goes on to affirm that children who are attachment parented go on to become extra-sensitive to injustices and have strong social consciences. According to Sears, kids who enjoy attachment parenting grow up to become "kids who care" (in Granju xx).

In order to successfully emerge with these parenting miracles, attachment parents take on certain tasks. Practically, there are a number of tenets that are central to attachment parenting (often known as the five B's of attachment parenting):

- Birth-bonding: immediate physical bonding between mother (father?) and infant in the moments and hours following birth
- "belief in the signal value of your baby's cries": immediate response to baby's cues
- Breastfeeding
- "baby-wearing": carrying the baby in a sling or other device as frequently as possible
- "bedding close to baby" (adapted from Sears 6).

In addition to the five B's, attachment parenting philosophy attempts to minimize reliance on arbitrary deadlines for milestones (weaning, toilet training, sleeping through the night).[1]

Attachment parenting includes the above tasks, but goes beyond this simple list to instead act as a parenting philosophy. Proponents of the theory argue that attachment parenting is both child- and parent-centred. The child-centredness is born of the theory's focus on children as respected partners in the parent-child relationship. Children ought to be taken seriously and their cues ought to be responded to quickly and lovingly. In addition, children have the right to frequent, loving access to primary caregivers. This includes both parental attention and physical contact. The parent-centredness of attachment parenting is somewhat more difficult to locate. Attachment parenting advocates argue that while this style of caregiving may sound exhausting, "in the long run, it's actually the easiest parenting style" (Sears 10). By focusing on the needs of the child, parents will begin to understand their babies' cues, thus ending the frustration and confusion often associated with new parenthood. In addition, because children are incorporated into every aspect of parental life, parents may have more freedom and flexibility than non attachment-style parents—simply put the baby in the sling and go out for dinner, as Dr. Sears advocates (Sears 299). Finally, attachment parenting gurus argue that attachment parenting is the most natural choice for parents and children—and thus is actually the easiest and best choice for everyone involved.

So—what is the problem? Attachment parenting apparently provides excellent options for children and their parents and produces exceptional results. Of course, the reality of attachment parenting is significantly more complicated.

Who Are We Really Referring to When we Speak of Attachment Parents?

Though the theory is called "attachment parenting," and not "attachment mothering," even a cursory examination of the writing on this topic makes clear that the primary caregiver of attachment parented children is expected to be the mother. Although Sears argues that the work of caring for children should be shared by both parents, the discussion in both major attachment parenting "bibles" cited above is obviously addressed to mothers. While sections of the Sears' opus *The Baby Book* are addressed to attachment fathers ("Attachment parenting includes fathers, too" [10]) the majority of the book clearly takes mothers as the target audience.

This emphasis on motherhood is accomplished in a number of ways. The focus on breastfeeding as a critical tenet of attachment parenting requires mothers and babies to be in close proximity: the books make quite clear that even bottled breast milk result can lead to nipple confusion and will minimize the integral mother-child bond of breastfeeding (Granju 175). This exhortation to nurse immediately supposes that mothers will be the primary caregiver. Even in the case of bottle-feeding parents, Granju advocates the designation of a single feeder in the early days, reminding us that "nature designed *mothers* to feed their babies, not a rotating band of friendly helpers" (177). Likewise, in a discussion of mothers who must return to work, Sears asks mothers looking for alternative caregivers, "Who will mother your baby?" (411). This demotion of attachment fathers to "friendly helpers" typifies the philosophy of attachment parenting: Dad is an integral part of the process, because, hey, someone has to keep Mom sane! While adoptive parenting is peripherally discussed, neither text considers alternative families, such as same-sex parents, or families with more than two parents.

Dr. Sears does consider the possibility of mothers who, for one reason or another, cannot be with their babies around the clock. Regarding mothers who return to the work force, however, he cautions mothers to evaluate priorities: "Are there desired luxuries that can be temporarily put off? No material possessions are more valuable to your infant than you are." Sears goes on to explain that "...baby will ultimately have a voice in this decision, too. If you are blessed with a high-need baby ... full-time mothering for a longer time may be your only real option" (413). Statements such as these put the lie to the notion that attachment parenting can be simultaneously both child and parent focused—children are clearly the absolute priority in this parenting style. Likewise, the above statements decode the euphemistically-termed attachment parenting, and explicitly position mothers at the centre of this theory.

Criticisms of Attachment Parenting

If done by the book, attachment parenting has the potential for extremely regressive gender implications. By arguing for the universal and natural privileging of mothers as essential (and largely solitary) caregivers, attachment parenting forces families to return to a male breadwinner/female caregiver model. This gender discussion of the family unit is not explicitly discussed, however.[2]

One of the most disturbing aspects of attachment parenting theory is its reliance on the argument that this parenting technique is both natural and obvious. Sears writes that "When I first began using the term 'attachment parenting'…I felt ridiculous giving a name to a style of baby care that parents would naturally practice if they follow their own intuition rather than listening to the advice of others" (Sears in Granju: xix). Sears bolsters his claim by discussing the numerous indigenous people, who, uncorrupted by Western ways, simply respond to their babies' needs intuitively, thus raising untroubled and somehow superior (though obviously uncivilized) children. This focus on attachment parenting as a biological imperative is sufficiently troubling from the perspective of both race and gender, that a thorough critique must be left for another time. It is the "natural" character of attachment parenting that is meant to bolster claims of this theory as mother-centred. Simply put, if left to their own devices and given the opportunity to shake off the anti-family messages prevalent in Western society, all mothers would *want* to breastfeed, co-sleep and subsume their own needs to that of their children. Find yourself resenting attachment parenting? The theory is not flawed: you are simply unnatural, or, alternately, oppressed by capitalist (and probably feminist) notions of progress.

Both Sears and Granju assure us in the introductions to their books that attachment parenting ought to incorporate flexibility and that parents should pick and choose aspects of attachment parenting that fit their lives and values. Nonetheless, the overwhelming "evidence" of good outcomes presented in favour of attachment parenting leads to one insurmountable conclusion: any decisions that don't comply with attachment parenting will "naturally" lead to bad outcomes. Basically, a focus on the biological underpinnings of attachment parenting allows the theory to very rapidly assume the status of dogma.

So Why on Earth Would We Do This?

Based on the above criticisms, it may be difficult to imagine why any woman would choose attachment parenting as a method of raising children. For many women, however, the focus on attachment parenting as natural may be very empowering. Women who choose to stay home with their children may find validation in this theory. The theory is also couched in terms subtly suggesting the exaltation of natural motherhood as superior to fatherhood. The many sacrifices that virtually all new mothers must make are given integral value. For many women, the decision to attachment parent is an essentially feminist decision.

Now is perhaps the correct time for me to situate myself with respect to this topic, and to reveal my true perspective. In many respects, I am an attachment parent. I continue to breastfeed and co-sleep with my toddler, bonded with both of my children skin-to-skin after their midwife-assisted births, and haven't slept through the night in years. My sling is in the car. My community of mothers (admittedly, an unscientific sample), largely young, educated, professional women, co-sleep, babywear, breastfeed and home birth. How can these decisions be reconciled with the major gender critiques of attachment parenting? Specifically—why have we made these choices?

The superficial answer may lie in the alliance between natural parenting and other "natural" movements. Attachment parenting advocates may belong to movements that often draw feminist women: anti-globalization and anti-consumerist movements, environmental groups, etc. In common with feminism is attachment parenting's emphasis on the de-medicalization of childbirth. As a result, many women who choose to give birth in de-medicalized, "natural" ways may also enter into the realm of attachment parenting.

While this superficial answer satisfies some of the reasons why, in my experience, so many feminist mothers have chosen to attachment parent, the true answer is significantly more complex. Specifically, in the world in which we live today in North America, it is very difficult to come up with choices that are simultaneously child-centred and mother-centred. If we want to maintain our independence within the first year of our children's lives, at a time when there are only meagre social supports such as daycare and paternity benefits, many of us believe we do so at our children's expense.

The fundamental dilemma may not be about attachment parenting, when all is said and done. The fundamental dilemma is that, after a lifetime of being told that we have the right as women to demand the best for ourselves, we find that, given only limited support, we are required to put our children first. Perhaps feminist mothers choose attachment parenting because, at heart, the choice is already made. If the focus has shifted from woman-centred to child-centred, perhaps the details of the decision are largely irrelevant. Once we are solely responsible for these tiny, vulnerable lives, the decision not to let them cry through the night or not to make them eat on a schedule seems to only peripherally increase or decrease the impact of motherhood. When we are forced to choose between our own commitments and the needs or desires of our children—because we can't, as so many of us were taught, "have it all"—we may simply subsume our own needs and give ourselves whole-heartedly to our children.

Can Attachment Parenting be Detached from its Patriarchal Origins? Strategies for Change

I believe that it is possible for attachment parenting to become less patriarchal if we focus on the withdrawal of attachment parenting choices from attachment parenting theory. Ultimately the choices of attachment parents (particularly exclusive breastfeeding) place a great burden of parenting on mothers. Further, the patronizing and minimizing subtext of Dr. William Sears' writing and the focus on attachment parenting as a biological imperative are profoundly anti-feminist. Perhaps the ideal is a truly flexible model of attachment parenting that allows feminist mothers to undertake some of the tasks associated with attachment parenting without fearing the recrimination and "bad outcomes" threatened by Sears et al throughout their parenting guides.

The way forward—the strategy for change—in any response to the "experts" is in removing the hallowed air of expertise. Ultimately, attachment parenting undermines its message of instinctive parenting and biological imperative by suggesting that there is, in fact, One True Way to raise happy and healthy children. To redeem attachment parenting, then, its techniques must be perceived as flexible, and parents (mothers, fathers as well as countless other caregivers undefined within the attachment parenting model) must be allowed to trust their instincts in determining the right path for their child and their family.

A focus on flexibility and assessment of collective needs could promote the obvious commonalities between attachment parenting and other progressive movements while resisting the capacity for this parenting style to simply act as one more agent of guilt and prescription. Arguably, flexible attachment parenting would better describe the choices many feminist mothers are making, anyway. A possible project for feminist mothers, then, would be to devise a parenting manual that allowed the strengths of attachment parenting and its unique alliances with some feminist philosophies and feminist allies to shine while eliminating the guilt and dogma that pervade this philosophy in its current form.

A secondary consideration, however, would be the continuation of a provocative analysis of attachment parenting that examines its misogynist and bio-centric tendencies. Such a critique, however, must also take care to avoid alienation of mothers: an analysis which finds attachment parenting problematic, and therefore maligns the real choices of many women, is as anti-feminist as a wholesale alliance with the cult of AP. Rather, a feminist response to attachment parenting must consider all the nuances, the excellent reasons why a holistic and less medical approach to childbirth and parenting might find allegiances with feminism, while considering the ways that, in privileging biology, attachment parenting ossifies some very troubling gender roles.

[1]Not all attachment parents undertake all of these tasks. Likewise, many of these parenting techniques may be taken on by parents who do not self-identify as attachment parents.

[2]Sears writes with wife Martha and peppers his discussion with anecdotal evidence of how strong a partnership they had in parenting their eight children. Perhaps significantly, however, in an early footnote we read that "Throughout this book, unless stated otherwise, 'I' refers to Dr. Bill Sears; 'Martha,' naturally refers to Martha Sears" (3). Though motherhood is central and sacred, Martha's testimony is literally relegated to the margins.

Works Cited

Granju, Katie Allison. *Attachment Parenting: Instinctive Care for Your Baby and Young Child.* New York: Pocket Books, 1999.

Sears, William and Martha Sears. *The Baby Book: Everything You Need To Know About Your Baby – From Birth to Age Two.* 2nd edition. New York: Little Brown and Company, 2003.

Power to Mother

Attachment Parenting and the Patriarchal Model of Work

Nélida Quintero

Disentangling cultural norms and biological needs when it comes to childbirth, breastfeeding and infant rearing is a daunting task. Who is the trustworthy expert on these issues: the doctor, the midwife, the researcher, the mother of ten or oneself? Since, at a minimum, the right hormones, a uterus and breasts are needed to carry a pregnancy, give birth and breastfeed, these processes belong to women. This makes women's roles as caregivers both fundamental to parenting, and also problematic for the workplace. With the availability of baby formula, breastfeeding is no longer required for infant survival. Further, while breast milk might be nutritionally superior to formula, breastfeeding heightens an infant's dependency on, and attachment to a single caregiver, burdening her with an exacting around-the-clock charge. Why then choose to breastfeed? At the same time, why choose to leave the baby in the care of others?

Attachment parenting advocates are concerned with questions such as these. Their arguments, while sometimes based on a romanticized version of infant rearing practices in the Third World,[1] highlight problematic issues such as the unfriendliness of the workplace in industrialized countries toward the mothers of young children. While family-friendly workplace policies directed towards the needs of both parents—such as parental leave, part-time and flex-time—have been recently put forward, the reality is that mothers usually bear the bulk of responsibility for pregnancy, childbirth and infant rearing. Furthermore, such policies are often punitive in the long term. Part-timers generally do not receive benefits, flex-timers and home-based workers may be perceived as less serious workers, and long parental leaves often hurt career advancement. Mothers who want to have careers and practice their chosen professions, or who simply need to work, struggle to find strategies for parenting that allow them to participate in a patriarchal model of work while bearing and raising children. Attachment parenting is therefore not a feasible choice for working parents, even when parents want to care for their babies and young children in this way, since the demands and values of this model of work and attachment parenting practices generally conflict.

Attachment parenting challenges several widely accepted notions about how babies should be treated, such as, for example, the belief that good infant rearing requires strict scheduling and training. The "cry-it-out" or Ferber method of sleep training, which has served many frustrated and sleep-deprived parents, is based on this belief. Since eating and sleeping by oneself at an early age are highly desired goals in this view, bottle feeding, early weaning and separate room crib sleeping are requisite. This type of childrearing allows for babies to be cared for by others, freeing parents -mothers- to participate in other spheres of life, such as wage work.

In contrast, from the perspective of attachment parenting, the newborn has needs that can be best satisfied by one all-important caregiver, ideally, the biological mother. William Sears points out that attachment parenting can be practiced by other caregivers, but since it favors babywearing and co-sleeping as well as breastfeeding on demand, it is often the nursing mother alone who must be available around-the-clock to tend to her baby.[2] A babywearing mother carries her baby around in a sling or carrier as much as possible. If she is co-sleeping, she shares her bed with her baby. A mother who breastfeeds on demand follows her baby's cues instead of a breastfeeding schedule. This means she cannot easily take on any other responsibilities, and must retreat either partially or temporarily from her other pre-motherhood roles. This interlude can only be undertaken under specific circumstances, and at a price. Taking time off from work for pregnancy and infant rearing is both a luxury and a setback: a luxury, because generally, only those who can afford to give up an income, even temporarily, can choose to take this path, and a setback because careers truncated by infant-rearing years are often negatively assessed upon return to the workplace. Though on the surface, we seem as a society to extol parenthood and family, the practical aspects of daily life as a working mother belie such apparent respect. Because we undervalue motherhood and care giving, only some can make the choice to pay the price and take time off.

Further, work is practiced in much of the industrialized world today with a particular type of worker in mind, allowing only such a worker to succeed (Blum 1993: 295; Crosby, Williams and Biernat 677). Expected to have few demands outside work, she can't be personally available to care for her loved ones, interrupt her career for a few years and pick up where she left off, choose to breastfeed on demand, or carry her baby around at her will. Given the current model of work, it is unlikely that work settings and schedules would allow fathers or mothers to spend the energy and time attachment parenting requires to care for an infant.

Out of necessity then, parents encourage their infants to learn to separate quickly from their mothers. In an economic system where it is difficult for most families to live on a single income, doing away with a salary is a hardship, if not an impossibility. Even when putting aside such burdens, the intense work of caring for young children can be trying when shouldered primarily by one caregiver. Without the extended network of support often available in Third World countries, which attachment parenting practitioners hold up as a model, where families and community members are available to assist in the nurturing and caregiving of the young and elderly, attachment parenting, even for a mother without a full-time job, can be exhausting.

Some might argue that attachment parenting and breastfeeding are simply matters of personal choice—that all parenting choices are equal, and that parents and infants are not unduly hampered by workplace demands—but research has shown that the choice to breastfeed is closely connected to socio-economic class and employment. In Nigeria, educated working mothers usually breastfeed for a shorter time than lesser-educated, unemployed women, possibly because of workplace constraints (Davies-Adetugbo and Ojofeitimi 115-36). In the United States, college-educated women, who generally have more resources and higher household incomes than women with less education, tend to breastfeed for a longer time, since they have greater access to information, maternal-child support, and healthcare services (Blum 299-300). Breastfeeding and one-to-one infant rearing by the mother often go together, not only because the biological mother has the capacity to breastfeed and so it is generally impractical for another caregiver to look after a breastfed infant, but also because the demands of breastfeeding and wage work often clash.

As with most debates, the attachment versus non-attachment parenting discussion is framed as an oppositional dialectic that highlights the extremes. Advocates of attachment parenting list an array of negative consequences based on theory and medical and psychological studies. Feminist discourses challenge the motivation and cultural bias underlying such research. Jules Law contends that the literature on breastfeeding, for example, does not present the risk data clearly, but rather, favors breast milk, despite only a small or questionable margin of benefit over formula; and without considering other issues, such as personal or family priorities, values, and compromises (411).

Further, from a feminist perspective, the maternalist ideology inherent in attachment parenting and breastfeeding advocates, such as La Leche League, narrows the definition of woman, emphasizing biology as the determinant factor for her identity and the available range of roles in which she can participate. Law questions the arguments and research backing the benefits of breastfeeding and the essentialization of mothers (407-428). Faye Ginsburg et al. note that some researchers have made the claim that babies require the short and frequent breastfeeding sessions observed in hunter-gatherer societies, though such sessions are incompatible with sedentary urbanized life (324). Others remark that breastfeeding is often presented in simplistic terms, as a process that can take place naturally, without the need of support or other resources, and that this does not match the reality of most women.

In societies where breastfeeding is not commonly acceptable in public, mothers of breastfeeding infants may feel isolated while confined to their homes (Wall 598). Judith Galtry points out that, whereas both parents can be equally involved in rearing their infant, nourishing a breastfed baby is the sole responsibility of the mother (Galtry 17). An "equality discourse" that focuses on shared responsibility often fails to accept and recognize such differences. But underscoring women's difference, as is done in the maternalist discourse, can serve to highlight the fact that women are still not on equal footing with men (Blum and Vanderwater 297). As long as the ideal worker stereotype is upheld, mothers—and particularly mothers following attachment parenting practices—will continue to have limited work options. Due to the fact that the needs of mothers have not been reflected in the workplace, the equality perspective focuses on women's ability to participate and excel in a work model designed for men, instead of challenging it. Since the paragon of human experience is set by, and based on men, it undervalues the birthing, breastfeeding, nurturing, and care giving experiences.

The equality argument also tends to belittle the value and contribution of domestic and reproductive work historically assigned to women. Empathy, patience, multi-tasking and endurance are among the many abilities that need to be finely developed for this type of work. Caregivers need to be keenly attuned to the needs and feelings of others. These skills are often overlooked and undervalued in the contemporary workplace, though they are applicable and useful in most contexts in which people need to interact and work together.[3] While the motherhood wage penalty might be due in part to the fact that the skills developed while raising and nurturing a family are not valued by employers, mothers are often aware of the usefulness of such skills in the workplace. In a study by M. N. Ruderman et al., women managers noted that their multitasking and interpersonal skills in particular were strengthened by their work as mothers (381).

Attachment parenting does not propose that one need sacrifice the well-being of one family member for the well-being of another; it is circumstances outside the purview of this parenting approach, such as demands placed on wage earners by the workplace, that make it difficult to adhere to it. Sears refers to research showing that the mother-infant dyad is dynamic and interactive from both a biological and psychological perspective. Co-sleeping mothers and their babies synchronize their breathing, for example (Sears 644). By the same token, he notes that what's good for both mother and baby, is good for the family as a whole.[4] At the social level, greater respect for infant rearing is needed, as are policies that demonstrate an understanding of the value and complexity of such tasks. Particularly in the realm of wage work, the patriarchal model needs to be reassessed to include the experience of childbirth and infant rearing. Temporary, full, or partial retreats from the workplace to accommodate such experiences must be fully accepted and respected instead of punished. Government policies must challenge the current model of work by either requiring or setting incentives for employers to offer part-time schedules with proportional wages, training, benefits and advancement opportunities; working from home alternatives; longer maternal leaves for both parents, and penalty-free job options for mothers returning to work after an extended child-rearing break.[5]

It should be possible for a woman to contribute to society both as a worker and a mother throughout her life, not in the uninterrupted, single-focused, fixed-schedule, on-site mode that defines wage work presently. Workers who choose to have children, breastfeed, and care full-time for their infants during the first few years of life should be able to make that choice without penalty. Giving birth and nurturing early life are experiences that merit an equally prominent place in a worker's summary of achievements, next to degrees, awards and other educational and professional milestones. Whatever the parenting style one chooses, and however demanding in time and effort, one should proudly acknowledge childbirth and infant rearing as wondrous life events, valuable social contributions, and skill-building experiences in the life of a multi-faceted worker.

[1] For this perspective on Third World parenting, see William Sears, *The Baby Book* and Meredith Small, *Our Babies, Our Selves.*

[2] For a detailed explanation of Sears' perspective on attachment parenting see William Sears, *The Baby Book.*

[3] For a discussion on the interrelationship of work and family experiences and their potential beneficial interaction see Jeffrey N. Greenhaus and Gary N. Powell, "When Work And Family Are Allies."

[4] However, though Sears and La Leche League strongly stress the benefits of attachment parenting, both also underline the importance of finding a mode of parenting that works for the family. Attachment parenting practices may not work well for all mothers.

[5] See Joan C. Williams and Holly Cohen Cooper, "The Public Policy of Motherhood," for a discussion on policies that could promote better working conditions for mothers.

Works Cited

Blum, Linda M. "Mothers, Babies, and Breastfeeding in Late Capitalist America: The Shifting Contexts of Feminist Theory." *Feminist Studies* 19.4 (1993): 290-312.

Blum, Linda M. and Elizabeth A. Vandewater. "Mother to Mother: A Maternalist Organization in Late Capitalist America." *Social Problems* 40.3 (1993): 285-300.

Crosby, Faye J., Joan C. Williams, and Monica Biernat. "The Maternal Wall." *Journal of Social Issues* 60.4 (2004): 675-682.

Davies-Adetugbo A. A. and E. O. Ojofeitimi. "Maternal Education, Breast-feeding Behaviours and Lactational Amenorrhoea: Studies Among Two Ethnic Communities In Ile Ife, Nigeria." *Nutrition and Health* 11.2 (1996): 115-26.

Galtry, Judith. "Suckling and Silence in the USA: The Costs and Benefits of Breastfeeding" *Feminist Economics* 3.3 (1997): 1–24.

Ginsburg, Faye and Rayna Rapp. "The Politics of Reproduction." *Annual Review of Anthropology* 20 (1991): 311-343.

Greenhaus, Jeffrey N. and Gary N. Powell. "When Work and Family Are Allies: A Theory of Work-Family Enrichment." *Academy of Management Review* 31.1 (2006): 72-92.

Law, Jules. "The Politics of Breastfeeding: Assessing Risk, Dividing Labor." *Signs* 25.2 (2000): 407-450.

Ruderman, M. N., P. J. Ohlott, K. Panzer, and S. N. King. "Benefits of Multiple Roles for Managerial Women." *Academy of Management Journal* 45 (2002): 369–386.

Sears, William and Martha Sears. *The Baby Book: Everything You Need to Know about Your Baby: From Birth to Age Two*. Boston : Little, Brown, 2003.

Small, Meredith F. *Our Babies, Ourselves: How Biology and Culture Shape the Way We Parent*. New York: Anchor Books, 1998.

Wall, Glenda. "Moral Constructions of Motherhood in Breastfeeding Discourse." *Gender & Society* 15.4 (2001): 592-610.

Williams, Joan C. and Holly Cohen Cooper. "The Public Policy of Motherhood." *Journal of Social Issues* 60.4 (2004): 849-865.

Attachment Theory as a "Practice of Heterosexism"

Resisting the Psychologisation of Lesbian and Gay Foster Carers

Damien W. Riggs

The new millennium has witnessed a significant growth in academic research on attachment theory[1] and foster children. This has been intimately related to the increased acceptance of attachment theory as a valid argument in court cases seeking to secure long term foster placements for children (Gauthier, Fortin and Jeliu 381). Yet, whilst this may appear to be a productive development for both foster carers and children in terms of placement stability, it brings with it a number of negative implications for foster carers who identify as lesbian or gay. The majority of these arise from the legacy of attachment theory itself. Most notably, John Bowlby (the original proponent of attachment theory) developed his theories as a result of a directive from the World Health Organisation to investigate the needs of children who had been orphaned or rendered homeless as a result of the second world war, and who were thus in need of foster care (Satka and Mason 88). Whilst this was an important and necessary response to the needs of such children, it was nonetheless problematic in the sense that Bowlby drew upon his previous work which had focused upon the effects of removing children from their *heterosexual, biological* mothers. As a result, attachment theory is, in essence, a theory of normative mother-child relations as they are expected to look under heteropatriarchy.

With this critique of attachment theory in mind, I seek within this chapter to demonstrate some of the normative assumptions that continue to shape the application of attachment theory, and the implications of this for lesbian and gay foster carers in particular. In "talking back" to those who potentially (mis)use attachment theory in regards to foster carer provision, I examine research that looks at "issues of attachment" for lesbians and gay men, and I outline how notions of pathology continue to inform attachment research. In a similar way, I then focus on how normative constructions of the family adhere to attachment theory's construct of the "internal working model" (IWM), and I propose that the promotion of such models serves to position lesbians and gay men as having "unhealthy attachments." I conclude by suggesting that notions of attachment theory may be understood as "practices of heterosexism" that work to marginalise and exclude lesbians and gay men, and which require extensive rethinking if they are to be used at all in practice with lesbian and gay foster parents.

Running throughout this chapter are a number of critiques of heteropatriarchy and its institutions (e.g., psychology) as elaborated by lesbian feminists. These critiques are of central importance to understanding how attachment theory continues to be promoted as a useful way of understanding the world. Lesbian feminist critiques highlight the importance of questioning which groups of parents are privileged in attachment theory, and which frameworks are drawn deployed to warrant its authority. In writing this chapter I am mindful of how attachment theory promotes a view of "human development" that privileges not only the heteronorm, but also the values of the white middle-class (of which I am a member). This chapter, however, represents a singular reading of attachment theory that focuses on its heteronormativity, and thus elides an explicit focus on the racism and classism that adheres to it. Further research is required to elaborate the ways in which attachment theory operates to marginalise a wide range of people.

Psychology and Heterosexism

In their reading of feminist psychology, Celia Kitzinger and Rachel Perkins suggest a number of interrelated points that locate psychology as a practice that contributes to the oppression of lesbians (and gay men, I would suggest, though in different ways). First, they suggest that "psychological approaches teach us to privatize, individualize, and pathologize our problems as women and as lesbians, rather than to understand these difficulties as shared consequences of oppression" (5-6). In this way, psychology attempts to reduce the political to the private, thus obscuring the fact that psychology is always already a political practice—it is simply based upon the denial of this. In other words, psychology is located within a normative (heterosexual) politics that disclaims its investment in maintaining heterosexual privilege by constructing it as universal.

Second, Kitzinger and Perkins suggest that psychology espouses itself as a "value-free" discipline—something that is reinforced by the claim that psychology is an "objective science" (66). As a result, the (heterosexual) value base of psychology is routinely explained away, and thus those of us seeking to challenge this base are positioned either as having "vested interests" or as making "moral judgements" about what are considered to be "personal issues." Such rhetorical strategies work to manage the critiques that lesbians and gay men make of psychology by reasserting the privileged position of psychology to arbitrate over what counts as "good science."

Finally, psychology typically prioritises an account of sexuality that focuses on "sameness." Such an approach constructs sexuality as being "just one aspect of an individual." This view of sexuality gives rise to a liberal response to same-sex attraction in that it suggests "we are all equal," and thus that everyone "should be tolerated." Whilst this may appear to be a positive account of sexuality, in that it purports to counter discrimination, it does nothing to challenge the power dynamics that underpin heterosexual privilege, and thus implicitly works to reassert the simplistic binary of hetero/homo, in which the former is taken to be a model for the latter (Riggs, "Re-Assessing" 135).

This logic of "sameness" is evident in research on the "attachment styles" of gay men. For example, Monica Landolt and her colleagues suggest that their research on gay men was aimed at "extending and replicating work with heterosexual samples," the implication being that it is possible to "extend the logic ... of opposite-sex relationships ... to gay relationships" (125-126). Monica Landolt and Donald Dutton employ a similar logic in their work on abuse in gay men's relationships. Also drawing in part on attachment theory to justify their conclusions, Landolt and Dutton *do* question the suggestion that gay relationships are "just like" heterosexual relationships; yet having done so, they nonetheless accept this comparison as a basis for their research. Indeed, in their conclusion, whilst they refute the notion that there is a "functional wife" (sic) within abusive gay relationships, they propose that "patriarchy should be seen not as a causal factor, but rather as a mediating (contextual) factor in intimate abuse" (356-357). In drawing this conclusion, Landolt and Dutton effectively deny the differential impact of heteropatriarchy upon same-sex and opposite-sex relationships, and thus ignore the ways in which heteropatriarchy often negatively shapes gay relationships.

Biology and Developmentalism in Attachment Theory

The extensive literature on attachment theory is replete with references to the supposedly biological or hereditary nature of parent-child attachment. Such claims to biology thus work to justify the hegemonic status of biological parenting through recourse to the notion that psychological constructs—such as "attachment"—represent universal, "natural" events. For example, Christine Tyrell and Mary Dozier suggest that:

> From an evolutionary perspective, the human infant is equipped with behaviours that promote proximity to caregivers under conditions of threat and, therefore, enhance the infant's chance for survival... Attachment theory suggests that different patterns of caregiver responsiveness are associated with particular infant attachment strategies. (50)

In this way, attachment is seen to be a child's "natural reaction" to threats, to which caregivers are "naturally" responsive (in whatever way). Similarly, in her examination of the history of attachment theory, Beverly Birns suggests that:

> It is now clear that babies are born with behaviours that may be determined by genes, intrauterine environment and other factors prior to birth, and that the infant's temperament codetermines the care provided. (11)

This recourse to notions of "inherited behaviours" works to legitimate certain relationships as being more valid than others: if a child is presumed to inherit their behaviours from their biological parents, then this positions such parents as being the only ones able to "properly attach" to the child. My point here is not to question these "behaviours" *per se*, but rather to question the usefulness of attributing behaviours (such as those labelled as "attachment strategies") to biological causes. My reason for doing so is to examine how notions of biology are used to justify particular normative assumptions about "human infants" and "caregivers"; and thus how they can be used to demonstrate the "deviancy" of those people who do not conform to these normative ideals (see also Riggs, "Developmentalism" 100). In relation to lesbian and gay foster parents, then, the privileged status of biological interpretations of "attachment behaviours" may be used to deny lesbians and gay men a role in foster care by demonstrating their "non-normative biology." Thus, as Diane Raymond suggests, "if it is true… that [as some lesbian and gay advocates suggest] we may never know the source of sexual orientation, then it would make sense—within a homophobic framework—to "play it safe" and refuse to let gays (sic) and lesbians parent or to deny custody to them" (118). Raymond's point is an important one, for if we are to follow the biological attachment logic (such as that demonstrated by Birns), and if same-sex attraction, or more specifically, same-sex parenting, is positioned as undesirable by society as a whole, then the implication is that lesbians and gay men will continue to be excluded as "inappropriate parents."

One of the ways in which gay men are positioned as inappropriate appears in research that promotes the notion that gay men are "gender nonconformists" (and are thus unable to model appropriate ways of being "good moral citizens"), something that is evident in research on gay men's "attachment styles." Thus, for example, Landolt and her colleagues suggest that the "gender nonconformity" that gay men exhibit as children may be one of the causes of their apparently poor attachment to their fathers (119). Not only does this work to blame gay men for their "poor attachments" (as a result of *their* gender nonconformity), but it also serves to reinforce the notion that normative gender behaviour is both desirable, and something that can be corrected, as in their claim that "the majority of gay males... defeminize (sic) by adulthood" (119). The implication of statements such as this is that being "feminized" is an unwanted attribute, and that the most desirable outcome is for young boys to "correct" such behaviours.

Whilst Landolt and her colleagues do not suggest that "poor father-child attachments" cause same-sex attraction *per se*, this proposition *is* made by Kurt Freund and Ray Blanchard in their work on gay men's sexual attractions and attachment styles. They cite research suggesting that "increased father-son distance [is] induced by... feminine boys (sic) themselves" (22). Here, and as in Landolt, the suggestion is that boys who are "gender nonconformists" cause their fathers to be distant. Freund and Blanchard take this further by suggesting that whilst it "is impossible, in practice, to test the hypothesis that physical or emotional removal of the father causes homosexuality" (8), this would be a desirable hypothesis to investigate, were it possible. Together, these two examples of research on gay men, "gender nonconformity" and attachment position gay men as inherently disposed to unhealthy attachment relationships (at least with their fathers), and that, as a result, gay men may be unable to engender "healthy attachments" with their children.

In addition to examples of attachment research which imply that gay men's sexuality causes us to have poor relationships with our fathers, there is the concept of "merger": a psychological description used to diagnose lesbian relationships as being "inappropriately attached." Thus, as Kitzinger and Perkins suggest, the concept of merger is used to position lesbians as having "ego boundary problems," and thus effectively unable to have "healthy relationships" (defined as each partner having a clearly defined, "separate" identity) (119-126). This concept is also employed to some degree by Landolt and her colleagues, who cite previous research to claim that "gay men's interpersonal difficulties [may be understood] in terms of overattachment and overseparation in close relationships." (118) Such constructions of gay men therefore serve to reinforce the notion that we are "inherently flawed," rather than looking at the reasons why lesbians and gay men may actively choose to closely associate ourselves with our partners or loved ones (for example for protection or safety from experiences of hostility and heterosexism on a day to day basis).

Normative Constructions of the Family

As discussed in the previous section, the notion that attachment is something we inherit is rendered more explicit in research on attachment theory that promotes an understanding of the concept of "internal working models" (IWMs). From an attachment perspective, IWMs are proposed to be the result of "actual interactions and interchanges with the primary caregiver, [through which] children begin to develop mental representations, or internal working models, of the parent-child relationship" (Pearce and Pezzot-Pearce 27). IWMs are thus seen to form the basis of the expectations that children learn to have of caregivers. Yet, whilst this may appear to be a fairly reasonable account of parent-child relationships, it points towards the normative model of attachment that is promoted through attachment theory. In other words, if children who come into foster care have been initially raised within a heterosexual-headed household (as the majority of children in care have been), then they bring with them "IWMs" of attachment that are founded upon a normative account of (hetero)relationality.

The notion of IWMs also deserves further examination for the gendered assumptions that adhere to it. As I suggested in the introduction, Bowlby's development of attachment theory was based on his assumptions about the importance of the normative heterosexual, biological mother-child relationship. Attachment theory, and in particular IWMs, are thus prescriptive models for who may be counted as a "real parent"—they privilege heteromothering over all others forms of parenting. Feminist researchers have long challenged the implications of this for heterosexual women (e.g., Bliwise 45; Franzblau 25) and have paid particular attention to the ways in which notions of biology are used to construct heterosexual mothers as being either "good" or "bad," according to their ability to "instinctually bond" with their children (Burman 125). Such constructions of hetero-mothering are thus used to police the boundaries of "acceptable parenting" and to reinforce the notion that parents should raise "good moral (heterosexual) citizens" (Riggs, "Locating" 95). The assumption that the category "mother" equates with the subject position "heterosexual" is evident in research on attachment in foster care placements. For example, Tyrell and Dozier implicitly conflate "parenting" with "mothering" throughout their article:

> The primary aim of the present investigation was to examine foster *parents'* understandings of children's insecure attachment strategies. *Foster mothers and biological mothers* were interviewed regarding the type of difficulties they experience with their children … [and] *parenting sensitivity* was assessed through videotaped observations of *mothers* interacting with their children during a free play session (emphases added). (53)

Here, Tyrell and Dozier start by talking about "foster *parents'* understandings," and then carry on to only talk about foster *mothers*. Again, they talk about *parenting* sensitivity, but only observe it through watching *mother*-child

153

interactions. This serves to reinforce the normative assumptions that attachment theory makes about parenting practices.

Yet I would take this further to suggest that Tyrell and Dozier's equation of parenting with mothering serves to reinforce a heteronormative understanding of parenting. By elaborating a seemingly metonymic relationship between biological and foster mothers, they would appear to assume that both of these categories are inherently representative of heterosexual women. I make this assumption for a number of reasons: first, Tyrell and Dozier do not report the sexuality of their interviewees, but they do report their marital status. At the time the paper was published (and indeed as is still the case in the majority of states), lesbians and gay men were unable to be legally married in the US. This would suggest that none of the participants were identifiable as being in a same-sex relationship. Second, and more explicitly, Tyrell and Dozier refer in the first instance to "foster parents" and "birth parents" in terms of "mothers" and "fathers" (as exclusive couples). This would suggest that their conceptualisation of parenting confirms the assumption that any child raised in a two-parent household will be raised by parents of "different genders." Thus Tyrell and Dozier's study, whilst not explicitly heterosexist, nonetheless fails to acknowledge that not all mothers are heterosexual, nor that all foster children are necessarily raised in households headed by heterosexual foster parents.

Finally, accounts that normalise heterosexual families are also evident in a paper by David Holtzen, Maureen Kenny and James Mahalik on lesbian and gay adult attachments and the self-disclosure of sexuality. They suggest that parental attachment may be "a possible protective factor that might buffer the negative impact of societal prejudices and reduce the risk for dysfunctional cognitions and, perhaps, depression" (353). It may well be the case that parental support is an important factor in a "positive coming out experience." The paper presumes that young or adult lesbians and gay men come out in the context of a heterosexual family, within which the *heterosexual* parents can protect their children from harm. There is obviously a problem when this logic is mapped onto the example of children who identify as lesbian or gay being raised in a lesbian or gay-headed household. The implication is that lesbian and gay parents cannot protect children in their care who identify as lesbian or gay as well as heterosexual parents could. In other words, Holtzen and his colleagues' statement suggests that lesbian and gay parents (who already potentially face "societal prejudices") may potentially be unable to protect our children from such prejudices, particularly if we are considered to be the "cause" of the prejudice itself (or at least part and parcel to it). Thus the heterosexual nuclear family is again taken to be the most appropriate place for children to be raised in, and indeed, lesbian and gay headed households are positioned as potentially placing children and young adults who identify as lesbian or gay at risk of "societal prejudice" or "dysfunctional cognitions and depression." The important point here is not to argue over whether or not lesbian and gay headed households are or are not "at risk" of "societal prejudices." Rather, my focus is to challenge why lesbians and gay men are (yet again) taken as the object requiring analysis, rather than examining the heterosexism that structures Western societies (Clarke 560; Riggs, "Proving" 250).

Conclusions

Throughout this chapter, I have provided an understanding of attachment theory that views it as a meaning making practice, rather than as something that reflects "real truths" about the world. Yet, at the same time, I have demonstrated some of the ways in which the psychologisation of parenting constructs certain worldviews as "objective truths." As such, psychological renderings of the family, and parenting, work to accord considerable cultural value to the heterosexual nuclear family, through the construction of lesbian- and gay-headed families as being inherently "pathological," "unhealthy" or "morally bereft."

The question that needs to be asked, then, is do those of us who identify as lesbian and gay foster parents want to relate to each other and the children that we care for through discourses of attachment? Can attachment ever be a productive way of understanding our families; and is it a useful way of approaching foster parenting? My answer to these questions is somewhat tentative. On the one hand, and following lesbian feminist critiques of psychology, I am wary of any attempt at "reformulating" attachment theory. Yet, on the other hand, I am mindful both of the powerful influence of attachment discourse, and more importantly, the power of attachments in our everyday lives. For children placed in foster care, there is a great deal to be gained from the attachments that they form with those of us who enter into caring relationships with them. Research tells us that this can assist children in combating previous experiences of abuse and neglect (Dozier, Stovall, Albus and Bates 1470). In regard to adults, parent-child attachments occur within lesbian- and gay-headed families in ways that meet the needs of adults for mutual, caring relationships, and these must be supported and celebrated.

What is required then, is an understanding of attachment that starts from the fact of each individual relationship, and which values not only adults' but also children's, understandings of attachment, and the meaning given to it. If we start from the meaning ascribed to each individual relationship, rather than from a broad set of assumptions derived from a particular group of (white, middle-class, heterosexual) people, then it is more likely that we will be able to validate the specificities of diverse family configurations, and the role they play in meeting the emotional needs of both adults and children (Riggs, "Becoming," Ch 6). As I have demonstrated within this chapter (and as this book suggests more broadly), rather than turning the knowledge of our experiences over to those who assert their status as "experts," it is important that those of us located outside the norm of heterosexual, biological, parenting, create our own opportunities to "talk back" about the attachment experiences that shape and enrich our lives with meaning. For it is these experiences that contribute significantly to countering the deleterious effects of both the heterosexism and homophobia experienced by lesbian and gay parents, and the abuse and neglect experienced by children that leads to them being placed into foster care.

I would first like to acknowledge the sovereignty of the Kaurna people, the First Nations people upon whose land I live in South Australia. As always, thanks go to my co-parent Greg for support and proofreading; and to our foster children Gary and Jayden, for helping this all make sense. This research was conducted as part of an ARC Discovery Grant: DP0666189.

[1]Not to be confused with "attachment parenting," "attachment theory" provides an account of the adaptive tendency that is thought to exist amongst human infants (and some animals) that functions to maintain proximity to a figure who provides protection and safety for the infant.

Works Cited

Birns, Beverly. "Attachment Theory Revisited: Challenging Conceptual and Methodological Sacred Cows." *Feminism and Psychology* 9 (1999): 10-21.

Bliwise, Nancy G. "Securing Attachment Theory's Potential." *Feminism and Psychology* 9 (1999): 43-52.

Burman, Erica. *Deconstructing Developmental Psychology.* London: Routledge, 1994.

Clarke, Victoria. "'What About the Children?' Arguments Against Lesbian and Gay Parenting." *Women's Studies International Forum* 24 (2001): 555-570.

Dozier, Mary, K.Chase Stovall, Kathleen E. Albus and Brady Bates. "Attachment for Infants in Foster Care: The Role of Caregiver State of Mind." *Child Development* 72 (2001): 1467-1477.

Franzblau, Susan H. "Historicizing Attachment Theory: Binding the Ties that Bind." *Feminism and Psychology* 9 (1999): 22-31.

Freund, Kurt and Ray Blanchard. "Is the Distant Relationship of Fathers and Homosexual Sons Related to the Sons' Erotic Preference for Male Partners or to the Sons' Atypical Gender Identity, or to Both?" *Journal of Homosexuality* 9 (1983): 7-25.

Gauthier, Yvon, Gilles Fortin and Gloria Jeliu. "Clinical Applications of Attachment Theory in Permanency Planning for Children in Foster Care: The Importance of Continuity of Care." *Infant Mental Health Journal* 25 (2004): 379-396.

Holtzen, David W., Maureen Kenny and James Mahalik. "Contributions of Parental Attachment to Gay or Lesbian Disclosure to Parents and Dysfunctional Cognitive Processes." *Journal of Counselling Psychology* 42 (1995): 350-355.

Kitzinger, Celia and Rachel Perkins. *Changing our Minds: Lesbian Feminism and Psychology*. New York: New York University Press, 1993.

Landolt, Monica A., Kim Bartholomew, Colleen Saffrey, Doug Oram and Daniel Perlman. "Gender Nonconformity, Childhood Rejection and Adult Attachment: A Study of Gay Men." *Archives of Sexual Behavior* 33 (2004): 117-128.

Landolt, Monica A. and Donald G. Dutton. "Power and Personality: An Analysis of Gay Male Intimate Abuse." *Sex Roles* 37 (1997): 335-359.

Pearce, John W. and Terry D. Pezzot-Pearce. "Psychotherapeutic Approaches to Children in Foster Care." *Child Psychiatry and Human Development* 32 (2001): 19-44.

Raymond, Diane. "'In the Best Interests of the Child.'" *Homophobia: How we all Pay the Price*. Ed. William J. Blumenfeld. Boston: Beacon Press, 1992.

Riggs, Damien W. "Locating Control: Psychology and the Cultural Production of 'Healthy Subject Positions.'" *Culture, Health and Sexuality* 7 (2005): 87-100.

Riggs, Damien W. "Developmentalism and the Rhetoric of 'Best Interests of the Child': Challenging Heteronormative Constructions of Families and Parenting in Foster Care." *Journal of GLBT Family Studies* 3 (2006): 87-112.

Riggs, Damien W. "'Proving the Case': Psychology, Subjectivity and Representations of Lesbian and Gay Parents in the Media." *News and Sexuality: Media Portraits of Diversity*. Eds. Laura Castañeda and Sharon Campbell London: Sage, 2006.

Riggs, Damien W. "Re-Assessing the Foster Care System: Examining the Impact of Heterosexism on Lesbian and Gay Applicants." *Hypatia* 22 (2007): 132-148.

Riggs, Damien W. *Becoming Parent: Lesbians, Gay Men, and Family*. Teneriffe, QLD: Post Pressed, 2007.

Satka, Mirja and Jan Mason. "Deconstructing post-World War II Conceptualisations of Children and Child-Adult Relations." *International Journal of Critical Psychology* 11 (2004): 87-110.

Tyrell, Christine and Mary Dozier. "Foster Parents' Understanding of Children's Problematic Attachment Strategies." *Adoption Quarterly* 2 (1999): 49-64.

Half-Time Parenting

A Creative Response to Sears and Sears

Laura Camille Tuley

When I first heard about "Attachment Parenting" (a concept coined by Dr. William Sears and his wife Martha, authors of the oft-cited book series on infant development), the memory of my nine-month-old son's relentless every two-hour nursing schedule during the first six months of his existence was still fresh in my exhausted mind. Hence, when I began to "listen in" on discussions on the feminist pregnancy listserve about "wearing one's baby," and later read Sears' formal description of the biological and psychological need for rigorous infant attachment, summarized in his cavalier observation that "the continued presence of the mother, as during babywearing, is a necessary regulatory influence" (303), I felt, as both a feminist and a professional academic, vaguely incensed.

First of all, I wondered, how can a father effectively bond with his baby if the mother is, more or less, constantly "wearing" him or her? I have always held a strong belief in egalitarian parenting, convinced that, if only men desired to participate more actively in infant care and were enabled to do so by a sensitized public sphere, it would be theoretically possible for men to bond with their babies, just as do women. Shared bonding, I would argue, could potentially revolutionize both heterosexual partnerships and the development and socialization of children; after all, would not both boys and girls grow up with a greatly expanded view of gender roles if the responsibilities of childcare, specifically, and the domestic sphere, more generally, were handled fluidly by both sexes? The fact of mothers who maintain careers is not, I argued, sufficient to even the score. Dads need to get in on the act of "mothering," too. And then there was the difficult matter of *my* working life, in particular.

At the time of my son's birth, I was teaching for a small liberal arts college in New Orleans where I was bound to a four/four teaching load that afforded me only the standard six weeks of paid maternity leave. Granted, I was only required to teach a half-time schedule for the duration of the semester in which I returned to work. This comparatively small amount of teaching provided me with a welcome dose of strikingly "adult" conversation and intellectual exercise (in contrast to my life at home as instinctive maternal vessel). However, even six weeks off and a half-time schedule would not have accommodated what Sears refers to as "the art of Attachment." Moreover, to be entirely honest, the brief periods between breastfeeding in which my husband was able to relieve me by holding and rocking our baby, were vital to my sanity. Thus, while I cannot, obviously, speak for all mothers (many of whom, I feel certain, are more patient, focused and devoted than I, who could not allow a day to pass without reflecting on what I was *not* doing professionally or "creatively"), I can say with conviction, that Sears' proscription for laboring mothers of infants or toddlers sounded to *me*, on first hearing, to be as much a form of bondage as a vehicle of bonding. And it is perhaps this contradictory "truth" about Attachment Parenting that captures the heart of my experience of motherhood: that it is marked by a fundamental ambivalence, or intricately painful joy.

When I returned to Sears' literature on Attachment Parenting in order to begin rethinking this conundrum with greater detachment, my son was approaching a year and a half. I say this to note that as my baby was careening around the house on colt-like legs, learning words, and developing a forcefully individual personality, the memory of our initial struggle was miraculously starting to fade. Whatever the cause (nature's way of igniting one's desire to have another baby, or the effect of extended sleep deprivation), it allowed me to look afresh at Sears' much touted wisdom, and at least for a moment, to re-evaluate and qualify my feelings.

My son was what Sears cheerfully terms a "high-need baby"—one that is more often than not, fussy or colicky, extremely sensitive, and generally difficult to please (for no scientifically known reason)—my husband and I spent many hours attempting to assuage his seemingly disconsolate moods. In retrospect, when I read Sears' proscribed treatment for the high-need baby, I feel a vague nostalgia, and mild regret. I am readily able to imagine my baby's appreciation of, and gratitude for, the intensive care and focus recommended by Attachment Parenting. As I remember my son's moodiness through the Sears lens, it seems obvious that my baby was pleading for greater intimacy and deeper sensitivity than I, who so often handed him off to the care of my exhausted husband, was prepared to offer.

Specifically, Sears divides his doctrine of Attachment Parenting into seven essential tenets, all of which he formulates with a word or phrase that begins with the letter "B." He thus creates a catchy resonance likely designed to combat the inevitable onset of amnesia in the tired, new mother's overtaxed brain. These seven B's are *Birth Bonding; Belief in Your Baby's Cries; Breastfeed Your Baby; Babywearing; Bedding Close to Baby; Balance and Boundaries;* and, finally, *Beware of Baby Trainers.* My beef, qualified though it now is, was primarily with two of his tenets, to which I have already alluded: Breastfeeding and Babywearing. The others were more or less "givens" for me. I planned a natural childbirth which may have increased my closeness with my baby during labor (though it seemed, mainly, to increase my pain). I tried, as did my husband, to listen sensitively to my baby's cries in order to discern every need and desire to which they were, allegedly, a cue. My husband and I ended up bedding very close to our baby for most of 15 months, primarily because it was easier to do so while night nursing (itself a subject of controversy) than to rise repeatedly to pick him up from and put him back into his neglected crib. We always strove and continue to strive, with mixed success, to achieve "Balance and Boundaries," that is, in a nutshell, to set aside time for ourselves and each other—the kind of time that theoretically rejuvenates your commitment to and enjoyment of your child. And, finally, while I consulted various baby "trainers"—veteran mothers, doctors, and books, such as the Sears literature[1]—for advice, we both tended to rely on a combination of our instincts, interests and abilities in choosing how to tend to our baby. For example, we elected to put him in a good full-time daycare center by the time he was eight months old; chose not to let him "cry it out" at any point; and began to feed him cereal at four months, solids by six; and weaned him completely by 15 months.

To me, what this highlights is the fact that most of Sears' sacred "B's" came naturally to my husband and to me, as they probably do to most reasonably sensitive and well-informed parents. Babywearing and Breastfeeding, however, represent a difficult ideological juncture between nature and culture, one that haunted and continues to haunt me by virtue of their fluctuating histories and ambivalent relationship to women's role and responsibilities within and beyond the home. First, both concepts, as Sears defines them, clearly privilege the mother/infant relationship as essential to the infant's (and toddler's) healthy and normal development: "In recent years there has been a flurry of research validating, almost down to the cellular level the importance of the mother's presence. Fascinating findings (for example, infant animals separated from their mothers have higher levels of stress hormones and lower levels of growth hormones) are beginning to open a lot of eyes about the value of attachment" (412). According to Sears, breastfeeding is best when practiced on demand, and for an extended period of time (from one to three years). The multiple benefits of breastfeeding in an infant's first year of life are now common knowledge. What is not generally agreed upon, by either health officials or mothers, are the benefits of long-term breastfeeding (i.e., beyond one year). And, although one can, theoretically, go back to work full-time during the first year of the infant's life by pumping the baby's required milk supply, Sears' recommendation is that, if at all possible, the mother should stay at home full-time (or work only part-time) for the duration of the baby's infancy, and ideally, toddler-hood. Further, as any woman who has tried to work full-time and pump her breastmilk knows, the labor and time required to maintain the necessary backlog of milk is daunting.

Sears' counsel, moreover, assumes both a husband who makes an adequate salary to support his budding family, and a woman who is willing and able to put her career on the backburner. Hence, gender inequity, or the status quo, is the not so golden flip side of breastfeeding to the extent that Sears enjoins. Yet, those mothers who choose to work full-time, in the face of pressure to be "good" (read: stay at home) moms will invariably suffer from guilt and depression at the prospect of depriving their infants of the breast full-time, and insisting selfishly upon the value of a working life outside the home. Moreover, would not a woman whose own needs intellectually and emotionally are satisfied by other work—be that part or full-time—likely provide better or more quality care (as an extension of her own contentment) than a mother who feels compelled to sacrifice her livelihood? The fact of the matter is that women are expected to have lives and goals of their own, over and above maternity. Consequently, today's children will likely grow up to expect that, as with a "good" or "normal" father, a truly "good" and accomplished mother is not one who stays at home full-time, but rather, one who is also educated and contributes to the public sphere. Moreover, who is to say to what extent a baby might benefit from being fed by and consequently connecting with her father at least half of the time? While Sears evokes compellingly the age-old notion that women are and should be natural and primary caregivers, the effects of intensive paternal presence and infant care are largely untested and therefore not understood. In effect, Sears' conventional conflation of sex and gender enables him to claim that a sexual division of labor is essential to healthy parenting.

Sears begins his discussion of "babywearing" (a feat performed with the aid of a traditional sling), by citing various nonwestern or non-industrialized cultures as authentic models for pristine maternal behavior: "The mother of a patient of ours visited the island of Bali, where she witnessed a ground-touching ceremony. The Balinese babies are carried, or worn, for the first six months of life. The mother [or some other caregiver in the extended family] wears the baby all day long, and baby is put down to sleep next to the mother. The baby literally does not touch the ground for the first six months, at which time a ground-touching ceremony is held"(281).[2] Sears goes on to recount what he sees as the benefits of nearly constant babywearing. First, he claims, babies cry less, and develop better because "the energy they would have wasted on crying is diverted into growth." Further, a baby learns a great deal in the arms of an active parent by observing her as she maneuvers objects, and interacts with other individuals. Moreover, wearing a baby throughout the day makes life easier for the mother, who is able to complete a variety of other household chores, responsibilities, and errands, while simultaneously attending to the needs of her infant.

Finally, Sears reiterates, women respond hormonally to a high level of contact with their babies (thus making them more nurturing, i.e., more "natural" mothers). Again, however, "good" mothering construed in the form of nearly constant physical contact pretty much precludes going back to work other than part-time, at which point, Sears concedes, either the father or a good babysitter may wear her baby. The lifestyle required by babywearing is particularly inconvenient for academic women whose work revolves around the act of *writing*, work that cannot be completed to any significant degree while "slinging" one's baby. Thus, the academic mother must choose *either* to almost entirely sublimate her creative energies and desire into crafting a new human being, or not to mother at all. Not only does this interpretation of mothering confine both individual women and their partners to conventional gendered types, but it could lead to discontent, lowered self-esteem and resentment on the part of those women whose livelihoods involve not just working, but creativity, and the exchange of ideas. Again, is not a woman who exercises her intellectual passions and talents for some portion of every day better equipped to mother without reserve—that is, to act as a "good" mother, than a woman who has repressed or severed an essential facet of her identity?

Perhaps as significant, is an academic woman's choice to forgo her work could well endanger her career as a "serious" academic, if she is, in fact, on a tenure track. In their study "Marriage Baby Blues: Re-defining Gender Equity," Mary Ann Mason and Marc Goulden expose the stark, and persistent absence of mothers in the academy. They observe that 77 percent of men who have babies early in their careers are likely to get tenure, versus 56 percent of women who have babies at the same time. Most women who have babies before obtaining tenure either leave their track position to become what Mason and Goulden term "academic gypsies" (i.e., part-time lecturers or adjuncts). In contrast, single mothers, women without children and women who have babies later in their careers are far more likely to achieve tenure. Mason and Goulden further note that the majority of women who achieve tenure are not married with children 12 years out from receiving their Ph.Ds. For men, it is the opposite: being married with young children is the dominant model for success. 70 percent of tenured men are married with children versus 44 percent of women. The article suggests precisely what Sears both assumes and recommends: that a sexual division of labor is necessary to the successful formation of families.

Still, as I mentioned previously, despite my reservations, I am unable to wholly dismiss Sears and his emphatic advocacy of Breastfeeding and Bodywearing. As disturbed as I was and am by both the essentialist implications of his theory and the real concrete statistics that attest to the consequent social inequality (i.e., men get rewarded for their labor, academic or otherwise, while women are increasingly excluded from the public sphere and/or creatively stifled), I know, intuitively, that my high-need baby would have done well in a sling, as he did at my breast, which was available to him on demand for much of a year (and part-time after that). And, while I do not regret putting him in daycare, which has facilitated his development on many levels, I wonder how much calmer, more trusting and more nourished he may have felt had I not worked for at least six months. Even now, I recognize how much he values attention and closeness—to be held and carried—and wonder whether my husband and I might not have profoundly limited his many fitful hours of colicky discontent as a newborn had I worn him through my afternoons. It is clear that my focused presence does make a difference to him emotionally, and may have made a difference to him developmentally in those early months.

And, yet, this choice did not fit me. I could not have "worn" attachment parenting in a comfortable sling. I do need to write and I gain vital inspiration from teaching. Moreover, I value a partner who is willing to participate in every aspect of childcare, with the obvious exception of breastfeeding. Of course, by virtue of breastfeeding alone, a mother's relationship with her baby cannot be reproduced precisely by a father or partner, but this is not to say that the labor of parenting, like "real" labor in the "real" world, cannot be generously shared. Greater support in the public sphere for parenting, by both sexes, would likely relieve much of the tension around women's choices.

In the end, however, ambivalence at what might be lost in the process of trying to sculpt a balanced life (one of Sears' "Bs") is, I suspect, a natural and inevitable aspect of motherhood. Perhaps less natural is the impulse to cleanse or sanitize the experience, to devise a scientific formula with which to tackle the job. Ambivalence is, after all, simply a reflection of the human condition, which, like any newborn, must be attended to passionately and individually. I can appreciate the common sense logic of the Sears way, as with any "baby trainer," and as per Sears' own advice, only to the extent that it does not contradict the mysterious wisdom of me interacting with my child.

[1]Despite Sears' cautionary stance on baby trainers, it is my contention that he and his texts function, paradoxically, as "trainers" for many an uncertain new mother in how to parent one's baby appropriately.
[2]Sears ignores the salient fact that we do not generally romanticize or attempt to adopt social rituals valued by non-industrialized cultures simply because, as idyllic as they may seem, such practices would not cohere in the context of our highly mechanized, fast-paced and medically advanced culture.

Works Cited

Mason, Mary Ann and Marc Goulden. "Marriage Baby Blues: Re-defining Gender Equity", *The Annals of the American Academy of Political and Social Science*, 596.1 (2004): 86-103.

Sears, William and Martha Sears. *The Baby Book: Everything You Need to Know About Your Baby From Birth to Age Two*. Boston: Little, Brown and Company, 2003.

4.
Mother Guilt

Being "Good" Mothers

Instinctual Mamahood

How I Found the Mama

Janni Aragon

My travels as a mother cause the intersections of class, race, and feminism to clash at times and then, at other times, to run seamlessly together as even parts of my identity. I experience motherhood as a feminist, Generation X'r, Latina, educator. In terms of class and education, I speak from a place of privilege, which affords me a glimpse into a different world. In terms of race, I traverse new territory as a mother. Motherhood has solidified my understanding and appreciation of my feminist politics.

Intersection of Sexism and Racism

There are different times in my life when I have realized the monumental effects of being a Latina, first-generation, college graduate. We are removed from Latino culture in Southern California. We are removed from my own family of origin, as well, and this has caused some misgivings on my part along with feelings of love (and, at times, loathing) for all the familial baggage. My education has caused upheavals in my family of origin, specifically between me and my parents, aunts and uncles. I broke new ground by moving out and going to university, and I know that this example was good for my younger siblings. However, it also created a silence between me and my parents and other adults. The silence says more than words could. The silence speaks to my lived experience in a house filled with machismo and misogyny and my understanding of injustice and violence. This sense of injustice makes me know what I do not want in my life or my daughters' lives. The flip side of this coin is that my family of origin is part of who I am; and as a woman of color, my sense of *Latinidad*[1] comes from my family and our traditions. My mamahood has made me come face-to-face with some of my own familial demons. I strive to be a better person, a better feminist, for my own sake, but more importantly for my girls.

I grew up in a traditional Latino household where the cultural mores of machismo prevailed. I recall the distinct moment when my father announced, "This is a Mexican communist household and I am the dictator." For my mother, and for most of the women in my family, marriage and motherhood were virtually synonymous, and usually happened at the same time.[2] My mother got pregnant with me when my parents were sixteen and seventeen, and I was born when they were seventeen and eighteen. They were just kids themselves, and my mother never did finish high school, while my dad took the GED. Years later, I found out that my four grandparents all got married by eighteen, as well; and only one of the four finished high school. However, while I was growing up, my parents made a point of telling me that I should wait until I was older to get married and have children. They would cite examples of aunts (never uncles) who blew their chance at going to college because of a teen pregnancy or poor choice in a mate. My parents, in their own right, raised a daughter whom they wanted to be good in school and independent in the world. However, this was contradicted by my home life, in that I was to fit into the traditional molds of the dutiful, eldest daughter. I was the first woman in my extended family to earn a bachelor's degree and advanced degrees, and these achievements forever alienated me from my family of origin.

While reading about motherhood when I was pregnant with my eldest, I tried to understand my mother, who had five children before she turned twenty-eight, and her own lack of choices. Here I was, one year younger with only one child. I did not feel overwhelmed as a mother per se, but I felt consumed by the expectations of motherhood, and the difficulty of trying to juggle work, writing, and parenting. I also came to a better understanding of the contradictions that motherhood presented me: My role as a mother gave me sudden prestige in my family of origin, and I could not shake off my disappointment that my parents were most proud of this achievement and my new status as a mother.

In addition to struggling with the competing demands of culture and gender in my family of origin, I am paralyzed at times when I come across the nexus of sexism and racism in the larger culture. I have felt out of place on campuses where I attended school and to which I then later returned as the professor, even though my long tenure at these institutions should have made me feel at home. As I continued through the academic pipeline, one thing became apparent: there were fewer and fewer women of color. These imposter feelings have resurfaced at academic conferences, especially when I do not see a soul who looks like me, or shares a similar experience.

I have found that initially racialized sexism was more harmful. It was easy at times to compartmentalize my identity as a woman at home visiting my family and then see that others would see me solely as a person of color. However, once

I had my first daughter it seemed as if my identification as a woman of color grew by my experiences. I also never realized how averse I was to confrontation when my baby girl was with me. My partner is not invisible in all this, yet I think his own upbringing as a white, heterosexual male makes it difficult for him to comprehend racism fully; whereas contemplating the problems of sexism is easier for him to understand.

My training as a social scientist taught me to analyze what I was experiencing, and I sought texts that dealt with feminist analyses of motherhood. I read as much as I could to help me with the benign cultural codes and the harmful influences on my life as a mother, as a parent of a daughter. What spurred my work was my sensitivity to issues of class and race. I am a feminist, social scientist, and cultural critic at heart. I take these attributes with me in my travels into the other areas of my life. I am influenced by the feminists who have gone before me, and by the generation of feminists today. I wonder, though, how best to arm my daughters, so that they do not feel out of place with their own mixed cultural legacy. How do I protect my daughters from sexism and its evil twin, racism?

One vignette illustrates well the social landscape I must navigate. I had taken my daughter to Wal-Mart. When we left the store, a woman had seen us walking to our car and had followed us, waiting for our parking space. I started to place the bags in the back of the car, carefully arranging the goldfish crackers and other fragile items while keeping an eye on Kennedy, who was sitting patiently in the cart. In the background, I heard the driver revving her engine. Within a few moments, the revving of the engine was accentuated by cursing because I was not moving quickly enough to satisfy the driver. At this point, I could feel the rage building inside of me. I was hurrying as fast as I could; however, my priorities were for my child and the crackers, and not the other woman's desire for my parking spot. I finally got Kennedy in her car seat, at which point she decided she wanted water and a snack. At this point, the car horn was honking repeatedly and the expletives were flying and becoming more vulgar. I made eye contact with the driver, and I saw that she had two school-aged children with her. She was another mother.

As I finished with Kennedy's needs, the woman found another parking spot. When I finally worked my way around to the driver's side of my car, she was walking toward me. Her body language was angry and she was not smiling. Without hesitating, I said, "You have set such a poor example for your kids." I turned my back and heard, "Well, at least I'm not a beaner slut." Her kids were laughing. I stood there stupefied, wondering if my daughter heard the comment. I got in my car, tears filling my eyes. The surreal nature of the situation escalated when I looked for a pen and paper to leave a response for her about the need for care and education; I could find only crayons and a coloring book.[3]

As this example illustrates, skin color is an ongoing issue in my life as a woman of color. Within the Latino community there is an adoration of lighter skin. Similarly, skin color privilege exists in other ethnic communities and of course exists within larger, mainstream society. In the community in which we used to live, there was a small park adjacent to a satellite library. Many have referred to it as the "nanny park" as there is often a sea of dark-haired women and their blond charges in strollers. It was at this park during my first month of motherhood when an elderly woman said, more as a statement than a query, "You're the nanny." She seemed surprised to find that I was not, given that I have dark hair, eyes, and darker skin than my daughter. Until my light-haired daughter was older and people could see the resemblance in our eyes, and her own hair darkened to a shade of light brown, I was often asked this question. In my readings about motherhood, even in the feminist texts, it was hard to find someone who wrote about navigating these sorts of issues. During my first daughter's early years, I also felt that my primary job was to protect her and I did not have the strength to get into a confrontation with another person. Thankfully, my unease passed, and it has become easier to explain that I had light hair as a child and that my partner was a towhead until he was ten. But I am still bothered by the queries of white people who feel entitled to ask such rude and personal questions, especially in front of my children. I work to not react angrily and hope that my eldest will not, as a result of these continual questions about race, develop a complex about being darker-skinned than her peers. I still remember the stories about a second-cousin wanting to take a bath in bleach, so she could make her skin lighter.

Avoiding Stepford: Coming to Terms with Motherhood in My Own Way

Within weeks of having my daughter, I sought other mothers. The hospital where my daughter was born sponsors a parent's organization[4] that publishes a monthly schedule of its various educational classes, social events, and classified advertisements. I joined the organization and looked for other mothers in my neighborhood. I started a neighborhood playgroup for my early 1998 baby. Before I knew it, I was the "captain" for this group, which evolved from a mothers' group to a kids' group as the infants moved into the beginnings of toddlerhood.

The majority of the women in the playgroup were a good 8-15 years older than I, primarily professional women who had taken time off from their careers to enjoy motherhood. The age difference between us was indicative of their financial capability to stay at home. Later, as the babies became toddlers, some returned to work part-time or full-time. While this parent organization and the playgroup itself were a place of friendship and support, they also caused me to shake my head in frustration at some painful vignettes about the triad of classism, racism, and sexism.

On one hand, this organization was a blessing with its free educational classes, social activities, and playgroups. On the other, its niche is for families that are predominantly white, middle class to upper middle class, and stay-at-home-mothers. While this is not a condemnation of the organization and all the good that it does for its 3,000 plus family members in the greater San Diego county area, I sometimes wonder if there is more that it could do for mothers who really need friendship, mentorship, and the free classes about sleep, teething, safety, discipline, and development. However, chances are that the women who need this organization most are working daily, and do not have time to make the morning or evening meetings.

I always left the playgroup with an unsettled sense of my reality. I have had many conversations about vacationing or traveling with other mothers from the playgroup. At the time, I could afford to enroll my daughter in enrichment classes at Gymboree and elsewhere because her grandparents have been so generous, paying for many of the classes. At the age of two, she has already been enrolled in more activities than I ever was. But in most parts of California, working class or middle-class families cannot afford to purchase a home. I have forgotten neither my class roots nor my appreciation for what I am able to do for my daughter.

Being a playgroup captain was gratifying, as I connected with a few younger mothers, and found some wonderful friends for my daughter. I also found that over the years the like-minded parents continued their friendships, and these enriched me as a mother and as a community volunteer. Overall, though, my participation in the parent's organization also felt like a social science experiment where I was a participant-observer.

Working Mama

My middle-class existence as a parent, and my status as a lecturer at various universities make me appear as a stay-at-home-mom (SAHM) to some. However, my reality is that while raising my first daughter, I was teaching part-time at a local community college, working as a Research Assistant for my mentor, and dissertating. This meant that I was working more than full-time. I found that late in the evening and during her naps was the only time that I was able to dissertate; when I was on campus I was either in "instructor mode" or "research assistant mode." When my daughter was approaching her second birthday, I found the pre-school at a local university was a blessing for my family, but this also meant that I was now teaching yet another course and not working on my own academic project in order to defray the cost of pre-school.

We need to look at the intersection of politics and personal life within the institution of motherhood. I still struggle with sexism and racism; however, my identity as a mama is stronger and I am both more patient and resilient. As a mother of two girls instead of just one, I have more faith in my own instincts. I believe in women and girls, and I know that my feminist philosophy has helped me be a better mama. The feminist in me has helped me navigate the occasionally rocky terrain where racism exists or where I feel uncomfortable based on my own class privilege, mixed cultural legacy or immigration status. Now living in Canada, I am hard pressed to find a good Mexican restaurant. When I am downtown and I hear tourists speaking Spanish, I feel myself eavesdropping, trying to discern whether these tourists are from Mexico, the US, or possibly South America. The dialect reminds me of home, of California, of my roots as a woman of color. The racial make up of our new home is primarily white, Asian, and some Native peoples. The predominant language is English with a smattering of French and some Chinese, Japanese or Vietnamese. There are times when I look around the park, the mall, the causeway near the harbor, at the sea of white faces and wonder what this will do to my daughters' identities. Will they still identify as Latina? Is place important to my own understanding and appreciation of race? My best friend just sent a bib for the preschooler that says, "Kiss Me, I'm Latina." I will take lots of pictures of the bib on my daughter. *Kiss Me, I'm Latina.*

I wonder about living in Canada where the issue of race seems more subtle and imbued within the framework of white and native or in some cases on the West Coast, white and Asian.[5] This is a change from the US, where most mainstream conversations about race are stuck in the white and black dichotomy. I anticipate having to discuss issues of race to my daughters. I identify as a woman of color and I already have seen that some people have a strong need to be able to "place" or identify me. My kids, too, get comments and compliments that are mostly innocent, but occasionally someone really wants to know why she looks so "exotic" or why my preschooler is blonde. I have a sense of wanting to hold onto my own culture and at the same time embrace Canadiana. I'm more comfortable with my responses to queries about "where are you from." But they're really trying to ask, "what is your race, what is your ethnicity?"

Today as a mother, I feel capable of dealing better with issues of racism and sexism than I did in the past. This is not the old, tired cliché that having kids has made my life better or that I am suddenly a more fulfilled person as a mother and now "enlightened." No. Having kids has caused me to better understand and practice my feminist politics, my antiracist politics. Having kids has made me daily practice my feminist politics. This makes my life interesting and at times complicated. Having kids has made me see the big picture and know that my identity as a mama is a work in progress.

[1] "Latinoness."

[2] Actually, pregnancy usually came first, then marriage.

[3] It was also ironic that I was in a Wal-Mart, the epitome of a globalized business that is well-known for purchasing goods from sweatshops and for supporting a political and evangelical agenda that I disagree with. I was there out of sheer convenience. After this incident, I promised myself not to step in another Wal-Mart.

[4] The organization will remain nameless in order to protect my friends and the actual organization. The organization's intent is to bring families together. It is a resource for families.

[5] This is my experience in the city that is now my home. If I lived in other parts of Canada, the discussion might be one of Anglophone versus Francophone.

Against the Law

Kimberly Chisholm

"IT'S AGAINST THE LAW! WHAT YOU ARE DOING IS AGAINST THE LAW!"

Is it? I suppose so.

Andie is four. It's 8:03 this Friday morning in late September, and we are late for school. She runs down the front porch steps and onto the lawn in only her little blue jeans. Wild haired, bare-torsoed, jumping up and down with her hands in small fists, voice worn by nearly an hour of screaming. "YOU CANNOT DO THIS TO ME!"

An hour before, three shirt choices had not been enough for her.

Downstairs at the breakfast bar, the boys had been eating their waffles. Xavier is two. Billy is six and has found a pen and laid it neatly below the permission slip I am to sign. He toys with his fork, mulling over a question. I try to maintain meaningful eye-contact even as I back toward the stairs where insistent Andie calls "Mommy!" above us.

"Is google," Billy asks, "really the highest number possible? Higher than a gazillion?" I move away, taking the first few stairs backwards. "Than a bazillion?"

"I'm not sure," I say, finally turning from him.

Upstairs Andie is awash in sartorial indecision. I lay out three shirt choices.

She stands with her chin down, tiny brows together. "Three…" It's not quite a whine but I am overwhelmed by the urge to sit on her bedroom floor, and give up before we've begun.

"THREE … IS NOT ENOUGH!" Andie is the one on the floor, writhing near the strewn Polly Pockets that she did not—I slump, resting a hand on her bureau—pick up last night.

"I'm giving you," my voice is unyielding, "three choices."

"THREE IS A FEW. A FEW! YOU SAID SO YOURSELF. I NEED MORE THAN A FEW SHIRTS TO MAKE A GOOD CHOICE!"

I come down to her level, the most elementary recommendation offered up by Penelope Leach and T. Berry Brazelton; Eisenberg, Murkoff and Hathaway; *Child* and *Parents* and *Parenting;* sage co-op preschool teachers and glossy BabyCenter.com. I believe it demonstrates respect for the child. I believe in the intimacy, but I lower myself also because this child exhausts me.

She ceases writhing. She looks at me askance, gauging my posture.

The roundness of her cheeks, a wideness in her eyes makes me recall the smooth warmth of her head against my chest as we read last night, how Xavier had tramped by in no more than Andie's plastic heels, and her pink checked apron, his pudgy bum visible under the bow in the back. Together, she and I had laughed. In the possibility this memory creates, I soften. She might just possibly sit up and choose one of the shirts.

"I NEED SIX CHOICES! I NEED HALF A DOZEN CHOICES—AT LEAST!" Fierce kicking joins the writhing. Her calculating heels flash within inches of my knees.

I could go ahead and offer five choices. Not Louise Bates Ames, not Vicki Iovine, neither of the Searses will witness my violation. I could defy the edict of every mom-friend and even my sympathetic pediatrician Dr. Greene who all say: never concede to a tantrum. Three choices must remain three choices. I give Andie five.

Writhing and kicking cease. She sits up, cross-legged. She tilts her head.

"TWO..." she flings herself back, "...IS A COUPLE! HOW CAN I MAKE A GOOD DECISION WITH A COUPLE!? I WILL NOT COME DOWN UNTIL YOU GIVE ME HALF-A-DOZEN CHOICES!"

I stand. She flays, kicks, thrashes. I stride out of her room. I channel Mary Sheedy Kurcinka, willing myself to think of her as spirited, persistent, self-assured. This tantrum could be considered a small price for a four-year-old who knows the difference between a couple and a few—a goddamned half-dozen. But anger rises red-black in me. I am rigid and distant. As I grip the stair rail she rushes after me then remembers her threat and darts back to her doorway, thin arms spread with a small hand on each jamb.

I descend.

"YOU HAVE TO WAIT! WAIT!!!! I HAVE SOMETHING VERY IMPORTANT TO TELL YOU!"

The very important thing will be that she needs half-a-dozen choices.

When I stride into the kitchen, the boys smile, placid and a little afraid of their sister's wildness. Andie's waffle is mush in its pool of syrup. The boys fork their strawberries, chew their waffles, take mindful sips of diluted organic apple juice.

To think I had wanted a trio of girls who would be as close to me as I am to my mom. Girls who would be "easier" or "harder" than boys depending on the expert you were considering. Girls, nonetheless, who would remain connected to me forever. And then I wish for something gross in its generalization and traitorous in its intent: I want a third sweet boy there on the empty stool.

"Mommy," Billy's voice is measured. "Don't you think that Bionicles would make great soccer players?" He's resolved the google question on his own.

"They'd be amazing soccer players."

Billy grins.

Lunches, sunscreen, milk for my coffee, permission slip signed, sweatshirts found. I gather backpacks, the library books, the sharing.

All this over the steady undercurrent of: "I HAVE SOMETHING VERY IMPORTANT TO TELL YOU! I HAVE SOMETHING VERY VERY IMPORTANT TO SAY!"

I move into a lull. If I were to let the unceasing shrill of it register, I would have to bound up the stairs and throttle her. My boys finish eating and the clock reports that we are an astounding six minutes ahead of schedule.

As the three of us troop by the foot of the stairs I call, "Andie!" tamping down a spike of anger at her failure to come down. I will not raise my voice, I will not run up the stairs muttering, "godammit." I will not drag her, thunking, step by step back down. Good mothers do not slam doors, or slap flat hands on counters. Good mothers don't damage their children with roiling, blooming anger. My mother did not. My mother held us close even in our rage, she let us sleep in the big bed and spoke in soothing tones. Well ahead of her time, she nursed all four of us for years, anticipating Sears and Bowlby, and infant attachment, intuitively reveling in each of Brazelton's "touchpoints."

"Andie. You need to come down now. We are walking out the door."

Across the terraced lawn, Billy vaults into the way-back seat of the car, saying, "Buckle up for love!" I struggle to put Xavier into his five-point restraint.

Behind us Andie jets onto the porch. I turn purposefully, tense in all the tranquility I force myself to exude. Her bare, stamping feet make more noise than should be possible on the cream-colored boards. Her fists, her red eyes, the horrible way her face is pulled into itself, her tiny, bare torso make me so so sad for her.

But she's not even half-dressed, and we are verging on late; because of her we will all be late. I stand rigid in seething, teeming fury.

She shakes her head and screams, "WHAT YOU ARE DOING IS AGAINST THE LAW! YOU WERE GOING TO DRIVE AWAY WITHOUT ME!"

Did I say I was leaving without her?

She jumps up and down, rage tight in her small rounded shoulders, her belly, her pale, bare feet.

"Andie. It's good you've come down. Now hurry over so we can get going."

Her hair is a mad-child's, her head thrashing. Then she's still. This, though, is a mere coiling. Her eyes squeeze shut and she screams, "YOU HAVE TO CARRY ME!!!"

Months and months of that refrain pump visceral fury through me. My voice is fatal. "I will not." I pause, and she renews her screaming. Anger propels me toward her. I raise my voice. "I will NOT carry you!" I take the steps two at a time.

"AAAAAAHHH!" rips from her round mouth. She runs from me, and slings her small arms, and one blue-jeaned leg around the wide brick base of the banister.

"YOU ARE NOT A GOOD MOMMY! I DON'T LIKE YOU AT ALL!" Then my own words in her ragged voice: "THIS BEHAVIOR IS NOT OKAY!!" She twists her head toward me, and spits a white glob of sticky saliva that clings to her chin.

The hot blackness in me glows red. I grab her upper arms to pry her from the post. How much pressure will bruise? *Parenting* tells me that bruises constitute abuse. I switch to her torso. I free one arm but the other leg is now around the thick brick base, and as I force the second arm from its hold, she begins to whack at me—hard.

"Mommy?" calls Billy from the car, "Do you think this might deserve a time out?"

I look up and try to smile at him, thinking how impossible it seems to facilitate the non-punitive regrouping I have carefully built into each well-crafted time-out. I smile at Billy, because the boys need to know that all is fine, that Mommy's got it under control.

And in my upward glance, Andie detaches herself, twists and leaps up, clawing at my face and arms.

"This! This behavior ..." I will not repeat her mockery of me and yet I can think of nothing else. "This ... is NOT OKAY!"

She kicks and writhes. I force her arms to her sides—bruises be damned. "AAAAHHHH!"

I pin her under my arm with far more force than necessary, her little body sideways, legs flung up behind. I sputter, "Godammit! Godammit!"

As I storm across the lawn I notice a minivan down on the road—it's my friend Joan. Joan is waving, the window gliding down. I want Joan to witness this. Someone has to believe that my generous, and kind, and well-behaved daughter is capable of savagery. I glower, and hitch her backwards on my hip. Joan's brows rise. Her mouth draws down. A little half-wave and the window glides back up. Joan drives on.

I throw Andie into the car with force that rings through my body, and I am appalled at how satisfying this feels. I slam the door as hard as I can, dying inside because Xavier's carseat is closest. But she has pushed me too far. I take deep breaths as I race, careening around the car. I yank myself up and jam the key into the ignition.

"Godammit," I mutter. Look out, all of you, I think, because Mommy has precious little under control. Not even Mommy knows what she's capable of. And realize, realize! It's you, Andie who has sunk me this low.

"I'M NOT BUCKLED!!" Her tattered voice fills the car. "YOU CAN'T DRIVE! I'M NOT BUCKLED!!!!"

I gun backwards down the sloped driveway, willing deep, calming breaths, smiling at Xavier who frowns and grips his sippy cup. I ask if his invisible friend Mr. Ainya is with us.

"Mmhm." He nods, unsure Mr. Ainya should be.

And for good reason. Out on the road I halt abruptly and jam the gears into place. We lurch forward. Andie is thrown back but scrambles forward screaming, "I WILL NOT BUCKLE! YOU CANNOT DRIVE!! I WILL NOT BUCKLE!!"

Anger blazes in me.

She clambers forward. She tugs the neck of my favorite sweater. She smacks at my face. Small fingers scratch my jaw and temple. She takes a handful of hair.

I swerve onto the side of the road, and I am screaming, the same horrible "AAAAAHH!" as my daughter. I am twisting and flashing. I grab Andie's bare shoulders, vaulting us both backward. I slam her into the middle seat on top of poor Mr. Ainya. I buckle the seatbelt, she unbuckles immediately. I slam my hand into the buckle, needing to hit something, screaming, "AAAAH-HHHH!"

I am horrified by how good this feels.

"THIS IS TOO HARD!" I scream. "WHAT AM I SUPPOSED TO DO?"

I bring my face to within inches of hers and Andie glares, stony, contained. And then she smiles. She has won. This, not half-a-dozen shirts, was what she wanted all along.

From beside us, whimpering. The effort is inhuman and yet for my littlest boy I soften. I lay a hand on his chest. "It's okay. You're okay. I'm just upset with Andie."

She wriggles free of the seatbelt and screams again, lurching toward me.

I stave her off with an elbow as I smile at my frowning toddler. A soothing hand goes to his knee but as I contort myself back into the driver's seat, Andie flails forward yanking and punching. I shove her away. Into the suicide seat.

She looks out the windshield, horrified to be in the forbidden front seat as I charge, steeled, onto the road. In the rearview mirror I watch her scuttle into the way-back and, miraculously, buckles up.

Silence.

I accelerate too fast, I stop too suddenly. I jangle, and smolder, and grip the steering wheel so hard my hands ache.

"So, Mommy." Billy's voice is a balm in the quiet.

I breathe. "Yeah, Billy?"

"I have a question." He gazes out the window, considering. Andie is staring at her older brother, her eyes glossy, her movements slow, as if under water. "Do you think when Shaq was six like me his body felt different, knowing it was going to be so tall?"

"What…" Andie's voice is worn. "What do you mean, Billy?"

He looks at her, wary.

"I'm not sure about that, Billy," I say quietly, watching.

"We should ask Daddy," Andie says. "He'll know." She faces forward. Her eyes close slowly then open again. "We'll ask Daddy later."

There is one space in the parking lot. I gather her shoes and her backpack. I pull a shirt over her head. She blinks. I exhale. I need her in her beloved classroom. She has had no toast, no juice, no sunscreen but I take no chances. I hurry across the parking lot behind Billy with Andie on one hip, Xavier on the other. At the door two crying kindergarteners wrap around their mothers. Andie slides down. She kisses me. "Bye, Mommy. I love you." She takes her place on the yellow letter "H" on the rug.

Mrs. Stella approaches, alarmed by the glossy, inflamed eyes. "Is she *al-right?*"

"Minor tantrum," I whisper.

"Andie?!"

"Yes. Andie."

Dr. Greene returns my call within the business day.

"Well!" he chuckles and I love him for sounding a little impressed. "We need to remember that she is extremely bright, extremely articulate, and somewhat controlling."

"And that the controlling part comes," I add, "from anxiety." This seems important. "Or fatigue, or hunger, or frustration … "

"I wonder," he says, "if we need to remind ourselves of the compassion piece. Something like, 'Andie. I know it's hard to watch the clock in the morning and make so many decisions. But you are really happy once you get to school.'" Dr. Greene suggests I unfurl a list of every task I need to accomplish each morning to give her a visual sense of my responsibility. I am to use my calm voice, not to defend myself, but to remind her of her part of the deal. I am to get down on her level. "And of course," he reiterates, "never concede to a tantrum. What's important," he finishes, "is compassion."

It appears I forgot the compassion.

Armed with my professionally-endorsed script, my list of 72 morning tasks, and compassion, I lie in wait. The following Monday Andie comes downstairs fully dressed. She eats her toast and eggs and melon and asks for more. She helps Xavier pull up one of the heavy stools for Mr. Ainya.

The parking lot. 8:12. We are almost late and the PTO check was left behind and there was only decaf and I forget, in the moronic parking job of the minivan next to me, just how prepared I am. While unbuckling Xavier I sense a stiffening within the car.

Andie's hands fly out to her sides and she sits up. "My *sneakers!* I left them in here yesterday. I *did!* I *know* I did, but now they're *gone!*"

Xavier grips onto me, eyeing his sister. Billy sits back, giving her a wider berth. Silently, I prepare: it's hard to remember so many things … you're doing a good job … it's frustrating when you're sure you left something somewhere. I pull Xavier to my chest and step up into the car, running a hand over the list of 72 tasks in my back pocket, the list Andie enthusiastically helped me compile one calm and rewarding afternoon. I peer down to where there are usually six or seven assorted shoes among the books, and action figures, and flung sippy cups. Andie glares at me and I see what she sees: a worn pair of flip-flops, cracked and crusty, a sick faded green.

I pause. I look at her very carefully, holding Xavier close while gathering compassion—she will be overcome with my empathy and consideration.

She looks at the flip-flops, then back to me. "These are great, Mommy," she says. "These shoes right here will be just fine."

Three mornings later she descends in green pants, green t-shirt, green hoodie, her hands wild at either side of her head. "ONE OF MY FAVORITE FLIP-FLOPS IS GONE! IT'S *GONE!*"

At long last! I am well-caffeinated and we are only barely behind schedule. I approach, I kneel. I settle empathetic hands on her hips. "Andie. I know it's hard when you can't find something."

"DON'T SAY IT'S HARD!"

Xavier and Billy stand at the door, watching as their sister thrusts her hips back and away—not soothed, it appears, by my compassion. I press on: "I'm sorry this is frustrating. I know they're your favorites, but you love your sneakers too. It's time to go now. You need to wear your sneakers and we will find your flip-flops after school."

"WE'LL NEVER FIND THEM. THEY'RE LOST! I WON'T GO!"

I ease the list from my pocket.

"DON'T TAKE OUT THAT DUMB LIST! YOU'VE DONE ALL

THOSE THINGS ALREADY—I WATCHED YOU DO THEM! YOU HAVE TO HELP ME!"

She jumps up and down, her hands in fists. I sit back on my heels. I look at Billy and Xavier, huddled together. Then I look at Andie, who has paused, but then glares, and jumps up and down again for good measure.

I sigh. I let my head fall back then look to her again. "My god," I say, with something close to wonder. I am very present, very aware of how she has stopped jumping up and down and is watching me closely.

Compassion, lists, soothing tones at children's eye-level—try them on someone else's kid. This child could get over on masterful Dr. Greene himself. All at once I see that I can give up. This cannot matter so much. I remember vaulting between the seats, screaming, smacking the seatbelt. Sudden laughter bursts from me.

Andie is still.

I sit back on my bottom. She stares saucer-eyed, then remembers herself, and stomps one histrionic foot.

I laugh more, thinking how really tough this kid is, and how this strength will serve her well out in the big wide world. Laughter comes pouring from me, and this feels even better than screaming or jamming her into my hip or throwing her into the car.

I'm laughing so hard that there is no sound. I brace myself with hands on the floor. I cannot stop. I take a deep breath and manage, "So much for compassion. So much for my goddamn list."

Near the door, a burbling giggle from Billy. I smile and Xavier joins in.

"So much for strategy and perfect parenting—my God!"

Andie looks to her laughing brothers, then back to me and she grins. She giggles, and then she laughs. I sit there on my bottom before my daughter, and we laugh.

Hip Mamas, Playful Imperfections and Defiant Voices

Resisting Fantasies of the "Good Mother" in Ariel Gore's Survival Guides

Susan Driver

In *The Hip Mama Survival Guide*, you'll find an "expert" quoted here and there, but mostly you'll find stories from other moms. Stories that have helped me through and made me laugh. Stories that will, I hope, remind you that you are not alone, and offer a few tools that will come in handy as you invent motherhood all over again.
　　　　　　　　　—Ariel Gore (*Hip Mama Survival Guide* 7)

…when most books for parents preach mommy martyrdom, Ariel Gore's approach is like a hand reaching out to pull you from the quicksand of guilt.

　　　　　—Julianne Shepard

These are parenting manuals for Gen X mothers who want to see the edgiest parts of their youth reconciled with their new status as parents.

　　　　　—Amy Benfer

Ariel Gore's mothering guides defy categorization. *The Hip Mama Survival Guide* and *The Mother Trip* give advice, and admit there are no clear answers; they offer help and suggest doubts; they make fun of conservative reformers, and laugh at ordinary maternal mishaps; they ambitiously call for revolution, and reveal the details of both pleasure and exhaustion in parenting. Pigeonholing Gore's project is impossible from the start. Mixing serious social statistics and research with anecdotes, comics, interviews, to-do lists, quizzes, fictions, autobiography, political satire and activist strategies, Ariel Gore's books are wildly hybrid. These books replicate the spontaneous juxtaposition of texts and images that make up the collaborations of Gore's zine *Hip Mama* into the coherent organization of a personalized self-help book. It is this combination of intimate confession, and political analysis of mothering as an experience, and institutional matrix that forges the unique blending of these guides as a cross-over genre that refuses to divide and specialize myriad dimensions of mothering into neat containable compartments. The polyvocal style of Gore's mothering guides constitutes critical and creative dialogues back and forth across differences and commonalities of advice by, for and about mothers. Here are scattered fragments of support and information that throw into question the very boundaries between those giving and receiving instruction.

Offering advice to mothers in ways that simultaneously subvert and reinvent expert knowledges, these texts are intrinsically ambivalent about the very possibility of providing truths that might guide moms through their "treacherous" journeys once and for all. Yet, it is precisely Gore's wry enactment of insights and suggestions that gives rise to a transformative style of discourse engaging readers in an ongoing conversation. Gore talks back to dominant ideological powers while activating a grassroots movement of maternal advocacy and empowerment. Questioning the very validity of authorities that speak abstractly on motherhood, Gore compels discussion for and about mothers by mothers. Top down advice that seeks to control the perceptions and behaviors of mothers gives way to fractured local voices of mothers addressing their specific experiences. At the same time, Gore is the privileged advisor, mediating the stories of others through her writings. In this way, the status of the expert "knower" and guidance councilor to mothers has not so much disappeared as reemerged in a more self-conscious, reflexive, and responsive form. Gore turns back upon her role as maternal "guider" with playful irony, showing up her fallibility and imperfection as she encourages other mothers to join in as co-authors of new kinds of mothering methods. The point of advice in *The Hip Mama Survival Guide* and *The Mother Trip* is not to put forth fixed absolutes about what is right and wrong. Rather, it is to recenter the very production of ideas about "good enough" mothering through a myriad of diverse and changing maternal perspectives in the flux of surviving and making sense of their respective life worlds. In the process, Gore makes moms laugh at themselves. And it is precisely this move to lift the moral weight of guilt-inducing knowledges from above, to foster the pleasures of shared insights from below, that enables Gore's books to radically depart from the historical protocols of expert advice to mothers.

Disrupting Fantasies of Maternal Perfection:
Embracing Messy Maternal Knowledges

This journey we are on as mothers is treacherous. Instead of clear road signs we get questions we don't know the answers to. The path is marked with joys and dangers, laughter and wrong turns, glorious views and insults of all kinds. (Gore, *Hip Mama* 247)

The distinctiveness and impact of Ariel Gore's guides stand out for me as a researcher overwhelmed by the dominance of popular, scientific, political and policy texts about motherhood constructed through the detached voice of reason. Depicting motherhood as an idealized and universalized social function, the dominance of mainstream manuals obscures the nuanced details and contradictions of mothering. Not only is a single image of the "good mother" continually projected as a fantasized figure, but haunting images of "bad" and "unworthy" mothers also pervade literature seeking to regulate and define motherhood as an identity. Molly Ladd-Taylor and Lauri Umansky write that "fundamentally the 'bad' mother serves as a scapegoat, a repository for social or physical ills that resist easy explanation or solution" (22). The problem at stake here is one of representational closure, wherein maternal subjectivity becomes inscribed within either/or frameworks wherein particular articulations of experience become seen or unseen, remembered or forgotten, evaluated as appropriate or not. It is the rational containment and hierarchical regulation of the maternal self as good/bad, sexual/asexual, heterosexual/lesbian, black/white, normal/perverse that precludes ways of understanding the ambiguities through which mothers live and speak themselves in all their complexity. Devising ways of representing and rethinking those dimensions of mothering overlooked and prescribed within dominant knowledges becomes the critical task. Yet, it is paradoxically a task that subverts the coherence of critical reason. Against the controlled rhetoric of science and philosophy, the experiential voices of mothers mark a subversive rupture. The trick becomes rendering the sensuous, mobile and unruly practices of mothering into a collectively meaningful dialogue.

Ariel Gore's guide-books mark a creative departure point for an alternative popular culture of mothering that begins within the contested world of institutional and discursive control. Positioned on the side of those who are devalued, ignored or attacked by hegemonic powers, Gore portrays maternal experiences as always bound up with surrounding institutional frameworks and common sense assumptions. Static images of the controlled, perfect and uniform maternal subject insinuate themselves throughout Gore's work as the backdrop against which mothers resist and negotiate meanings. In Gore's words, "the modern mama fantasy includes layers of the 1980s Super Mom, the 1950s housewife, the early twentieth century domestic scientist and the Victorian fountain of moral purity" (*Mother Trip* 4). Offering advice that actively confronts the limitations of maternal ideologies, Gore helps mothers to develop an actively political stance through which their specificities become recognizable. Acknowledging the power of media-constructed maternal fantasies to shape present realities, Gore pursues a project of de/reconstruction: "Whichever make-believe families fueled the maternal dreams and nightmares of your youth, we're all reinventing motherhood together now, and it's no easy task" (*Hip Mama* 3). While there is no escaping the prevalence of media ideals, fantasies and myths, there are ways of talking about, and sharing experiences that turn attention and emotional attachment away from static ideals towards the gritty contexts of mother care, work and love. An important part of Gore's guide for reinventing motherhood is the demystification of maternal perfection. Confronting the allure of the mother who knows and does it all without error or complaint, Gore writes that "if there's one thing I've learned about mothering, it's that there are a million ways to raise good kids, and none of them is perfect" (*Hip Mama* 247). Gore undertakes her role as an advisor with caution and skepticism, making it clear that there are no perfect solutions or plans.

Perhaps one of the most cleverly articulated ways Gore navigates around controlling images of motherhood is through parody. Gore mimics the conventions of social scientific surveys and pop culture quizzes, repeating their structured lists of answers and numerical results with playful excess. Inserting a quiz "How Crazy Are You?" in a chapter on the arrival of the baby, Gore approaches the emotional health of mothers with wry humour. Twisting an approach that would clearly separate the sane from the psychotic, the normal from the sick, Gore leads us through an exercise in which all positions verge on "insanity." Stereotypes from June Cleaver to Roseanne are what is up for grabs here, each burdened by biased judgment and binary oppositions. The result is a questioning of the very attempt to measure and evaluate mothers on a scale from imperfect to perfection. Participating in these quizzes pushes the reader to consider whether it is the very questions asked by mainstream advice manuals that need to be interrogated. Parody allows Gore to deal with difficult issues with insight into the manufacturing of maternal guilt, shifting responsibility onto those who categorize and guide mothers in the name of scientific and moral truth. Mothers are both distanced and included within these parodic exercises, creating spaces of inquiry and reflection that allow for ambiguity.

Gore's books pivot on the edge of serious practical know-how and ridiculous absurdity. And it is the unclear relationship and proximity between them that is precisely the point. Motherhood is inexorably ambivalent and imperfect. Gore uses her book to both uplift mothering as a complex, wonderful relationship and expose it as deeply contradictory predicaments of culture. And rather than merely reject ideal fantasies of perfection as unattainable, Gore embraces the joys of uncertainty as she unfolds "the chaos theory of mothering" in all its conceptual uncertainty and pragmatic heterogeneity. Chaos becomes the lynchpin of Gore's approach, advocating ways of embracing the loss of control rather than trying to prescribe or regulate new techniques of mastery. Gore writes that "chaos is good news. It's movement. It's change. It's revolution. It's scary. But like intuition, I think we can trust it" (*Mother Trip* 9). In other words,

Gore creates an affirmative discourse that faces up to the fallibility, difficulties and struggles of mothering in contexts of poverty, racism, homophobia and isolation while refusing sanitized images of maternal happiness, writing that "we prefer the real and lived in all its scary imperfection to the glossed over and bogus" (*Hip Mama Survival Guide* 7). Embracing the value and complexity of mothering on the margins of mainstream social, economic and cultural systems, Gore frames "other" mothers in terms of their capacity for ingenious survival and honesty. Gore pays tribute to "rebel moms" as those willing to privilege knowledges honed through experiences that rarely get public attention and value. There is undoubtedly an inspirational tone running throughout Gore's books which recasts the ordinary characters and mundane aspects of mothering into a transformative project to change the world.

Feel Good Advice: "Better Than a Double Prozac Latte"

Ariel Gore provides an unremittingly honest account of the raw daily grind of mothering without adequate social supports combined with a joyful pleasure in quirky interactions. Gore renders the painfully challenging real life dimensions of mothering interesting, fun and engaging. There is an obvious attempt to entertain and draw readers into the unpredictable pleasures of mothering from the margins. *The Hip Mama Survival Guide* does not only grapple with the nitty gritty details of taking care of kids but also provides mothers with a sense of social power, value, belonging and pleasure. Constructing an empowerment discourse that rests on a plurality of desires and circumstances, rational individual models of accomplishment give way to easy-going, do-it-yourself praxis. Ariel Gore positions herself as a kind of mother/friend figure who nurtures moms, encouraging them to take care of themselves, indulge in personal whims, relax and let go, forget the responsibilities of mothering and focus on their longing to be more than merely moms. She suggests that it's OK to be both a "selfish" and adoring mom. Advice turns towards fostering desires that push open narrow identity expectations of mothering, into erotic, community, educational, artistic and friendship realms of connection and exploration. Self-empowerment messages take on interesting meanings outside a normatively controlled context of being an all-sacrificing yet fulfilled mom. What emerges are not images of women who are blissfully content, have everything and are enviously successful, but rather the possibility to forgo such images for new ones where risks are taken and differences embodied without comparison or hierarchical standards.

Against social pressures that isolate individual moms, compelling each one to become a better mom than everyone else, Gore addresses mothers as a supportive and inclusive community:

We are married, single and partnered. We range in age from fourteen to sixty-four. We are city girls, suburbanites, and country folks. We are gay, straight and bi.... We are black, brown, peach colored and every hue in-between. But in spite of all our differences, we have the basics in common: We know our rights; we enjoy our kids; we don't identify with Kathie Lee Gifford anymore than we do with the six-foot-tall, ninety-pound supermodels who dominate the pages of women's magazines. (*Hip Mama* 6)

Speaking on behalf of a broad network of moms works to break down barriers dividing mothers but also disrupts the discrete voice of the advice giver. Gore invokes a collective "we" throughout her advice books. Performing a collectively-honed common sense guide to mothering, Gore replaces the universalism of dominant ideologies with the collectivism of insubordinate opinions. The "we" threaded throughout *The Hip Mama Survival Guide* constructs an imagined community fostering a sense of belonging based on open-ended mothering experiences that variously diverge and converge according to temporal situations rather than ascribed characteristics. Mothers are invited to identify with the "we" as a locus for resistance and dynamic self-representation. Gathering the informal words of mothers, many stories and tips on mothering by other women enter into this text. Interwoven throughout each chapter are quotes and insights, passed on by word of mouth, detailing diverse areas of mothering. At the end of each chapter, a "rebel mom" is interviewed, delving into the unique conditions of her political, family, work, academic or artistic insights into mothering. A central goal of Gore's guide books is to promote personalized and collectively articulated powers and pleasures. She accomplishes this by speaking from her singularity as a mom writer, investigator and critic to involve other mothers in community of alternative maternal know-how. Community provides a social and political context through which to shift emphasis away from individual maternal wrongdoing and guilt onto shared conditions, alternative visions, and political actions of mothering. Gore's survival guides perform and solicit community as a given while pedagogically leading moms to reorient their relations with each other. She impels mothers to find their "own village":

So get out, already. Go to the park, go to your local café, find a La Leche League meeting in your area, go to your local senior center and adopt a grandparent ... sign up for a class, check the "Bulletin Board" section of your community newspaper for support groups ... advertise about starting a new group, subscribe to on-line and print zines ... whatever! (*Hip Mama* 124)

At the same time that Gore constructs a participatory project linking mothers, advocating social change and activism, she simultaneously gives permission for personalized soul searching, meditation, and wandering, and dreaming. An individualized therapeutic ethos pervades Gore's books, valuing a process centered on the maternal care of the self. Instead of restructuring the obligations and responsibilities of motherhood in determined ways, emphasis is put onto forgetting the rules, letting go of structured schedules, enjoying the moment in whatever way is chosen. She compels a mom to "allow yourself to follow the day wherever it takes you. Allow yourself to become mesmerized by the follow of event, by the uninterruptedness of it all." (*Mother Trip* 122) Encouraging the importance of following subjective pleasures and desires in whatever forms they take, Gore shifts the very parameters of maternal guidance away from what mothers "should" do towards what they feel like doing. This is not to say that material realities, physical labor and cultural obstacles are forgotten in a flight of new age maternal fancy, but the burden of totalizing ideological conformity gives way to partial intimate spaces of creative control and enjoyment as a promise accorded to moms, for moms, by moms. In a culture that positions independent will and desire as the antithesis of good mothering, such a move of unapologetic self-care and interest marks a bold departure for advice given to mothers. Gore affirms the experiential desires of mothers without falling prey to the ways maternal bodies have become extensively commodified and fetishized within mainstream mass media.[1] Whereas celebrity mothers have become a spectacle of glamorized white middle-class heterosexuality, Gore shifts attention onto the extraordinary lives of mothers beyond commercial image systems. No longer the reserve of the privileged rich and glamorous moms of Hollywood, Gore positions pleasure and agency as the right and need of all moms. The challenge becomes enabling such emotional, sensual and spiritual realms of possibility in the midst of women's everyday working lives of taking care of others. Gore's power as writer here is inspirational rather than analytical; she both gives mothers permission to follow their desire from within the imagined community of hip mamas and suggests small ways of making it happen.

Reading Unruly Maternal Subjects with Reflexive Care

What strikes me as a reader of Gore's mothering guides is the very constitution of mothering discourses from embodied locations of ambivalence that also represent a bold do-it-yourself righteousness "from the trenches" of everyday mothering. Yet, following the subversive pedagogical/experiential lines of Hip Mama Survival Guides is not a transparent or neutral process of exegesis. There is no position from which to evaluate these narratives and self-help knowledges outside the vulnerable questioning they ask of themselves and others and the locations from which they speak and are received. The challenge is to return the ethical respect they accord the words of mothers, to follow them, connect them, comment upon them without violating their integrity or rationalizing their feeling words. Achieving this is difficult, especially in the context of making academic arguments. Taking responsibility for how I mobilize these texts, I borrow their tools and strategies for moving between theory/fiction/experience. Staying as open as possible to these movements across discursive borders is not an arbitrary choice, but a necessary tactic, reorienting theoretical practice through the changing patterns of a text's desiring voices. And this is precisely what makes engaging with them so unsettling and intriguing. The status of desire is both the subject and the process of reading Gore's books, which are themselves an effect of a personal reading of contemporary worlds of mothering as always already elicited in-between selves and others. Collectively styled grassroots dialogues for, by and about mothering are about risking a multiplicity of intersubjective meanings while speaking through and about specific social, cultural, economic and political relations of mothering.

What emerges throughout Ariel Gore's *Hip Mama* project is not a prescribed content or form of maternal subjectivity but an attempt to explore multiple counter-styles of mothering that resist dominant forms of representation that seek to judge "the good mother" as an entity bound by either a lack of desire or a rigidly contained definition. In either case, what is disturbing is the extent to which those judging extricate themselves from processes of investment and identification. Working to undo such detached normative models of representation, Ariel Gore enacts a vulnerable process of questioning and personalizing interpretation. The dialogical modes of maternal knowledge Gore develops can be linked up with broad-based networks of variable discourses. An expansion of accessible and innovative community forums, through which the intimate details of maternal lives are addressed and circulated, indicates popular movements toward self-representational practices that compel and push further the ideas I have been exploring throughout this essay.

Gore's project does not stand alone. Concerted attempts to challenge devaluations of motherhood positioned above the fray of embodied feelings and labor can be traced across a range of contemporary popular cultural texts. Today, we can witness a proliferation of do-it-yourself maternal discourses including autobiographical manuals, advice books that playfully undermine authoritative genres of truth-telling,[2] collaboratively created self-help books such as *The Mother's Guide to Sex*, internet blogs and groups, community workshops, TV documentaries such as *Sexy Mamas*, video diaries such as Laurel Swenson's *Your Mother Wears Combat Boots* and *Marking the Mother*. Mass media technologies are being utilized to reach across audiences and readers, providing forums for discussions between mothers on mundane and "taboo" topics:

> The legions of mothers who visit sex-related discussion boards on parenting Web sites—swapping tips on everything from waning desire to remaining kinky—reveal a profound hunger for an explicit discussion of sexual issues. (Semans xii)

Many mothering groups and publications are organized to encourage interactive forms of communication that affirm and complicate what mothers have to say about their lives and how they say it. Spaces open up in which mutually reflexive experiential conversations begin to blur oppositional maternal and non-maternal identities. What is remarkable is the extent to which these projects are contingent upon collaborative processes involved in exchanging advice, sharing stories, and critically analyzing dominant ideologies. Their ethical and political impetus toward democratic plurality is forcefully articulated against "expert knowledges," often parodying them and talking back to them by playfully reiterating the fears and anxieties they perpetuate. At the same time, desires and pleasures are interwoven into these texts in heterogeneous ways that refuse unification and hierarchical valuation. Such popular maternal texts produce smart, practical and sensual knowledges activated as convergence points of subjective and collective cultural processes of resistance.

It is important to acknowledge broad popular cultural fields of grassroots maternal guides so that individual subjects and the narratives they tell do not become isolated as rare extraordinary examples of quirky difference against an abiding hegemonic sameness. Recognizing the ways multifarious cultural practices and dialogues inter-articulate identities and desires that exceed idealized maternal images becomes crucial for dispelling universalizing myths and totalizing theories. This destabilizes good/bad, giving/selfish, normal/perverse, hetero/queer divisions through wide-spread contradictory discourses that have no singular origin or exclusive effect or meaning. It is precisely these public assertions of diffuse and unpredictable relations of maternal meaning that pose the greatest threat to formations of power based on the regulation and containment of maternal differences. A future task becomes opening up ways of reading and thinking through ephemeral, ambiguous, playful and politically signifying activities through which maternal self-representations elicit socio-cultural recognition beyond normative prescriptions.

[1]For a concise discussion of the sexual fetishization of celebrity moms and the demonization of welfare moms in popular media see Susan Douglas and Meredith Michaels.

[2]There are a few very interesting examples of manuals that break the heterosexual mold including Rachel Pepper's *The Ultimate Guide to Pregnancy for Lesbians*.

Works Cited

Benfer, Amy. "Generation S-E-X, Contrary to Ancient Doctrine—and the Neighborhood Pimp—Mommies Can Be Hotties." *Salon Magazine*, May 2, 2001. <http://archive.salon.com/mwt/feature/2001/05/02/mother_sex/index.html>.

Douglas, Susan and Meredith Michaels, "The Mommy Wars: How the Media Turned Motherhood into a Catfight." *Ms Magazine*. Feb/March 2000: 62-68.

Gore, Ariel. *The Hip Mama Survival Guide*. New York: Hyperion Press, 1998.

Gore, Ariel. *The Mother Trip: Hip Mama's Guide to Staying Sane in the Chaos of Motherhood*. CA: Seal Press, 2000.

Ladd-Taylor, Molly and Lauri Umansky. *Bad Mothers: The Politics of Blame in Twentieth-Century America*. New York: NYU Press, 1998.

Pepper, Rachel. *The Ultimate Guide to Pregnancy for Lesbians*. New York: Cleis Press, 1999.

Semans, Anne and Cathy Winks. *The Mother's Guide to Sex: Enjoying Your Sexuality Through All Stages of Motherhood*. New York: Three Rivers Press, 2001.

"Sexy Mamas." City TV episode of *Sex TV*. 1998.

Shepard, Julianne. "Book review of The Mother Trip" *The Portland Mercury*. June 15, 2000: Vol. 1 No 3. 5 Jul. 2007 <http://www.portlandmercury.com/portland/Content?oid=22301&category=22148>.

Swenson, Laurel. *Marking the Mother: Tattoos, Mothers and How We All Break the Rules of Motherhood*. Video Out. 2000.

Swenson, Laurel. *Your Mother Wears Combat Boots: Dyke Moms Rant*. Video Out. 1996.

Intensive Motherhood Ideology

Shaping the Ways We Balance and Weave Work and Family into the 21st Century and Beyond

Angela Hattery

Ideology is a set of inter-related beliefs concerning an area of social life. One may hold a gender ideology, a religious ideology or a political ideology, for example. Often a set of behavioral expectations flows directly from an ideology. The degree to which a specific ideological content will affect the behavior of the individual is dependent upon the strength with which an individual person subscribes to a particular ideology. According to Goran Therborn, "The operation of ideology in human life basically involves the constitution and patterning of how human beings live their lives as conscious, reflecting initiators of acts in a structured, meaningful world" (15). In this essay, based on my book *Women, Work and Family: Balancing and Weaving*, I will explore the power of the hegemonic ideology of intensive mothering in shaping the ways in which women balance and weave work and family, and in shaping their evaluations of the choices other mothers make as they strive to do "the right thing" both at work and at home.

An Historical Context

Although the "Leave it to Beaver" era of the stay-at-home mother[1] is limited in both time (the relatively short historical period, the 1950s and 1960s) and was available only to White, middle class women, this form of mothering—intensive mothering—came to dominate the ideological landscape and came to be synonymous with being a "good mother." This model of intensive mothering has pervaded motherhood ideology in the U.S.[2]

Motherly love and devotion were considered essential elements of child rearing. And, mothers who did not devote themselves entirely to the nurturing of their children were accused of practicing maternal deprivation.[3] Maternal deprivation refers to the belief that anything less than 24-hour, seven days a week attention by a mother of her children was considered deprivation of maternal attention and care similar to deprivation of food or shelter.

I argue throughout this essay that intensive motherhood ideology remains the dominant motherhood ideology in the United States. Despite the clear pockets of resistance to the ideology of intensive mothering, it holds hegemonic power. Intensive mothering dominates maternal labor force participation decisions as well as mothers' evaluations of their own employment and childcare situations.

Turkey Cookies

I illustrate this point with an example from my own experiences with work and mothering. In November, 1998, one of the room parents from my son's second grade class called. She asked me if I could bring a treat for the Thanksgiving celebration that his class was having. Of course, I said yes. As the week of Thanksgiving approached, I asked other mothers if they had any suggestions for a creative treat to bring for Thanksgiving. One of the other mothers from my son's class suggested turkey cookies. A turkey cookie is constructed by "gluing," with chocolate icing of course, a striped fudge cookie to an Oreo. The striped cookie serves as the tail and the Oreo as the base. Then a chocolate mint is "glued" to the Oreo for a head and a candy corn is "glued" to the mint for the beak. Because I was the room parent for my daughter's class and responsible for her Thanksgiving snack, as well, I decided to make 50 turkey cookies, enough for both classes. The night before the Thanksgiving parties I was up until midnight making turkey cookies. As I was grumbling in the kitchen, my then-husband questioned my motives. "Why are you going to so much trouble? Why don't you just pick up something cute at the bakery?"

Both my deciding to construct turkey cookies and my then-husband's reaction to this endeavor illustrate poignantly several very important points about gender and parenting. First, I am a career woman. At work, I am respected for my career successes. However, on the elementary school terrain, I am evaluated based on my mothering. Because I have internalized intensive motherhood ideology, I evaluated my own performance on this particular mothering task in reference to all the other Thanksgiving treats that would be contributed by other mothers. I came to the conclusion that if I really wanted to be taken seriously as a mother, I was required to deliver a creative, labor-intensive treat that would meet the standards set by mothers who stay at home full time. As a point of reference, it's important to note that though nearly three-quarters of all mothers with school-aged children are employed, in the affluent, predominantly White elementary school my children attended, the rate was significantly lower. In fact, I would estimate that fewer than 25 percent of the mothers were employed at all, and of those employed, few were employed full-time. Of all the mothers of the children at this elementary school, only a handful, maybe a dozen or so, were professional, career women.

My own internalization of intensive motherhood ideology had created in me a sense of guilt, a sense that I had better show that I could compete with those mothers who are not employed. In addition to my desire to be perceived as a successful mother of elementary school children, I also felt that my own evaluation of myself rested on my ability to produce this creative snack. In my evaluation, my ability to produce this creative snack reflected my commitment to motherhood, not my ability to be creative with snacks. Although I am a reasonably good cook, I am *not* at all creative in this sort of way. Yet, it did not occur to me that my success at this task reflected my creative ability. To me, it clearly reflected my commitment to my children. The guilt that I hold because I am an employed mother reared to the surface and kept me working well into the night to produce what I considered to be the kind of snack that stay-at-home mothers make.

Secondly, the interaction with my then-husband speaks very loudly about the gendered nature of parenting ideology. My then-husband believed that agreeing to bring any treat at all was a testament to my parental commitment to my children and their school experience. He felt that it was, in fact, going beyond the call of duty to volunteer at all. Furthermore, he considered it preposterous that I thought I had to stay up half the night creating this snack when I could have picked up something at the bakery on the way to school that very morning. Given that men's parenting behaviors are evaluated next to those of other men, he felt that, were he simply to bring something he had picked up at the last minute, he would be viewed as a successful father. Men, he said, would never feel guilty nor go to so much trouble. This is, I think, because their standard is that of the employed parent. When fathers manage to get off of work to attend an afternoon sporting event or a field trip, they are applauded. Yet, this behavior is expected of all mothers, whether they are employed or not. Thus, the turkey cookie episode illustrated, in my household, the differential expectation of fathers and mothers. And, it verified in my own analysis just how susceptible most mothers are to tenets of intensive motherhood ideology.

For me, the turkey cookie episode is an example of "doing gender" (West and Zimmerman 137). My own determination to produce a homemade snack was an action designed to create a gendered sense of self, that of a "good" *mother*, rather than a good *parent*, as defined by intensive motherhood ideology. In contrast, my then-husband's actions were also an example of "doing gender." His inaction and the lack of concern he felt about the snack were congruent with at least one definition of a "good" father. Each of us behaved in specific, scripted ways that both reflected and created gendered parenting.

Divisiveness Among Mothers

The turkey cookie story illustrates far more than my own insecurities about being an employed mother or the pressure I personally feel to keep up with stay-at-home mothers in "snack competition." It is indicative of a much more serious and pervasive issue. Both anecdotal stories and informal interviews as well as my research on women's work and family balancing and weaving acts[4] suggest that there is a growing tension between mothers who are employed and those who choose to stay at home. Susan Walzer refers to this as the "mommy wars."[5]

For their part, stay-at-home mothers tell me and write in letters to parenting magazines that they feel that they must pick up the slack for employed mothers. Because of the flexibility inherent in the academic schedule, I volunteer weekly at my children's school and drive frequently on their field trips. Although some of the mothers who are volunteering and driving are employed, the vast majority are mothers who stay at home. Often the discussion turns into a complaining session in which the stay-at-home mothers report that they feel burdened because they are always the ones to drive on field trips, volunteer in the classroom, and bring in the snacks. They complain that employed mothers just do not carry their portion of the load at school. Employed mothers, they contest, want all the privileges for their children, but they are unwilling to help to make the special events happen. Interestingly, neither group complains about fathers who don't share the load.

For their part, many employed mothers often report that they feel guilty that they are unable to leave work for afternoon field trips. They comment that they feel so overburdened by work and the proverbial "second shift" at home that they simply do not have the time to drive on field trips or engage in turkey cookie construction. They feel guilty when they arrive for a class party with food they have just picked up at the bakery and see all the homemade treats the other mothers have contributed. Finally, they frequently say that they feel resented by the stay-at-home mothers.

This conflict between employed mothers and stay-at-home mothers was strongly evident in the interviews that I conducted. Cheryl, a mother I interviewed, believed so fiercely in intensive motherhood ideology that she stayed at home full-time despite the fact that doing so meant relying on her husband's meager income, which meant that her family hovered just above the poverty line. Emily, a career woman I interviewed, believed that mothers like Cheryl, who felt called to stay at home at any cost, were depriving their children of necessities and over-valuing their own contributions at home. Cheryl, on the other hand, asked, "I mean, is a child going to be better off if they have a new bike rather than having you at home?" She and the others strongly committed to intensive motherhood ideology believed that employed mothers were selling their children short and ignoring their responsibilities as mothers.

The data in *Women, Work and Family: Balancing and Weaving* illustrate two important points: that employment status is dynamic and that employment and "staying at home full-time" are not necessarily mutually exclusive. Many of the mothers were engaged in a constant reevaluation of their employment status. Those who are sensitive to economic need and structural factors were likely to experience changes in employment status throughout their children's youth. For example, many of these mothers "timed out" when a baby was born, then they returned to work part-time, then full-time, then they timed out again when another baby was born and the cycle repeated itself. For these mothers, employment status is anything but static. Moreover, the cases of many mothers illustrate the non-mutual exclusivity of employment and staying at home. Women who worked part-time, who worked from home, or who worked non-overlapping shifts were employed *and* stayed at home—they did both.

Secondly, as with most issues affecting minorities, an ideology that serves to pit one group of mothers against another only serves to weaken the position of all women. When women are resentful and critical of each other's choices they will fail to support each other in these choices. For example, employed mothers may not support stay-at-home mothers in their fight for an equitable division of household labor or access to resources because employed mothers might suggest that if stay-at-home mothers want shared roles at home, they had better be willing to go to work. Likewise, stay-at-home mothers may be less sympathetic to the fight for longer and more adequately-funded maternity leaves and more flexible work schedules because they believe that mothers who want to be with their children should just stay home.

The conflict, as we enter the 21st century, is not limited, as it may have once been to stay-at-home mothers and employed mothers. With a growing number of women choosing to remain childless, the situation has now grown to include all three groups of women. Employed mothers are particularly vulnerable to conflict and tension with women who are choosing childlessness. Recent workplace discussions that have been made public[6] suggest that some women who are choosing childlessness feel discriminated against by "family friendly" policies which they perceive as advantageous to those who have children to the exclusion of those who do not. In fact, on my own campus there has recently been agitation over just these sorts of policies, including the funding for the building of on-site childcare, the financial burden to the university in contributing to family health insurance premiums, and tuition remission. Again, I would argue that this sort of division only serves to weaken the power of all women. As we women continue the painstaking climb to be recognized for our merits, not our wombs, and yet be equitably treated despite our ability to reproduce, our divisiveness only harms all of us. Until we recognize the links between home and work, between employment, fertility, and motherhood, we will not achieve equality in any realm. Until women support and affirm each others' choices, we will continue to shoulder the burden of the second shift, and we will continue to earn 70 percent of men's wages and face growing, not lessening, workplace discrimination.

Women evaluate their own choices. Women evaluate the choices of other women. And, experts and non-experts make claims in public forums about motherhood in general, as well as commenting on the mothering of specific, high profile, mothers. These evaluations, both public and private, reflect the belief that balancing and weaving work and family is a private, individual matter for mothers, and sometimes fathers, to negotiate. When mothers are not successful in balancing and weaving, *they* are blamed. This divisiveness among groups of women both reflects and recreates this notion that balancing and weaving work and family is an *individual* endeavor.

This attention to individual behavior diverts attention away from the role that social structure plays in balancing, and weaving work and family. As long as issues of mothering and balancing and weaving work and family are defined as individual issues and women's issues then those in positions of power in the society will not have to address the structural constraints, such as the lack of high quality, affordable childcare, responsible family leave policies, and accommodations in the workplace that inhibit successful balancing and weaving of work and family. Moreover, as long as stay-at-home mothers and childfree women view balancing and weaving work and family as problems reserved for employed mothers then divisiveness will continue to build. Women will continue to lack the power to define these issues as structural issues and structural solutions will not be proposed. Inequalities at work and home are intertwined and will not be eliminated unless we recognize this relationship.

The Power of Ideology

Therborn suggests that ideology exists to serve those in power. As long as the links between home and work, such as the ones I've discussed above, continue to be obscured by gender ideologies, women will not be able to resolve the dilemmas posed by gender inequality.

Therborn, following Karl Marx, notes that ideology defines what exists, what is good, and what is possible, and he postulates that within a given culture there may be several different ideologies, regarding any one of a variety of social issues, vying for hegemonic position. The ideology that is held by those in power and/or that which is beneficial to those in power will reign in the dominant, hegemonic position. Thus, those in power control ideology.

Secondly, because those in power control systems of discourse, the dominant ideology will be pervasive, whereas alternative ideologies that threaten the power structure will have fewer avenues for dissemination and thus will be less accessible. Marx put it best when he notes that "the ideas of the ruling class are in every epoch the ruling ideas" (49).

Furthermore, by defining what exists, what is good, and what is possible, the power in ideology lies in the fact that ideology defines behavioral expectations. Controlling ideology is a way to control behavior. In the U.S. at the beginning of the 21st Century, the motherhood ideology holding hegemonic position is that of intensive mothering. Despite strong pockets of resistance to this ideology, contemporary mothers, simply by living in this culture, are exposed to this dominant form of motherhood ideology. Thus, the labor force decisions of mothers with young children will be affected by this dominant motherhood ideology.

In addition to the outcomes of this hegemony that are discussed above, ideology can also result in false consciousness;[7] thus, mothers will be likely to accept the dominant ideology even when this runs counter to their own self-interests. In a culture dominated by the ideology of intensive motherhood, some mothers will trade economic independence to stay at home because they believe this is in their best interest. The question of whose interests are best served by the model of intensive mothering is contested terrain. However, as long as the ideology of intensive mothering retains hegemonic dominance, it will affect the labor force participation decisions of mothers with young children and subject their decisions to evaluation by themselves and others.

Finally, the power of ideology is not simply its power to dictate behavioral expectations but also its power to result in self-imposed and external judgments of behavior. Those who successfully resist the dominant ideology may still experience negative affect and cognitive dissonance as a result of the power and dominance of the hegemonic ideology that results in its internalization.

Shifts in Ideology?

However, none of the above discussion of ideologies presumes that they are static. In fact, I argue that ideologies can change at both the individual and institutional levels. Based on Therborn's argument, ideology at the micro level can undergo change. An individual may adjust his or her adherence to a particular ideology when the material conditions change such that a shift in ideology is warranted. For example, a mother who reluctantly returns to work because of an increased need for income may come to adhere less to traditional beliefs about motherhood than while she was staying home. This change in ideology may be an attempt to rationalize her change in employment status, or it may result from various influences at work such as friendships with female co-workers who hold alternative ideologies. Similarly, a mother who decides to stay at home after initially returning to work may become more committed to intensive motherhood ideology than she had previously been. She may find self-fulfillment and rewards in being at home that increase her commitment to the tenets of intensive motherhood ideology. However, it is illogical to assume that huge swings in ideology are likely.

Ideology can also undergo change at the macro level. In fact, one ideological perspective may supplant another. For example, Hays (1996) traces the content of motherhood ideology across the 20th Century and demonstrates that the ideology of intensive mothering replaced a less intensive ideology of child rearing that had existed during the agricultural and early industrial periods in the U.S. However, these sorts of shifts are only likely when they will benefit those in power.

Thirty or forty years ago, when women's labor force participation rates were at their lowest, at around 32 percent, the majority of mothers with young children adhered to intensive motherhood ideology, and they stayed at home raising their families. Among those women interviewed for *Women, Work and Family: Balancing and Weaving*, only one-sixth (n=5) of the mothers did so. At the other end of the ideological continuum only one-tenth (n=3) of those interviewed adhered to alternative motherhood ideologies and were true career women. The small percentage of these women suggests that outright rejection of the ideology of intensive motherhood has *not* become dominant. However, the shift away from strict adherence to intensive motherhood ideology, in attempts at balancing and weaving work and family may reflect *some* shift in ideology.

Alternately, the current political economy in the U.S. has produced a situation in which *most* mothers must be employed. Perhaps the shift is not from one extreme position on the ideological continuum to the other, but rather reflects the moderating of intensive motherhood ideology; there is no movement toward dominance by alternative motherhood ideologies but merely a response to the current economic climate.

Conclusion

When I first began this study I was a mother with two pre-school-aged children. Ten years ago I truly believed that the issues I was exploring were limited to mothers with young children. I thought that balancing and weaving work and family would become easier as my children grew and required less supervision. I can confidently say that I could not have been more wrong. In fact, what I now see is that although the process of balancing and weaving work and family changes as families enter new stages, it is in no way eliminated. In fact, certain issues are much harder. For example, our middle school day ends at 1:45 PM, and unlike at the elementary school, no "after school" program exists. This hardly conforms to the work schedule of most employed parents. As another example, the children are off two weeks around Christmas, one week in the late spring, and two and a half months during the summer. Not even a university professor has this much time "off." In North Carolina, school is closed when it *threatens* to snow. Occasionally, school is also closed when it is too hot. Most employed parents do not work for companies that close under these conditions.

With most mothers and fathers employed during standard hours, the solution to achieving a balancing or weaving of work and family is not simply to encourage fathers to be more involved in the daily care of children. These issues require solutions at the structural as well as the individual level. As both a scholar and a mother, I have seen very little research on the issues that face families with school-age children. Thus, I strongly recommend that future research and social policy debates consider issues facing families as their children grow up, and not just those facing families with infants and small children.

This study has raised several important questions about ideological shifts and changes in families as the children mature. What I know is that there are as many different stories as there are mothers, and that balancing and weaving work and family continues to be one of the most complex and important issues that families of the new millennium must resolve. Finally, if women are to reach true equality in the workplace and at home they need to begin to see their shared self-interests as *women* rather than identifying only with those women who make similar decisions about balancing and weaving work and family. This requires, first and foremost, an end to the divisive judging of other women's strategies for balancing work and family life. As long as women remain divided along work and family lines, we will never find true equality at work or in our intimate relationships and family lives.

[1]As many feminist scholars of work have noted, women's work is not limited to that which is paid a wage or done outside of the home in the formal labor market. I use the term "stay at home mother" to refer to women who do all or most of their work at home as opposed to "employed mothers" to refer to women who spend at least some time in the formal, paid labor market. Of course as I and others have demonstrated, because of the complex ways many women weave paid work and "family" work (such as by providing fee-for-service daycare in their homes), even these terms do not adequately capture

the complexities of weaving work and family. See Joan Acker's *Class Questions and Feminist Answers*.

[2]For a discussion of alternative motherhood experiences see Patricia Hill-Collins; Denise A. Segura.

[3]See Linda Gordon. Also see Sharon Hays.

[4]The project is detailed in *Women, Work, and Family: Balancing and Weaving* (Hattery).

[5]Some researchers also argue that the "Mommy Wars" are a fabrication of the media. See contributions by Jane Smiley and others in Leslie Morgan Steiner's edited volume, *Stay at Home and Career Moms Face Off on Their Choices, Their Lives, Their Families*.

[6]For one example, see Nicki Defago.

[7]Or, as Georg Lukács defines it as "phantom objectivity."

Works Cited

Acker, Joan. *Class Questions and Feminist Answers*. New York: Rowman & Littlefield, 2006.

Defago, Nicki. "Civil War Rages in the Office." *Daily Mail* 14 Feb. 2007. 21 June 2007 <http://www.dailymail.co.uk/pages/live/femail/article.html?in_article_id=436035&in_page_id=1879>.

Gordon, Linda. *Heroes of Their Own Lives: The Politics and History of Family Violence*. New York: Penguin, 1988.

Hattery, Angela. *Women, Work and Family: Balancing and Weaving*. Thousand Oaks, CA: Sage, 2001

Hays, Sharon. *The Cultural Contradictions of Motherhood*. New Haven, CT: Yale University Press, 1996.

Hill-Collins, Patricia. "Shifting the Center: Race, Class, and Feminist Theorizing About Motherhood" in *Mothering: Ideology, Experience, and Agency*. Ed. Glenn and Chang. New York: Routledge, 1994.

Lukács, Georg. *History & Class Consciousness*. London: Merlin Press, (1920) 1967.

Marx, Karl. 1993. *The German Ideology*. Reprinted in *Sociology: An Introduction. From the Classics to Contemporary Feminism*. (Ed.) Don Mills, Oxford Press, 1993. 49-50.

Segura, Denise A. "Working at Motherhood: Chicana and Mexican Immigrant Mothers and Employment." In *Mothering: Ideology, Experience, and Agency*. Eds: Glenn and Chang. New York: Routledge, 1994.

Steiner, Leslie Morgan. *Stay at Home and Career Moms Face Off on Their Choices, Their Lives, Their Families*. New York, Random House, 2006.

Therborn, Göran. *The Ideology of Power and the Power of Ideology.* London: Verso, 1980.

Walzer, Susan. *Thinking about the Baby: Gender and Transitions into Parenthood.* Philadelphia, PA: Temple University Press, 1998.

Relentless Rebuke

"Experts" and the Scripting of "Good" Mothers

Motherhood is one of the most dramatic and far-reaching social transformations in a woman's life. What makes it so powerful a force of change is not simply a matter of biological process or maternal response to the child. Equally important is the matter of cultural processes which attempt to shape the identity of the woman to replace it with the identity of mother. The cultural forces come in part from "experts" who attempt to impose cultural scripts on mothers by shaping the series of practices through which mothers are governed and come to govern themselves. These scripts are linked to the rules and regulations that aim at making mothers socially adapted and useful. The acts of power involved here do not render us merely passive and compliant. But whether mothers embrace the model, or reject it and therefore feel compelled to justify that rejection, these rules and regulations shape the material practices of mothers, and so help to shape mothers' experiences of their bodies, their subjectivities, and their possibilities.

Using Michel Foucault's notions of disciplinary practices as found in everyday habits and activities of individuals, I argue that prescriptive texts from "experts" such as physicians, psychiatrists, and psychologists produce discourses that shape material practices, including the physical care mothers take of themselves and their children, and their demeanor, as well as such "choices" as part-time jobs or jobs with flexible hours, late nights of housework, and the giving up of their own activities when they conflict with their children's schedules or activities. The cultural representations of "good" mothers as nurturing, selfless, and always available to whomever needs them, are crucial aspects of the process by which mothers constitute their selves and their lives and come to establish goals, aspirations, and relationships. These goals, aspirations, and relationships may appear to be personal and natural—but, in fact, are shaped by the discourses that regulate society and culture, which makes them political and contestable.

This article will focus on prescriptive texts which are part of the deployment of cultural scripts—that is, prescriptive texts in the forms of mass-market books that provide both descriptions of "good" mothers and advice on how to achieve that status. These texts are in the mainstream and, for the most part, use the standard of white, middle-class motherhood. Millions of mothers and others read them and, in the process, learn how to judge mothers. These texts are part of an explosion in the last 25 years of prescriptive advice that also appears in magazines, pamphlets, videotapes, websites and other internet sources—all of which claim to be about parenting but are aimed mostly at mothers. This influence by "experts" on women is not new but, in fact, continues a trend started more than a century ago.

Disciplining Mothers

Today, there are more than 20,000 books on parenting and two dozen parenting magazines with a combined circulation of over 20 million.[1] These numbers provide evidence that the reign of the "expert" has returned. In their book, *For Her Own Good: 150 Years of the Experts' Advice to Women*, first published in 1978, Barbara Ehrenreich and Deirdre English concluded that the reign of the expert was over. No doubt it appeared that way in the late 1970s after conscious-ness-raising and mutual ties among women were strengthened through the efforts of the Second Wave Women's Movement. But from the vantage point of nearly three decades years later, any decline in the power of experts seems short lived. Today, the pattern looks much like what Ehrenreich and English document—including a field of experts who present themselves as authorities on the "problem" of childrearing, who secure legitimacy through "science," and who seek not what is true but to "pronounce on what is appropriate" (28).

But just as the science that drew women in also betrayed women in the Eh-renreich and English account by turning consumer education into consumer manipulation, it has the potential to betray women again (181). Today, instead of empowering themselves, many women who seek expert advice more often are disciplining themselves in ways that curtail their freedom and their choices. The science of childrearing for mothers, which uses the language of liberation and personal fulfillment, actually confines.

Scholars locate the emergence of the takeover of childrearing by science around the turn of the twentieth century.[2] The assertion was that professionals knew how to care for babies better than mothers did. But as anthropologist Sheila Kitzinger points out, there is no evidence that detailed information about how to perform the tasks of childrearing makes women better mothers. In fact, she says, such information often results in dissatisfaction and resentment (10). In her view, forcing information on mothers in order to shape their practices has at least three additional flaws: intellectualizing makes the job of mothering harder; "experts" have biases; and "experts" often focus on restricted areas of behavior, taken out of the context of the whole or other behaviors (10).

It is in their daily practices that mothers try, and sometimes fail, to measure up to "expert" advice. They try to measure up in their daily answers to such questions as whether to spank or not, speak frankly or censor language, cuddle more, read to their children more, work for pay in or outside of their homes, and so on. When expert advice is used as an objective standard, mothers necessarily fail because they cannot measure up to the ideals presented. The prescriptive texts are powerful influences on mothers because they do two things: they assert their "expert" authors as essential to solving the "problems" of motherhood; and, in laying down authoritative rules or directions, they help construct and recreate particular kinds of identities and practices to solve those problems. That is, there is a self-perpetuating logic in the way that prescriptive texts work. The prescriptive texts make "experts" necessary by defining the problem mothers must solve; they make the existence of "experts" possible by supplying the underlying rationale for mothers' practices; and they make prescriptive texts effective by providing the practical knowledge mothers then believe they require.

That is, the experts present descriptions and advice that produce "truths"—or what appears to be "true" at a particular time and place. In this process, the experts produce aspirations and desires. Once desires are there, the experts have established a relationship of power from which they can act on bodies and thoughts in a way that shapes mothers' behaviors and practices. According to Foucault, this happens at the level of ongoing subjugation, at the level at which subjects are constituted as a result of the effects of powers. The "experts" and their discourses help construct maternal bodies that are socially appropriate. After pregnancy and lactation, maternal bodies thus are less the result of biological difference than the effect of socially and historically specific practices. That is, maternal bodies and practices are based on relations of power.

Analyzing the influence of prescriptive texts on maternal bodies and identities from a Foucauldian approach allows a focus not only on how women are turned into mothers but also on how mothers are turned into individuals of particular kinds. For Foucault, the emergence of disciplinary techniques such as surveillance, examination, and discipline, makes it possible to obtain knowledge about individuals, and with that knowledge comes power. Disciplinary practices are involved in such divisions as sane/insane, as well as "good" mother/"bad" mother, which are used for the purposes of normalization and social control. Motherhood is constructed in three ways: as a social institution, as an ideology, and in its practices which implicate it in the "complex and multiple practices of a 'governmentality.'"[3] Foucault uses the term "policing" over the course of his early work as a positive intervention in behavior that creates a frame of mind that seeks explicit definitions of what behavior is appropriate. This process paved the way for the self-discipline required in his later concept of governmentality, in which individuals may be seen as policing themselves, disciplining themselves as they constitute themselves as subjects. The emphasis thus shifts from government through society to government through individuals—for our purposes, through mothers—as they exercise what appears as "free choice" but, in fact, is limited by the narrow possibilities at any particular moment in time (Cruickshank 342).[4] Mothers become subjected when their goals come to match the goals set out to fulfill the social good, when they mobilize themselves in the interests of society—such as staying home with their children or working part-time, providing unpaid labor at home. Yet, individuals are not victims or passive consumers; they are active participants. The "power" in the "technologies of power" always presupposes capacity as an agent. According to Foucault, power is addressed to individuals who are free to act. But it is the sacrifice of the subject's own will that constitutes the new technology of the self; the sacrifice is made willingly, to constitute a new or "better" self (Foucault, "Technologies of the Self" 45, 49). Thus, mothers can break away from the cultural scripts by questioning, challenging, and reinterpreting the identities and values that the scripts assign to them. Although Foucault does not explain the source of this freedom to act, he suggests that it lies in our way of thinking, which is linked to tradition. He suggests changing our relationships with tradition: if we think differently about what has happened before, we can think differently about our possibilities. Without such challenging and reinterpretation of cultural scripts, mothers often help fulfill objectives of experts through the construction of themselves as social subjects with particular desires (Rose 72).

Defining Needs and Practices

Prescriptive texts are based in both narratives and science. The narratives, or stories of mothers' successes and failures, work as a kind of shorthand through which readers make sense of the world of motherhood and learn the difference between "good" and "bad" mothers. Cultural scripts teach cultural values which we internalize, and give us our sense of the world around us.[5] The scripts position us socially, and organize that process that strives to reproduce a universal "good" mother in each individual mother. The scripts exclude certain interpretations and perspectives of motherhood, and privilege others. The scripts are enabled by narratives and institutions that get their strength, not from force, but from their power to structure our lives (Marcus 389).

The science that is used makes claims to objectivity and truth, but in the process produces "truths" so that certain choices are seen as natural, self-evident, indispensable. For example, Benjamin Spock's most popular book, *Baby and*

Child Care, is presented in encyclopedia form, with detailed prescriptions on how to respond to infant and child behavior at each stage of development. T. Berry Brazelton's books tend to rely more on narratives about a few specific families and their children, yet he also offers detailed prescriptions on what to do with and for children. The prescriptions from these physicians represent and define mothers' needs, fitting them into what appear to be objective categories, then define the practices mothers should use to satisfy those needs.

Women often seek such advice even before conception so that they can do the most to produce a "perfect" baby. Texts are recommended to pregnant women and new mothers by their doctors and hospital staffs in part to make up for the lack of support and advice from extended families. Prescriptive texts also help make up for drastic reductions in hospital stays after birth, which for a while sent new mothers home with their babies within 12 or 24 hours of the birth. First, mothers are bombarded with the message that they cannot give birth to healthy babies without lots of help, which causes them to lose trust in their bodies; then, they are offered prescriptive texts to provide that help.[6]

Today's experts again define themselves as objective and above special interests. Their prescriptive texts define needs ranging from nutrition and exercise during pregnancy and breastfeeding, to schedules for feeding, bathing, and sleep for infants and young children. While diet and exercise are important to a healthy pregnancy, they are used to introduce mothers to the discipline that will be expected of them in their new role in areas in which such disciplinary practices could more easily be contested. For example, mothers are now encouraged to breastfeed (a reversal from the 1950s), and those who do breastfeed are encouraged to count for at least the first several weeks the number of wet diapers (6-8) and bowel movements (2-5) each day to make sure they are producing enough milk for their babies. The message is that the way to know your baby is thriving is to count and measure; the only measures considered valid are those entrenched in the authority of the "experts." This practice feeds the anxiety that is produced when "experts" suggest mothers may not be able to produce enough milk, an anxiety which, in turn, may reduce milk production.

In another example of defining practices, Deborah Shaw Lewis, in *Motherhood Stress: Finding Encouragement in the Ultimate Helping Profession,* advises mothers to make changes in their practices at dinner time so that toddlers do not get over-stimulated and become behavior problems. Shaw Lewis and other psychologists who offer advice on motherhood practices tell mothers to do most meal preparations ahead of time—when the toddlers are napping and before older siblings get home from school if the mother is at home; the night before, after the children go to bed, if the mother works outside the home during the day. Mothers are told to stay off the telephone during the late afternoon and evening hours so they will have more time to devote to their children.

Or mothers are encouraged to keep diaries of their children's behaviors, and their own responses to the behaviors, to help them see patterns of their own practices that they might address. Yet, as Ann Phoenix and Anne Woollett argue, such social and psychological constructions of "normal," "good," or "ideal" mothering run counter to the reality of most mothers' lives (13). They argue that psychology has been instrumental in constructing motherhood as extremely difficult, and mothers as pathological.

These elements of surveillance and examination fit Foucault's model of disciplinary power, which entails knowledge and power. In the case of counting wet and soiled diapers, the "experts" exploit the mother's desire to have a healthy baby; they attach to the mother the identity of being ultimately responsible for achieving a healthy baby; and they establish norms against which the mother measures whether she has achieved a healthy baby. The question is not whether mothers want healthy babies. The question is whether they really need to keep a chart of wet and soiled diapers and then use it to prove to the doctor that their bodies measure up by producing enough milk to meet the "norm." In the case of keeping a diary of child behaviors, the "experts" exploit the mothers' desires to have "civilized" children and peaceful time with them; they attach to the mother the identity of being responsible for achieving these goals. Even the desires behind the practices are constructed.

Breastfeeding mothers count diapers and weigh their babies, not under threat of force, but because they desire healthy babies, and they know that, as mothers, they are held responsible for producing healthy babies. They compare themselves and their babies to the norm, adjusting their own behavior when they or their babies do not measure up. As children get older, mothers are bombarded with advice on how to develop good eating and sleeping habits, and model behavior in their children by disciplining the mothers' own behavior and responses to their children. For example, current prescriptive advice calls for mothers to remain calm and in control of their emotions at all times. The psychologist Sylvia Rimm, offers this "ultimate tip" on childrearing in her book, *Dr. Sylvia Rimm's Smart Parenting*: "if you don't feel in charge, pretend you are" (39). The emphasis is on control, or the illusion of control.

In fact, mothers often are presented as out of control and in need of training to discipline themselves. For example, Penelope Leach, in the concluding chapter to *Children First: What our Society Must Do—And Is Not Doing—for Our Children Today*, emphasizes the need for parental training (241). "Bringing up children is probably the most difficult life task people undertake, yet society offers less preparation for it than for any other," according to Leach (241). She reports, "Private domains (families) are now too limited and fragmented to be relied upon as sole conduits for information" (240). Leach reassures new parents that their uncertainty about their new lives is typical. Her message is the same as that from many other experts: it is normal to be confused; I can help.

Brazelton, in his *Infants and Mothers*, takes a different tack on training and intensive mothering, calling mothering "too complex and instinctive to teach," then spends hundreds of pages telling mothers how to be better at that job (42). In *Infants and Mothers*, he presents a month-by-month description of the stages of infancy, predicting the wants and needs of children. In *What Every Baby Knows*, Brazelton urges parents to seek help from experts such as pediatricians, child psychologists, and social workers whenever they feel it is necessary (38, 264).

One of the problems is that the measure of the quality of mothering is limited: the prescriptive texts say that women are fit mothers if they conform to the normative ideal, or they are unfit mothers if they do not conform. Yet, even conforming does not always save them from guilt and shame. If they do not spank and their children still are not well-behaved, for example, they feel disappointment in the behavior of their children, which results in anxiety and guilt at not having done well enough. Alternatives to spanking, such as those recommended in Alvin Price and Jay Parry's *Discipline: 101 Alternatives to Nagging, Yelling, and Spanking*, require self-control, consistency, and other self-disciplining practices, not to mention time and space (to separate children from each other, or yourself from them, for example) (159-172). Although their advice is among the least judgmental, the underlying assumptions are the same: mothers have better-behaved children when they possess self-control and self-discipline.

The details of prescriptive texts and responses to them vary by race and class. K. Sue Jewell points out, for example, that African-American women often ignore or resist the normative ideal presented by American culture writ large, and instead define themselves according to their own micro culture (68). But, according to Jewell, not all African-American women reject all western cultural images of womanhood since they, too, want to obtain the rewards that result from conforming to cultural images.

Barbara Christian shows that, in many African-American communities, "the idea that mothers should live lives of sacrifice has come to be seen as the norm" (239). This is perpetuated by black men who, in the interests of patriarchal domination, create this controlling image when they glorify black mothers as embodying devotion, self-sacrifice and unconditional love, according to Christian.[7] Many poor mothers who come into contact with the macro culture through government agencies and their experts often have to conform in order to receive government benefits.[8] In fact, the American welfare system has regulated the lives of women in many ways—from efforts to discipline and Americanize the urban poor and immigrants, to restrictions which have changed the makeup of poor families.

But no matter what race, class or time period is involved, and no matter whether mothers are forced to take the expert advice or pay top dollar for it, the standard used in prescriptive texts is, for the most part, that of white, middle-class motherhood.[9] This standard is produced in symbolic representations which carry messages that say that mothers are nurturing, caring, sacrificing, and, although heterosexual, they are asexual. Mothers are responsible for their children and the men in their lives. This means they are easy targets for blame when anything goes wrong, and for the burden of making the sacrifices to make everything right.

Conclusion: From Sick to Incompetent

Ehrenreich and English said that the normal state of women in the late eighteenth century was sick, which was justified because such a state disqualified women as healers and qualified women as patients. Today, the normal state of mothers is incompetent, which disqualifies them as equals and qualifies them as objects of childrearing experts. The century-old ideological message resounds: a "good" mother is one who lives like the American middle-class mother lives or aspires to live, with the aspiration constructed by the "experts." Mothers continue to be seen as the major obstacles to childrearing. Children with problems still are traced to failed mothers. The prescriptive advice, warnings, and instructions are still designed to be consumed by each woman in isolation—making available the script so that they may be "good" mothers, so that they may "be" nurturing and efficient, so that they may fill the role of self-control and self-sacrifice, so that no structural changes in society are required. Prescriptive texts offer an illustration of one of the ways in which power constructs bodies and subjectivities, which has to be understood in order to be challenged. That is, motherhood is scripted not just by cultural images but by texts produced by "experts" and aimed at governing mothers. Such texts can be seen as imposing specific identities and practices on mothers. Changing this depends on mothers, and others, who know that the scripts can be contested, the performances can be interrupted, and the possibilities for mothers can be expanded.

[1]For books, see Amazon.com. For magazines, see *The 2000 Working Press of the Nation*. For how many mothers consult childrearing manuals, see Sharon Hays, *The Cultural Contradictions of Motherhood* (51).
[2]See, for example, Barbara Ehrenreich and Deirdre English, *For Her Own Good: 150 Years of the Experts' Advice to Women*; Philippe Aries, *Centuries of Childhood: A Social History of Family Life*; and Jacques Donzelot, *The Policing of Families*.

[3]For more on Foucault's notion of governmentality, see Foucault, *The Use of Pleasure*, and Luther H. Martin, Huck Gutman, and Patrick H. Hutton, *Technologies of the Self: A Seminar with Michel Foucault.*

[4]See also Michel Foucault, "On the Genealogy of Ethics."

[5]For more on the notion of cultural scripts, see John H. Gagnon and William Simon, *Sexual Conduct: The Sources of Human Sexuality*, and Sharon Marcus, "Fighting Bodies, Fighting Words."

[6]For more on women losing trust in their bodies, see Robie Davis-Floyd, *Birth as an American Rite of Passage.*

[7]This was the image presented by Louis Farrakhan for the Million Man March in October 1995. Black women were expected to offer physical, emotional, and financial support, but were not welcome to join the men at the march.

[8]For more on the behavior of low-income mothers and mothers in poverty, see Mimi Abramovitz, *Regulating the Lives of Women: Social Welfare Policy from Colonial Times to the Present.*

[9]Alice Adams offers details on this point in "Maternal Bonds: Recent Literature on Mothering."

Works Cited

Abramovitz, Mimi. *Regulating the Lives of Women: Social Welfare Policy from Colonial Times to the Present.* Boston: South End Press, 1988.

Adams, Alice. "Maternal Bonds: Recent Literature on Mothering." *Signs* 20.2 (Winter 1995). 414-427.

Amazon.com book search on parents, January 2005.

Aries, Philippe. *Centuries of Childhood: A Social History of Family Life.* New York: Alfred A. Knopf, 1962.

Brazelton, T. Berry. *Infants and Mothers.* New York: Delacourt, 1983.

Brazelton, T. Berry. *What Every Baby Knows.* New York: Ballantine, 1987.

Christian, Barbara. *Black Feminist Criticism: Perspectives on Black Women Writers.* New York: Pergamon Press, 1985.

Cruickshank, Barbara. "Revolutions Within: Self-Government and Self-Esteem." *Economy and Society* 22.3 (August 1993): 342.

Davis-Floyd, Robic. *Birth as an American Rite of Passage.* Berkeley: University of California Press, 1992.

Donzelot, Jacques. *The Policing of Families.* New York: Pantheon Books, 1979.

Ehrenreich, Barbara and Deirdre English. *For Her Own Good: 150 Years of the Experts' Advice to Women.* New York: Anchor Books, 1978.

Foucault, Michel. "On the Genealogy of Ethics: An Overview of Work in Progress." *Michel Foucault: Beyond Structuralism and Hermeneutics.* Ed. Hubert L. Dreyfus and Paul Rabinow. Chicago: University of Chicago Press, 1983: 229-252.

Foucault, Michel. "Technologies of the Self." *Technologies of the Self: A Seminar with Michel Foucault.* Ed Luther H. Martin, Huck Gutman, and Patrick H. Hutton. Amherst: University of Massachusetts Press, 1988: 16-49.

Foucault, Michel. *The Use of Pleasure: The History of Sexuality.* Vol. 2. London: Penguin Viking, 1985.

Gagnon, John H. and William Simon. *Sexual Conduct: The Sources of Human Sexuality.* Chicago: Aldine Publishing Co., 1973.

Hays, Sharon. *The Cultural Contradictions of Motherhood.* New Haven: Yale University Press, 1998.

Jewell, K. Sue. *From Mammy to Miss America and Beyond: Cultural Images and the Shaping of U.S. Social Policy.* New York: Routledge, 1993.

Kitzinger, Sheila. *Ourselves as Mothers: The Universal Experience of Motherhood.* Reading, MA: Addison-Wesley Publishing Co., 1995.

Leach, Penelope. *Children First: What Our Society Must Do—And Is Not Doing—for Our Children Today.* New York: Alfred A. Knopf, 1994.

Marcus, Sharon. "Fighting Bodies, Fighting Words." *Feminists Theorize the Political.* Ed. Judith Butler and Joan Scott. New York: Routledge, 1992. 385-403.

Phoenix, Ann and Anne Woollett. "Motherhood: Social Construction, Politics, and Psychology." *Motherhood: Meanings, Practices and Ideologies.* Eds. Ann Phoenix, Anne Woollett, and Eva Lloyd. New York: Sage Publications, 1991. 13-27.

Price, Alvin and Jay Parry. *Discipline: 101 Alternatives to Nagging, Yelling and Spanking.* Salt Lake City: Brite Music Inc., 1983.

Rimm, Sylvia. *Dr. Sylvia Rimm's Smart Parenting: How to Raise a Happy, Achieving Child.* New York: Crown Publishing, 1996.

Rose, Nikolas. "Beyond the Public/Private Division: Law, Power and the Family." *Journal of Law and Society* 14.1 (Spring 1987): 61-76.

Shaw Lewis, Deborah with Gregg Lewis. *Motherhood Stress: Finding Encouragement in the Ultimate Helping Profession.* Dallas: Word Publishing, 1989.

The 2000 Working Press of the Nation: Magazines and Internal Publications Directory. Vol. 2, 50th ed. New Providence, NJ: R.R. Bowker, 1999.

What Mothers Don't Say Out Loud

On Putting the Academic Self First[1]

Jessica Nathanson

I have a memory of being four years old and watching my mother, in a fury, tear up one of my stuffed animals. I had done something disobedient—neither of us remembers what, exactly. But both of us remember that moment clearly, and both of us recognize that moment as a failure, as something that a parent should not do. What I also see in that moment, however, is the effect on my mother of full-time mothering. Now that I am the mother of a two-and-a-half-year-old who has discovered willful independence and temper tantrums, I can understand that moment better than I want to admit. I have done many things as a mother that I am not proud of, and I have reacted out of anger and frustration. The distance between where I am now and where my mother was at that moment in my memory is not far—it is within walking distance. What has saved me from reaching that point thus far is my academic life.

This essay had its conception in my confused reactions to what I was hearing from other academic mothers around me. I knew that there were scores of feminist treatises on the difficulty, tedium, and challenges of motherhood. Yet, when I looked to my colleagues and friends, I found no one who would admit that she felt what I felt: that being a mother poses a danger to my intellectual, creative self. However, nurturing this self is what allows me to move past the difficult moments of motherhood: privileging my academic self makes me a better parent than I would be otherwise.

Relationship between Mother Self and Academic Self

I am acutely aware of how the demands of motherhood negatively affect my academic life. At the end of the day, on my way to pick up my son at daycare, I sometimes imagine what my evening would look like if I were not a mother. I could take my time over dinner, maybe read the paper or watch t.v. before heading back to my study to work (there would be room for me to have a study). Or I could head to a café and do my grading and class preparation while I had supper. My evenings now look quite different. After bathing our son and getting him into bed, I often lie down with him until he falls asleep, which can take over an hour. Given the fact that I'm almost never very well-rested, this sometimes ends as it did the other night—with me falling asleep right along with him. Our early morning class and daycare schedules also make it difficult for me to work at night. Thus, unlike my pre-motherhood days when I could work at all hours, my work schedule now is much more concentrated. I have lost the freedom of time that many writers name as a creative prerequisite—not necessarily forever, but for now.

Motherhood has also meant a redirection of energy I might otherwise put into my work. Applying for jobs with an infant, then a toddler, has sometimes made me feel schizophrenic. The process requires that I think and write as if I am a well-functioning scholar who is in touch enough with her work to be able to talk easily and intelligently about it without being distracted by a diaper that needs changing. The truth is, I can't shift gears so quickly—I can't move from potty training to talking about my research in one breath.

Mothers—even feminist mothers—are ashamed to speak these feelings. Certainly, feminist mothers have *written* volumes about them. But only rarely in my *discussions* with feminist mothers does anyone echo these concerns, frustrations, and fears. When they do, they express guilt and shame. For example, I once told an academic friend and mother that I felt drained by the hard work of spending a lot of time with a very young child, that I was a better mother when I had significant time to myself to read and write and think. I said that I needed to be re-energized by my work in order to be a full person, and in order to have anything to offer my child. My friend, struggling with having to go back to work after the birth of her child, could not understand why I would have a child if I didn't want to spend this time with him. Her reaction surprised me—I had assumed that she would understand my feelings within the context of the large body of feminist literature that expresses similar ideas.[2]

In contrast, I shared my feelings with a close academic friend who has no children. Not only did she understand me immediately, but she also said, "some of the most mind-numbingly boring times I have spent have been those playing with children. Sometimes, when I play with children I just get so tired; I ache to sleep." I suspect that not being a mother let her speak this truth easily: no one would hear her and worry for her children, and she would not lie awake at night wondering if this made her a bad mother.

Relationship between Mother and Child

When I think of the relationship between my academic and mother selves, I think of the struggle for a life of the mind. But when I think of the relationship between myself as a mother and my son, I think of my/our body. Whether pregnant, giving birth, or breastfeeding, my body is no longer something to which I alone lay claim. Shirley Nelson Garner writes eloquently of the shift in body she experienced on becoming a mother. She recounts the sense of ownership of her body that her two children have in a moment when each insisted on sitting in her lap: "One of them cried, '*I* get the lap!' Then the other shrieked, '*No*! I get it!' Then they both begin [sic] to insist, 'It's *mine*!' ... I was a contested piece of property" (70). My son's need for my body, both as a physical source of gratification through our extended nursing and as a simple presence, is still strong. When he wakes at night, it is me he wants. While he has become comfortable being away from me at daycare for hours at a time, and even wants sometimes to stay at daycare rather than leave with me, he is clear about his desire for me to be with him. Several months ago, I worked all afternoon on the notes that became this essay. It was the first time in months that I had had time to write. When I got home, he was restless and tearful until I finally suggested we get out his sling, a cloth wrap that allows me to carry him close to my body. At the mention of the sling, his face lit up, and he ran to the closet where it is kept, shouting "Sling! Sling!" I carried him around in it, tight up against me, for close to an hour, until this closeness had, in some part, made up for my earlier absence.

And, for my part, my body needs him. When he was younger, I needed him to nurse, or my breasts became full and uncomfortable. And every so often, I crave him. Anne Lamott writes about the "jungle drums" that beat in her blood and her head whenever she was away from her infant in his first year (88). Leaving aside the problematic nature of using "jungle drums" as a metaphor for uncontrollable, primal emotion and longing, there is a raw moment for me just before seeing my son again at the end of the day. Attachment parenting for me means, in part, a claiming of each other's body. Until recently, he slept next to me. I was there when he woke. Frequently, I woke before he did, anticipating him. The first nights when he slept in his own bed, I slept fitfully, literally jumping out of bed at the slightest sound. I couldn't feel his toes or his ears or the back of his neck to see if he was too warm or too cold. I could faintly hear his breathing, but I had to strain to listen. Mothers whose children slept happily in their own beds in their own rooms thought I was crazy.

Our bodily connection, too, can interfere with my professional activities. Because I was teaching part-time and working on my dissertation after my son was born, I never needed to pump in order to breastfeed him. So, when it came time to go on job interviews, beginning when he was nine months old and still solely breastfed, I was unwilling to start pumping and introduce bottles. I didn't want to risk lessening my milk production, often a side effect of pumping. My solution was to bring my son and partner along on two campus interviews, during which I took a breastfeeding break. Because I was interviewing for Women's Studies positions, my interviewers did not bat an eye when I made these requests (one even continued the interview informally during lunch, as I breastfed). But the second of these interviews occurred when my son was 17 months old—surely old enough, in the eyes of many others, to be away from me for a couple of days. And yet, being away for that long would have meant his drinking breastmilk from a cup or bottle for the first time and not having my warm, soft flesh to nestle into. Almost as significantly, *I* was not ready to be away from him for that long.

I want to believe that most academics are prepared to accept the breastfeeding mother as a necessary accommodation on job interviews and will accord her time to pump. However, Emily Toth's "Ms. Mentor" in *The Chronicle of Higher Education* draws the line at a woman who breastfed her baby during her interview, implying that it was inappropriate for the candidate to reveal herself in this way. By "reveal," I mean both to show her breasts (which isn't always necessary but is sometimes unavoidable during breastfeeding) and to show her non-academic self, her "unprofessional" side.

Extended breastfeeding poses another problem. When my son was 2, I left him home but brought a breast pump along on an interview and requested a pumping break. Eventually, his age came up in conversation, and I have to wonder about how the news that I was breastfeeding a two-year-old was received. Many people see extended breastfeeding as unavoidably sexual in nature and therefore deviant. However, the American Academy of Pediatrics and the World Health Organization both encourage extended breastfeeding; the World Health Organization even recommends it past the age of two (CDC). I have no doubt that continued breastfeeding is the right choice for my child. But despite all of this, I anticipate that my extended breastfeeding may have raised a few eyebrows on search committees. And yet, I do not want this aspect of my relationship with my son to be determined by the academy.

Relationship Between Academic Mother and Child

I have an academic friend who says that in her mothering and teaching and writing, she feels that she never does anything well enough. In truth, it is impossible to do anything well enough—it can be a huge task even to finish anything. The work demands a concentration and singularity of thought that is difficult to sustain. The child demands the same kind of presence and focus, a "being there" that leaves little room for other thought. It often feels as though these two roles of mother and academic simply cannot co-exist. Susan Griffin describes exactly this impossibility: "In these months while I am so intensely absorbed in my thoughts...when I am tired, never free from work, teaching, deadlines…my daughter keeps asking me, 'Mommy, do you like me'" (43)? It's not an easy balance. The summer I spent finishing my dissertation was hard for us. I was anxious, and distracted, and less available than usual; and my child expressed his need to be with me quite clearly. There were times when I had to take a few days off writing completely just so I could be physically present for him. But this is just the kind of flexibility that academic work often provides, making it possible for me to spend more or less time in each of my roles, as needed. It's only when that ratio gets out of balance (too much work time away from him, or too much mommy time with him) that things become difficult for one or both of us.

If my academic self struggles for a life of the mind, and my mother self is rooted in a contested body, then allowing myself to be an academic mother helps to resolve this split. It also makes me a better mother. Teaching and research give me a creative and intellectual outlet. Because I am engaged in activities that support my selfhood, challenge my intellect, and provide a creative outlet, I can come back to mothering refreshed and energized. If I can live my own life for part of the day and then spend time with him, I can really *be* with him, and enjoy him, and be a better parent to him. I am not an engaged mother when I don't have this time. I run out of steam and end up crashed on the couch watching mindless daytime television, playing catch with him but not really paying attention to him. He, in turn, can tell that I am not really there with him, and will begin to act out in attempts to gain my attention.

I remember one day when the balance wasn't right and I was home and bored, watching "Dr. Phil," a show targeted specifically at women, many of whom are home with children. On this one afternoon, the show was titled, "Mom vs. Mom." Predictably, Phil pitted SAHMs[3] against WOHMs[4], and viewers were treated to the worst extremes of these two factions. The WOHMs were on the defensive, their voices muted by the production. They did not say what I was hoping to hear: "I work because I am fulfilled by my work, because if I stayed home with my kids I would lose my mind." But they did point to specific ways that their working affected their children positively. One mother noted that her working fostered independence in her child, who had learned to make his own breakfast, and to get dressed on his own. A daughter spoke of having watched her mother complete her master's and doctoral degrees, and of the pride she felt in her mother's achievements. As my son played beside me, I was reminded that he, too, would benefit in such ways from my intellectual and creative life.

Being an academic mother means putting my academic self first, making my own well-being my top priority in order to be the best parent I can be. I see this as similar to the emergency instructions one receives on an airplane: I must put the oxygen mask over my own face, first; *then*, assist my child. Finding the balance that allows me to be a fulfilled person makes me a better mother. As even "Dr. Phil" pointed out in defense of WOHMs, "a race horse has to run." I think of my mother as a race horse in traces, as someone who needed but didn't have access to a creative life. We need to speak this truth to ourselves and to each other: the sacrifices involved in motherhood do not need to be complete and self-annihilating. Putting the academic self first is not selfish. It is an honest investment in mothering.

[1]An earlier version of this chapter was presented at the NWSA in 2003. I want to thank my mother for encouraging me to leave my memory of her in this piece, despite her concern that readers might think she was a bad mother (she wasn't). Thanks also to Amanda Erdman and Rebecca Flynn for their honest and helpful feedback on drafts of this piece.
[2]As just one example, Doris Lessing wrote: "There is no boredom like that of an intelligent young woman who spends all day with a very small child" (7).
[3]Stay-At-Home-Mothers.
[4]Working-Out-of-the-Home-Mothers.

Works Cited

CDC. "Breastfeeding: Frequently Asked Questions." Department of Health and Human Services, Centers for Disease Control and Prevention. 17 June 2007 <http://www.cdc.gov/breastfeeding/faq/index.htm>.

Garner, Shirley Nelson. "Maternal Boundaries; or Who Gets 'the Lap'?" in *Mother Journeys: Feminists Write about Mothering*. Ed. Maureen T. Reddy, Martha Roth, and Amy Sheldon. Minneapolis: Spinsters Ink, 1994. 65-76.

Griffin, Susan. "Feminism and Motherhood." *Mother Reader: Essential Writings on Motherhood*. Ed. Moyra Davey. New York: Seven Stories Press, 2001. 33-45.

Lamott, Anne. *Operating Instructions: A Journal of My Son's First Year*. New York: Fawcett Columbine, 1993.

Lessing, Doris. "Excerpt from *Under My Skin: Volume One of My Autobiography, to 1949*." *Mother Reader: Essential Writings on Motherhood*. Ed. Moyra Davey. New York: Seven Stories Press, 2001. 3-11.

"Mom vs. Mom." *Dr. Phil*. KELO, Sioux Falls, SD. 10 Nov. 2003.

Toth, Emily. "I'm Perfect, So Why Won't Anyone Hire Me?" *The Chronicle of Higher Education*. 22 Jul. 2002. 30 Nov. 2003 <http://chronicle.com/jobs/2002/07/2002072201c.htm>.

Contributor Notes

Janni Aragon has a Ph.D. in Political Science. She teaches Political Science and Women's Studies courses at the University of Victoria. Her research interests are Third Wave feminism, Women and Politics, and Women and Technology. Janni has two daughters, Kennedy and Trinity.

Chris Bobel is Assistant Professor of Women's Studies at University of Massachusetts Boston. Currently, she is writing a book, *When the Private Become Public: Menstruation, Resistance and Doing Feminism*, which examines continuity and change in the U.S. women's movement through examination of the menstrual activism movement.

Rachel Casiday earned her Ph.D. in medical anthropology at Durham University (England) and now teaches in the Department of Voluntary Sector Studies at the University of Wales, Lampeter. She is also the mother of four children (who have, incidentally, received the MMR vaccine).

Kimberly Chisholm earned her Ph.D. in Spanish and French Literature at the University of California, Berkeley. Her work has been published in academic journals and magazines including *The Believer*, *The Threepenny Review* and *Brain, Child*. Her book, *Hump: The Sticky Intersection of Sex and Parenting*, will be published by St. Martin's Press in 2008.

Denise A. Copelton is an Assistant Professor of Sociology at SUNY Brockport. Her research interests include gender and health behavior. Her current research examines how people with food allergies negotiate their diet within a social landscape of food replete with food allergens.

Susan Driver is Assistant Professor at York University. She has published a book on *Queer Girls and Popular Culture* (Peter Lang, 2007) and is about to publish an edited collection on *Queer Youth Cultures*.

May Friedman is a student at the York University School of Women's Studies. May is currently working on a dissertation about mothering and blogging which provides an ideal justification for her endless websurfing. In addition to thinking, reading and writing about motherhood, May is currently mothering two young children, Noah and Molly.

Angela Hattery earned her Ph.D. from the University of Wisconsin-Madison and is the Zachary Smith Reynolds Associate Professor of Sociology and Women's & Gender Studies at Wake Forest University. With Earl Smith, she recently authored *African American Families* (Sage 2007).

Amber Kinser is editor of *Mothering in the Third Wave* (Demeter Press). She holds a Ph.D. in relationship communication from Purdue University and is director of Women's Studies at East Tennessee State University. Her research interests are in feminist parenting and third wave feminism. She is the mother of a daughter and a son.

Stephanie Knaak is a Ph.D. candidate in Sociology at the University of Alberta in Edmonton, Canada. Her most recent article is "The problem with breastfeeding discourse," published in the *Canadian Journal of Public Health* (2006). She is a mother of two.

Catherine Ma (eatatmoms@yahoo.com) is an adjunct lecturer in Psychology at the College of Staten Island, CUNY, and a Ph.D. Candidate in Social-Personality Psychology at the Graduate Center, CUNY. Her research interests include social constructions of breastfeeding and breastfeeding ideology. Her inspiration stems from her three children.

Karen MacLean has a Ph.D. in Comparative Literature with a minor in Gender Theory, and has co-edited an anthology of essays by third wave Danish feminists. She is American, but lives in Denmark, and currently divides her time between parenting her daughters, Ingrid and Asta, and her work as a translator, writer and birth activist.

Laura Major recently completed her Ph.D. in English Literature at Bar Ilan University in Israel, focusing on contemporary pregnancy and childbirth poetry. Other research interests include: religion and literature, South African Literature and autobiography. Laura, a mother of four, currently lives in Israel.

Marsha Marotta, Ph.D., is Associate Professor and Chair of the Department of Political Science at Westfield State College in Westfield, Massachusetts, where she teaches political theory and in the Women's Studies Program. She is at work on a manuscript that examines the spaces of mothers' everyday lives.

Meredith Nash is a Ph.D. Candidate in Gender Studies at the University of Melbourne in Australia. Her current research, *The Baby Bump Project*, examines experiences of 'fatness' and body image during pregnancy. Meredith is a regular contributor to *Cosmopolitan Pregnancy* magazine and a range of other pregnancy publications.

Jessica Nathanson received her Ph.D. in American Studies from SUNY at Buffalo and is Assistant Professor of Women's Studies and Director of the Women's Resource Center at Augsburg College in Minneapolis. Her research interests include hybrid identities, reproductive rights, and feminist pedagogy; and she is the mother of a six-year-old son.

Laurie Ousley is Director of Liberal Arts at Trocaire College in Buffalo, NY. She has recently published in *Legacy: A Journal of American Women Writers*, and has recently edited a collection of essays on the political uses of children's literature, *To See the Wizard: Politics and the Literature of Children*.

Susan Racine Passmore is a feminist anthropologist who received her doctorate from Southern Methodist University and is currently working on managing motherhood and career. She is the mother of two daughters and an independent consultant and researcher on topics of health disparities in public health and child welfare.

Nélida Quintero is mother to a wonderful young girl. She is also a registered architect in New York and a doctoral candidate in Environmental Psychology at the Graduate Center, CUNY. Her research focuses on the socio-cultural aspects of architecture, currently exploring the relationship between virtual and physical space. She may be reached at quintero@alumni.Princeton.edu.

Damien W. Riggs is an ARC postdoctoral fellow in the School of Psychology, University of Adelaide, Australia. He has published widely in the areas of lesbian and gay psychology and critical race and whiteness studies. His newest book, *Becoming Parent: Lesbians, Gay Men, and Family*, was published in 2007 (Post Pressed).

Laura Camille Tuley is an Instructor in English and Women's Studies at the

University of New Orleans and a graduate student in Counseling at Loyola University. She received her Ph.D. in Comparative Literature at SUNY-Binghamton in 1998. She has written on feminist theory, art and culture, and has a regular column on mothering in *Mamazine*.